The Dialogue of Justice

The Dialogue of Justice

Toward a Self-Reflective Society

James S. Fishkin

*Yale University Press
New Haven
and London*

Designed by Nancy Ovedovitz and set in Sabon type by Tseng Information Systems. Printed in the United States of America by BookCrafters, Chelsea, Michigan.

Library of Congress Cataloging-in-Publication Data
Fishkin, James S.
    The dialogue of justice : toward a self-reflective society / James S. Fishkin.
    p.   cm.
    Includes bibliographical references and index.
    ISBN 0-300-05112-3 (cloth)
        0-300-06639-2 (pbk.)
    1. Justice.   2. Liberalism.   3. Social justice.   I. Title.
JC578.F56   1992
320'.01'1—dc20   92-15494
                                                                 CIP

A catalogue record for this book is available from the British Library. The paper in this book meets the guidelines for permanence and durability of the Committee on Production Guidelines for Book Longevity of the Council on Library Resources.

10   9   8   7   6   5   4   3   2

Contents

■■■■■■■■■■■■■■■■■■■■■■■■■■■■■■■■■

Part Three
The Ideal of a Self-Reflective Society

Illustrations

■■■■■■■■■■■■■■■■■■■■■■■■■■■■■■■■■■

Tables

Figures

Acknowledgments

■■■■■■■■■■■■■■■■■■■■■■■■■■■■■■■

The beginnings of this book were supported by the John Simon Guggenheim Foundation during a research leave I spent at the Institution for Social and Policy Studies at Yale University in 1984–85. The book was revised and expanded as part of my research during a year spent as a fellow at the Center for Advanced Study in the Behavioral Sciences at Stanford in 1987–88. I completed the book after my return to the University of Texas at Austin with support from the Darrell K. Royal Regents Chair in Ethics and American Society. All of this assistance is gratefully acknowledged.

I would especially like to thank the following people for their help over the period I have worked on theories of justice: Bruce Ackerman, Richard Arneson, Brian Barry, David Braybrooke, Robert Dahl, Bill Galston, Peter Laslett, Sandy Levinson, Ed Lindblom, Claus Offe, Doug Rae, Giovanni Sartori, Tom Seung, Michael Wald, and Bernard Williams.

I would also like to thank Tim Terrell for organizing a three-day symposium about this book at the Emory University Law School October 23–25, 1988. I am very grateful to all of the participants in that dialogue, which has greatly improved the final result. Arrangements are being made for the proceedings of the symposium to be published separately.

Part One

■■■

The Limits of Systematic Justice

1.1 Introduction

As once-repressive regimes crumble around the globe, we see them attempting to embrace liberal-democratic values. At the same time, Americans express extraordinary malaise with their apparently triumphant political ideals.[1] This unprecedented situation gives new urgency to the central question of contemporary political theory: Can we arrive at defensible and coherent ideals that ought to guide liberal-democratic aspirations?

This simple question has been the focus of almost three decades of intense work in contemporary political theory.[2] Yet this extraordinary level of activity, concentrated on philosophies of the ideal or just society, has yielded inconclusive results at best. I propose, first, to offer a diagnosis of the difficulties afflicting the contemporary dialogue about the just society, and, second, to offer a proposal that avoids those difficulties, a proposal based ultimately on the claim that justice requires a certain kind of dialogue. We will begin with the dialogue about justice and move to the claim that justice comes from dialogue in what I will call a "self-reflective society."

The viability of liberal democracy as a public philosophy has been held hostage by three false dilemmas. These overly constricted views of our possible options can be summarized as: *absolutism versus relativism, religion versus amoralism,* and *systematic theory versus intuitionism.* Leo Strauss and his popular disciple Allan Bloom would have us believe that without the certitude of rationally undeniable "natural rights," we can have nothing but "relativism," where the moral judgments central to Western civilization and democracy must be on the same footing as those of cultures which practice cannibalism.[3] Others would have us believe that unless religion is brought back explicitly into our public spaces, we will have "a naked public square" in which our society can profess to believe in nothing at all.[4] And within the camp of liberalism itself, those who would reconstruct a public philosophy aspire to systematic solutions, believing that anything less complete and determinate would amount to an "intuitionism" where, in effect, we each appeal to our personal tastes. When the new versions of liberalism fall short of such grand expectations, they wrongly appear to amount to nothing at all.

This book will chart a third way, to free the hostage from these false dilemmas. It proposes foundations for liberalism that fall into neither absolutism nor relativism, that are based on neither religion nor amoralism, and that amount, in the end, to something less than systematic theory and to something more than intuitionism. This third way, the ideal of a self-reflective society, combines the objectivity of morals asserted by the absolutists with the sensitivity to social context asserted by the relativists; it combines the value of neutrality on religion asserted by the secularists with the value of having values in public spaces asserted by the new religious right; and it combines the sensitivity to social justice asserted by the reconstructors of liberalism with the awareness of the controversiality and incompleteness of those solutions asserted by intuitionists.

Let us begin with the debate inside liberalism itself. Over the last two decades, those attempting to reconstruct liberalism have aspired to present us with a *systematic* theory of the first principles of the just society. However, there are serious impediments to such systematic theories. In the first two parts of this book I will examine those impediments, arguing that theories which ignore them fail to do justice to the true complexity and controversiality of the subject. Part 1 will focus on substantive impediments, part 2 on methodological ones.[5]

Part 3 will show how much can be done *without* systematic theory. It will offer a constructive argument for the first principles of a defensible liberal society—an argument that, within a more limited domain, avoids all of the difficulties discussed in parts 1 and 2.

What do I mean by a systematic theory? First, one that gives us a coherent picture of an ideal in clear focus, an ideal defined by full realization of one or more first principles that *hold without exception,* one or more first principles that solve what John Rawls calls the "priority problem."[6] Second, a systematic theory defines *moral progress* for us because we can measure how just a society we have by how close we are to the ideal. Even if we could never fully actualize such an ideal, our progress should be measured, asymptotically, by how closely we approach it. Third, a systematic theory should provide solutions that hold as a matter of general theory regardless of social context. They should offer the same prescriptions regardless of the differing beliefs or practices individuals or groups may bring to the issue of justice. They should, in other words, be *context-independent* rather than *context-dependent.* Given the availability of certain objective conditions such as resources and technology (and the lack of outside interference), the principles of justice offered by systematic theories do not vary in their basic substantive implications from one society to another. In particular, they do not vary with the beliefs and practices accepted by the people who live in the societies being evaluated.

I will argue that there are crucial impediments, both substantive and methodological, to this kind of systematic theory, and that the most plausible model for understanding the true complexity of political morality is not the systematic liberalism generally aspired to, but a different model that I will call "limited liberalism." On this construction, three main points should be made about the status of liberal political philosophy. First, we have competing first principles. There are fundamental moral conflicts among competing ultimate principles even under the best conditions to which we might realistically aspire. In other words, the pieces of our ideal solution don't neatly fit together even under the best conditions we might realistically imagine. We have competing "ideals without an ideal" rather than a solution to the priority problem that resolves all conflict among first principles. Second, we have fundamental moral conflicts in our identification of moral progress. It is possible, in other words, for each preferred state of affairs to be more just than the last but for us to end up in a cycle where we started, violating transitivity (or acyclicity). Third, instead of systematic solutions that are context-independent, we have limited solutions that are context-dependent. By this I mean that what is morally appropriate may vary significantly, depending on the social practices that are widely accepted in a given society.

Within limited liberalism, we will not aspire to resolve all moral conflicts. We will not presume to settle the priority problem among competing substantive principles. Indeterminacies and fundamental tensions among first principles are inevitable. To presume otherwise is not to do justice to the true complexity of political morality. But then how are trade-offs among competing principles to be arrived at? Can we get definite results when principles conflict and when theory does not seem to define systematic priorities?

Part 3 will propose a strategy that embraces these complexities, while at the same time offering a basis for definite prescriptions. Since Rawls, the crucial options for liberal theory have seemed to boil down to either systematic theory or "intuitionism." Intuitionism has been treated, essentially, as the absence of a systematic theory—a lack that seems to leave us all to trade off conflicts among principles as we see fit. In part 3, we will see that there are other options. It is possible to abandon systematic theory while offering definite conclusions—prescriptions that give far more specific guidance than would sheer intuitionism.

Briefly, I will propose a solution to the problem of political legitimacy by arguing that a self-reflective society produces obligations on the part of all its members. Instead of basing obligation on legitimacy, I will propose that we base legitimacy on obligation. The resulting notion of political legitimacy purports to solve the core issues confronting the liberal state without the necessity for a *systematic* theory resolving all the substantive issues of social justice. Within a more limited domain, this strategy supports first principles for an ideal theory of the liberal state. Instead of a systematic theory of justice, it offers a more limited theory of legitimate political institutions. Instead of one overall judgment of social justice, it decomposes justice into many morally appropriate decisions by many people in distinct roles in the requisite legitimate political institutions. Its distinctive prescriptions will focus, not on the substance of social justice, but on the conditions which must be satisfied by the institutions that must make the decisions. In that way, my proposal will avoid the full force of the conundrums of systematic justice to which we now turn.

1.2 *The Problem of Value*

Distributive justice can be thought of as a conjunction of three separate issues:

(a) The problem of *value,* or *what* is being distributed
(b) The problem of *structure,* or *how* that value is distributed—that is, its shape, impersonally considered
(c) The problem of *assignment,* or *to whom* positions in the structure are granted, or how those positions are rationed or given out

These three issues, together, define justice *within* a given society. In addition, there are, of course, issues about justice or injustice in the relations among societies. However, we shall see that the task is daunting enough, without the further complexities of international relations.[1]

My focus in part 1 will be on the true complexities of the substantive issues posed by the three problems. Part 2 will turn to the variety of possible decision procedures for resolving these substantive issues. In the end, I will argue for a particular category of decision procedure that can deal with these substantive issues to the degree necessary for limited liberalism. This decision procedure will contrast sharply with the hypothetical thought experiments that have formed the basis for all recent attempts at systematic liberal theory. While the substantive and methodological impediments to systematic theory are indeed very great, my theme in part 3 will be that a version of unsystematic theory can be developed that satisfies criteria for an acceptable theory that I will propose.

By the *problem of value,* I mean the problem of defining what we are distributing. Is it money, utility, or what Rawls calls primary goods? Is it prestige or self-esteem? Is it what Bruce Ackerman calls manna?[2] For there to be an issue about the structure of distribution, there has to be something that is being distributed—something whose distribution has a morally relevant effect on human interests.

In other words, to resolve the problem of value, we must have a theory for assessing human interests. I will pursue these issues in greater detail in sections 2.6 and 2.7, but it is worth pausing here to identify the basic issues. I will treat the problem of value in terms of two dilemmas, one that arises immediately and another that arises when time is considered. We'll turn to the second dilemma in the next section.

The immediate difficulty in assessing human interests is that if we use *want-regarding* criteria—that is, if we rely on criteria that identify interests with satisfaction of at least some actual preferences—we face various well-known difficulties about interpersonal comparisons of want satisfaction.[3] On the other hand, if we depart systematically from actual preferences, we face an alternative source of difficulty that is equally daunting.

Beginning with theories that rely on preference satisfaction, we can dramatize the problem by considering some empirical work of E. L. Thorndike, a psychologist who used dollars as place holders for utility in studies of Columbia University students in the 1930s. Thorndike tells us that for the sums of money specified, the Columbia students would—on average—agree to:

Have one upper front tooth pulled out	$5,000
Have one little finger of one hand cut off	$75,000
Eat a dead beetle one inch long	$5,000
Choke a stray cat to death (with bare hands)	$10,000
Have to live all the rest of your life on a farm in Kansas, ten miles from any town	$1,000,000

These dollar amounts were offered as the students' own precise assessments of their interests at stake in these possible events.[5] The implication is that if one of the Columbia students were stranded on a farm in Kansas for the rest of his life, it would amount to a deprivation equivalent to the mental suffering his peers would experience if they had to eat two hundred dead beetles, each an inch long. As in the later development of cost-benefit analysis, dollars are treated as place holders for utility.[6] Such conclusions seem startling to us today because they are entirely innocent of the difficulties that apply to interpersonal comparisons of the intensity of preference satisfaction, difficulties emphasized by Pareto, Lionel Robbins, and others.[7]

On the other hand, if we use criteria for evaluating interests that are not want-regarding, we can interpret a change as serving someone's interests even if none of that person's own preferences

agree with the assessment. Such criteria face a different fundamental challenge. They must justify paternalistic inferences that,
somehow, the theorist is a better judge of person X's interests
than X is. While we might all agree that paternalism may be justified in dealing with children (and in some other isolated cases), to
build paternalism into a general answer to the problem of value
would be to treat an entire adult population as if it were composed
of children—as if the theorist (or the state following such theories)
could routinely judge their interests better than they could.[8]

This dilemma appears to enmesh any substantively ambitious
assessment of human interests in one intractable controversy or
another. Later, we will see that the real force of this dilemma depends upon considering interests in a context-independent manner. It depends on the expectation that we should be able to assess
the interests of any individual simply by knowing how she ranked
on an index of primary goods, or on a utilitometer, or in her
shares of manna. For this kind of systematic theory of justice,
there is no need to know the social practices for dealing with
these matters that are generally accepted in a particular society.
My position will be that if those social practices satisfy certain
demanding conditions, then they are legitimate and, for purposes
of the relevant social choices by the relevant institutions, provide
a basis for appropriate judgment.[9]

Of course, there are also severe limitations to relying on what
is generally believed. Some of the worst injustices in history have
been largely accepted in their respective societies, even by their
victims.[10]

However, by specifying criteria for the development of shared
understandings, we can distinguish forms of consensus that are
suspect from those that have legitimacy. When victims of injustice accept the ideologies that rationalize their positions, it will
be obvious that the conditions under which they came to develop
those notions fall far short of our requirements. I will propose a
context-dependent strategy that is sufficiently demanding about
liberty of political culture that it plausibly clarifies the first pri-

orities of the liberal state. The institutions that have legitimacy—
in what I will call a self-reflective political culture—will specify
procedures more determinate than sheer intuitionism for dealing
with the inevitable fundamental moral conflicts. In doing so, they
will wrestle, in particular contexts, with the daunting problems of
value, structure, and assignment.

1.3 The Problem of Value Continued:
Future Generations

The challenge for systematic justice becomes much more difficult once time is introduced. Our notions of individual human
interests have not been refined to deal with problems involving
possible future people. However difficult the problem of value
may be when applied to the interests of the living, once the interests of future generations are taken into account, new sources of
intractable conflict emerge. If we consistently tie our conception
of interests to personal identity, we face one sort of conundrum;
if we consistently untie our conception of interests from personal
identity, we face another. To give up either conception consistently
would open us to bizarre and compelling counterexamples. But
we cannot rely on both simultaneously without tolerating fundamental moral conflict and fundamental pluralism. And we cannot
ignore this set of issues, because no defensible theory of justice
can neglect the facts that people are born and die and that our
actions may have serious effects on the interests of those yet to
be born.

The two conceptions of interests at issue are radically incommensurable; they do not fit together into a coherent image of the
interests of possible future people.[1] Once more, we get a kind of
broken image rather than a unified vision in clear focus.[2]

We would ordinarily assume that person X can be harmed if
and only if X is made worse off than X otherwise would have
been. For ordinary cases, this assumption works well enough. If
I punch you in the nose, you are worse off afterward than be-

fore (your nose is bleeding); that is what we mean when we say you were harmed. If, somehow, it could be shown that your nose would spontaneously have begun to bleed at exactly that moment, regardless of whether you had been punched, most, if not all, of the case for your having been harmed (by my punch) would evaporate. Let us call this the *identity-specific notion of harm:* X must be made worse off than X otherwise would have been for X to have been harmed.

Although the identity-specific notion of harm is both commonsensical and a central part of many legal notions (particularly in tort law),[3] it is inadequate for the evaluation of the interests of possible future people.

Consider two simple cases, one at the level of individual choice, the other at the level of social choice. First, a woman has a disease or is under medication for a given period such that, if she were to conceive a child during that period, it would have serious disabilities (perhaps, for instance, she has German measles and the child would be deaf). However, if she were to wait until after that period, she could reliably expect to conceive a normal child. Many of us would say that she should wait in the interests of the child. However, we cannot say so within the confines of the identity-specific notion of harm. The child who is born with serious disabilities is not worse off than it otherwise would have been, because if the mother had waited, it would not have *been*; another child would have been conceived instead, as differentiable from the first as one sibling from another. Within the confines of the identity-specific notion, the other child is not harmed by the mother's decision to conceive during the risky period.[4] Or, if it is harmed, we cannot formulate the harm with the identity-specific conception.[5]

Consider this social choice parallel: Let us imagine a third world country facing massive population problems. Suppose that demographers and economists together establish that if nothing is done about overpopulation, after several generations the country will face disaster—mass misery, malnutrition, starvation on a large scale. Let us call this the *laissez-faire* policy option. To simplify matters, we might imagine an alternative option—let us call it *restriction*—that would sharply curtail population growth over several generations. Without specifying how this might be accomplished, let us imagine that our demographers and economists tell us that great prosperity would likely be achieved after several generations of restriction.

It is worth noting that the population that *would* exist after several generations of population restriction is not merely a subset of the population that would exist after several generations of laissez-faire. In fact, after several generations, the overlap quickly fades to virtually nil. Consider all the contingencies involved in determining the identity of a particular generation (who marries whom, the timing of children, whom the children marry, and so on). My identity or yours would be different if any of these factors had been different (so that I could no longer speak of "my" identity in the same sense). I will accept Thomas Schwartz's calculations on this issue and conclude that after several generations, the overlap virtually disappears.[6] If this is the case, then we are in the same position trying to condemn the policy of laissez-faire as we were in attempting to condemn the decision of the woman to conceive during the risky period (leading to a child with serious disabilities). We cannot say of all those who would experience suffering and mass misery due to overpopulation that they are worse off than they otherwise would have been, because were it not for the laissez-faire population policy, *they would not have been*. If the other policy had been chosen, completely different people would have existed instead. Over several generations, the results of the two population policies—mass misery from laissez-faire versus prosperity from restriction—would be visited upon people with entirely different identities. Hence, whatever benefits or harms may be involved cannot be conceptualized within the confines of the identity-specific notion of harm.

This issue is not a mere philosopher's quirk. It is worth noting that a flood of litigation has bedeviled the courts on exactly this problem. Many "wrongful life" lawsuits have been brought on behalf of children whose prenatal defects should have been diagnosed by a doctor or a laboratory.[7] Typically, the contestants claim that the fetus should have been aborted—if the doctor or laboratory had only been sufficiently competent to inform the prospective parents of the child's probable disability. The difficulty faced by the courts has been very much the same as the one mentioned here. The ordinary way to conceptualize damages within tort law is to imagine returning the injured party to the position he would have been in had the injury not occurred. But in this case, that position is nonexistence. Nonexistence is, of course, not the same as death. Never to have existed is very different from having a life that is interrupted.

Given some of the bizarre implications of the identity-specific view of harm, one clear alternative takes on new attractiveness. Why not compare states of affairs by looking at the benefits and harms *disconnected* from any considerations having to do with the identities of the individuals? One theory has, of course, been particularly noteworthy for doing this: utilitarianism. Setting aside problems of interpersonal comparisons, let us suppose that we had a utilitometer, or that we could make at least rough interpersonal comparisons of the intensity of preference satisfaction.[8] This would permit us to compare the disutility experienced by the seriously disabled child with the utility experienced by the normal one, or to compare the disutility experienced by all those who suffer from mass misery due to overpopulation with the utility of those who experience prosperity from population restriction. Utilitarianism has the property that it permits us to look at any two states of affairs and compare the benefits and harms without having to know anything about how the identities of the people in one state compare to the identities of the people in the other. It is worth noting that while utilitarianism is the most notable example of this property, it is not the only possible one. Suppose we compared the two states in terms of an impartial distribution of

Rawlsian primary goods or of some other metric for benefits and harms that did not make essential reference to preference satisfaction. We can call such theories, utilitarianism included, *identity-independent* theories (for the assessment of interests). Derek Parfit is the most prominent theorist who has argued for some variant of utilitarianism precisely on the grounds that it is identity-independent, that it avoids the counterexamples to what I have been calling the identity-specific view.[9]

The problem with identity-independent theories is replace-ability. This point can be made most dramatically with a science fiction scenario. Suppose that I could painlessly and instantaneously *replace* all the readers of this book with others who will appreciate it more. Furthermore, as a general matter, the new readers—let us call them replacements—will get more out of life. On whatever identity-independent dimension of value we are talking about, they will achieve higher scores. To simplify matters, if we assume that the dimension of value is utilitarianism, then the point is that they will add more utiles to life each day than did their predecessors.

Note that I have not specified anything about *how* this transition takes place. Perhaps, as in the movie *Invasion of the Body Snatchers,* it occurs through creatures from outer space taking on your appearances and incorporating your roles and memories. Perhaps I have a machine that simply fabricates new copies. Or perhaps a new, miniature technology is contained within the book you are reading, a technology that will go into effect as soon as you reach a certain page. In any case, the reason for posing the issue in a science fiction scenario is that it clarifies the vulnerability of identity-independent views to replaceability arguments without raising empirical complications about the fear and disutility experienced by those who are eventually replaced. (For this reason, you will have to consider my example hypothetical or assume that you have already passed the crucial page.)

Of course, replaceability arguments are not limited to science fiction. Consider this dialogue about the collectivization of Soviet agriculture from Arthur Koestler's novel *Darkness at Noon* (Commissar Ivanov is addressing the prisoner Rubashov):

> "Yes, we liquidated the parasitic part of the peasantry and let it die of starvation. It was a surgical operation which had to be done once and for all; but in the good old days before the Revolution just as many died in any dry year—only senselessly and pointlessly. The victims of the Yellow River floods in China amount sometimes to hundreds of thousands. Nature is generous in her senseless experiments on mankind. Why should mankind not have the rights to experiment on itself?"
>
> He paused: Rubashov did not answer. He went on: "Have you ever read brochures of an anti-vivisectionist society? They are shattering and heartbreaking; when one reads how some poor cur which has had its liver cut out, whines and licks his tormentor's hands, one is just as nauseated as you were tonight. But if these people had their say, we would have no serums against cholera, typhoid, or diphtheria." [10]

The general problem is that for any identity-independent conception of interests, so long as the abstract structure of distribution, the payoffs to positions, is at least as good under the replacement scenario, there are no grounds for objecting within the confines of this kind of theory. In fact, if we are utilitarians and the replacement scenario would increase utility, we can be obligated to kill everyone and replace them with a new population of better utility-maximizers. On the identity-independent view, people are simply vessels for holding so much utility (or whatever else is our metric of value). It is the utility that matters, not the vessels. If a vessel breaks, it has no importance provided another vessel can be found or be created that will hold as much or more.

It is the very merit of the identity-independent principles in dealing with the earlier counterexamples to the identity-specific view—namely, that they *disconnect* the assessment of interests from the identities of the people affected—which renders them vulnerable to this replaceability scenario. Because the interests are viewed anonymously, such theories will permit us to object to production of the deformed child or to the miseries of overpopulation without worrying about whether the better-off people envisioned under the alternative choice are the same people. But the same anonymous consideration of interests leads these theories to neglect the question of whether the people under the replacement scenario are the same as the people in the original population. The general dilemma is that if we tie interests consistently to personal identity, we face the identity-specific counterexamples, but if we untie them consistently from personal identity, we face the replaceability scenario.

It may be worth pausing to consider two creative efforts to avoid one horn or another of this dilemma. The first, formulated by Peter Singer, aspires to avoid replaceability. I will argue that it does not. The second, formulated by Jonathan Bennet, seems to avoid the identity-specific counterexamples. I will argue that it does not.

Singer distinguishes his "preference" utilitarianism from the sensate classical version: "This other version of utilitarianism judges actions, not by their tendency to maximize pleasure or avoid pain, but by the extent to which they accord with the preferences of any beings affected by the action or its consequences." From this property of preference utilitarianism, Singer concludes: "Killing a person who prefers to continue living is therefore wrong, other things being equal. That the victims are not around to lament the fact that their preferences have been disregarded is irrelevant." [11]

Singer's notion is that some beings, such as animals, fetuses, and infants, experience utility only in the primitive sensate sense. Singer believes that replaceability arguments still apply in their case, and he explores the implications of this fact for the eating of meat and the permissibility of abortion and even infanticide. However, he believes that the applicability of utility to more developed children and adults in this second-higher sense of preference utilitarianism would block replaceability scenarios from being applied to such persons. It is in this way that his distinction between preference and sensate utilitarianism might be taken to get us out of our dilemma (when applied, at least, to older children and adults).

I believe that Singer's escape is illusory. Preference utilitarianism is, at bottom, identity-independent and thus vulnerable to some versions of the replaceability scenario. This becomes apparent if one thinks carefully about what the "other things being equal" clause might mean in Singer's solution. Recall that in our various scenarios, the replacements can also be imagined to have preferences in a self-conscious and reflective sense. Satisfaction of those preferences may easily turn out to balance the frustration of the life plans of the previously existing population.

More specifically, if we imagine, as Singer seems to, a special disutility in an ongoing life being interrupted (whether or not the person is around to regret the interruption), we might, symmetrically, imagine a special utility experienced by each replacement—for example, utility from the miracle of his or her being brought into existence. The new person may well experience an "existence bonus" that counterbalances the disutility from the previous person's existence interruption. Any reader of Walt Whitman's *Song of Myself* will have a vivid sense of such an existence bonus. There is no reason, in principle, why one of these must be greater than another. The theoretical vulnerability to replaceability arguments remains.

The vulnerability is built into the foundations of utilitarianism. It is unavoidably identity-independent because it is what might be called a purely structural principle. It defines the sufficient conditions for approving a change based entirely on information available from a listing of payoffs to positions under one alternative as compared to another.[12] If the total (or average, for some versions) is higher under one alternative, then it must be chosen. There is no reason for utilitarianism (or any other purely structural principle) to be concerned with the issue of whether the identities of the replacements are different from the identities of the originals.

Because utilitarianism completely unties human interests from personal identities, it avoids the counterexamples with which we started, but only by creating a vulnerability to replaceability arguments.

Consider a second strategy for avoiding our dilemma. It has sometimes been argued that we should only count the utilities of those who would exist were an action not taken. Bennett has developed one variant of this approach: "The question of whether action A is morally obligatory depends only upon the utilities of people who would exist if A were not performed."[13] This proposal helps with the particular examples we directed against the identity-specific view. For example, if the population planner compares the benefits of the restrictive policy with the misery experienced by those persons who would exist were that alternative not taken, then there is a clear case for the restrictive policy. Similarly, if the prospective mother compares the benefits of having a normal child with the disutility of the child who would exist if that alternative were not chosen, then there is a clear case for her waiting.

This strategy does not, however, offer a genuine way out of our dilemma. While it handles our two particular examples, it is still vulnerable to the same basic difficulty we encountered with identity-specific positions: on these views, it cannot be counted as a harm that someone is created to endure a miserable existence. Bennet's strategy is vulnerable whenever the *others* who would exist anyway are benefited by the misery of the newly produced person. For example, imagine a population considering whether to breed a race of test-tube–produced slaves. The persons who would exist were this policy not adopted are the present population. They would benefit overwhelmingly from having a race of slaves. The only ones who would suffer are precisely the ones who cannot be considered in this strategy—the ones who would not exist were the policy *not* adopted. They are the ones harmed by the policy, yet their misery could not be counted by this proposal.

The two horns of our dilemma are constructed out of partial pictures of the interests of possible future people. Each of the approaches has something to be said for it. But relying on one consistently to the exclusion of the other would lead to disastrous or bizarre results.

Consider a more mundane area where no exotic examples are required to make the point: procreational liberty. Procreational liberty defines a sphere of choice of undeniable importance where single-minded reliance on either identity-specific or identity-independent notions of human interest would lead to bizarre and disturbing results.

Identity-specific theories, if relied on consistently, give procreational liberty too broad a mandate, while identity-independent theories, if relied on consistently, give it an overly restrictive one. Identity-specific theories open up too broad an area of procreational liberty because they do not count as harms actions which, on other theories for the assessment of interests, might plausibly be counted as harms.

I am assuming that we are placing procreational liberty within some variant of the harm principle, namely, that people acting individually or together, consensually, can do as they please so long as they do not harm (or invade the rights of) others.[14]

Suppose families go ahead and produce seriously disabled or deformed children when they know perfectly well that after a waiting period they could produce normal ones (or be reliably likely to do so). Is that not sufficiently *irresponsible* that it raises basic questions about the appropriate breadth of procreational liberty? I am raising this primarily as a moral question, without getting into the complicated issue of legal remedies or restrictions. I merely want to make the point that there is something objectionable about producing a child under such (avoidable) conditions, and that what makes that action objectionable is some consideration of the interests of the child—once those interests are conceived in some way different from the manner permitted by the identity-specific notion.

On the other hand, if we were consistently to conceive the interests of possible children in the alternative, identity-independent mode, we would be led to other bizarre results. Our procreational liberties, in the negative-liberty sense of unconstrained personal choice, would be encroached upon by a host of new obligations and restrictions. Suppose we were consistent classical utilitarians and applied that position to the question of producing or not producing additional children. So long as the additional child would add (or was reasonably likely to add) more utility than disutility (including whatever utility/disutility was caused by the child but was experienced by siblings, friends, and others), then we would be *obligated* or morally required to produce that child. It would no longer be a matter of discretion or of personal choice. Once such issues are put in the category of moral requirement, they are no longer within the realm of procreational *liberty*. They are no longer in the area of life where we are permissibly free to do as we please so long as we do not harm or violate the rights of others. They are moved into the category of duty or requirement, where failing to perform the action in question is morally blameworthy and living up to the requirement is an obligation.

Consistently relying on the identity-specific view of harm overly demoralizes and broadens procreational liberty. Consistently relying on the identity-independent view overly moralizes and narrows procreational liberty. Each of these familiar and coherent approaches, approaches that work well enough in ordinary life, yields bizarre and unacceptable results for the interests of possible future people. We are left with conflicting, incommensurable images—images which do not fit together into a unified conception but which serve, at best, to identify conflicting moral considerations that can be balanced out in particular cases.

1.4 Structure: Problems of Progress

Let us turn to the second basic problem of justice, the issue of structure.[1] Suppose we were to have *perfect* solutions to the issue of how to measure people's interests (at least so far as these are at stake in questions of distributive justice), and suppose we were to have perfect solutions to the issue of how people ought to be assigned positions in the structure according to some viable theory of equal opportunity.[2]

Even with perfect solutions to the problems of value (what is distributed) and of assignment (how people get and maintain positions in the structure), the fundamental problem of structure would remain to be considered in its own right before we could arrive at a systematic, substantive theory of justice. Given a listing of payoffs (in our chosen value) to positions (n-tiles of the population defined by their shares of the chosen value), what can we say about the justice or injustice of any two alternative situations A and B? (See table 1.)

Merely from the information in two such listings of payoffs to positions, we can tell whether A or B has a higher total or a higher minimum, or is more equal or would benefit or disadvantage more strata of society. Many of the central issues of distributive justice can be stated within the confines of this pure problem. In an important article, Douglas Rae dubs this pure problem "simple justice."[3] While it is "simple" because many of the crucial complexities have been relegated to the problems of value and structure, it is, in its own right, even more difficult than has previously been realized. In fact, I will argue, no solution that passes certain minimum tests is possible. I will use these conclusions to raise some general issues about the kinds of answers we should expect from theories of justice.

Until relatively recently, there was a widespread consensus about the problem of structure, and indeed about answers to the entire issue of distributive justice. As H. L. A. Hart noted, there was "a once widely accepted old faith that some form of utilitarianism, if only we could discover the right form, *must* capture the essence of political morality."[4]

Why has utilitarianism fallen into disfavor? The most powerful arguments against it focus on the fact that it does not, in some sense, take seriously the "separateness of persons."[5] Most notably, it does not offer sufficient protections from the kinds of sacrifices that the greater social good can place on individuals. Consider

Table 1. The Pure Problem of Justice

| A | | B | |
Position Payoffs		Position Payoffs	
P_1	S_1	P_1	S_1
P_2	S_2	S_2	P_2
P_3	S_3	S_3	P_3
...	...	...	...
P_N	S_N	S_N	P_N

this stock example, which I will borrow from Gilbert Harman, Judith Thomson, and others:[6]

Imagine a doctor in a battlefield or other emergency situation who has to choose between saving five lives and saving one. The one life will take all of his time and resources. But if he neglects the one, he can save five others. We would not blame him for neglecting the one. Indeed, five lives saved at the cost of one lost, seems, on its face, a reasonable calculation. But now consider a second version. Our doctor, now a convinced utilitarian, has returned to the hospital, where he has five patients, each needing emergency donation of some vital organ. There are, unfortunately, no voluntary organ donors. But a patient in room 306 has checked in for a routine physical exam. He is a healthy specimen and, by himself, could supply all the organs necessary to save the other five. Our doctor cuts up the patient and redistributes the organs so as to save five lives. If the calculation (that five lives saved are worth more than the cost of one lost) was correct in the first case, why is it not also correct in the second?

Of course, some complexities must be accounted for in any utilitarian calculation applied to this case. If it is utility that is ultimately being maximized, we must assume that individual lives are place holders for future streams of utility. In this way, we can reach the conclusion that five lives are likely to yield more long-term utility than would one life. While the case might be modified so as to bring this assumption into question, it is not, on its face, an unreasonable assumption. Second, there are problems about the effect of such an intervention on social practices that do produce great long-term utility so long as people continue to rely on them—social practices such as the routine physical exam. However, utilitarians have always had a response for such objections. They can lie or deceive or just keep things secret if it will produce greater social utility. Without going into whether this strategy in itself constitutes further grounds for objecting to utilitarianism, we can see that it should be possible to preserve the inference that aggregate utility is served.

For our purposes, two main conclusions are worth drawing from this example. First, aggregate utility, even when supplemented by the fact that most people are made better off, hardly constitutes an adequate solution to the problem of structure. We must also deal with distributive objections focused on limiting the sacrifices that may be demanded in the name of overall social utility. Second, criteria for structure cannot be applied in isolation from criteria for assignment—criteria for who gets what position in the structure. There must be some fair process for determining who suffers and who benefits. The arbitrariness of picking out the patient in room 306 violates our implicit assumptions about fair assignment. We will return to the assignment problem below, but in the meantime, it should be emphasized that any solution to the structure problem can, at most, be necessary and not sufficient for an adequate solution, because criteria for fair assignment would be required as well.

In dealing with the structure problem, we must confront two distinct families of consideration. One focuses on the general welfare, the other on distribution. Following Brian Barry, I will say that one might be called "aggregative" and the other "distributive."[7] From each of these two families, I will take two basic considerations, to yield the following four:

1. The total welfare
2. The numbers affected

3. Equality
4. The minimum share (or the maximin principle)

When we think of the general welfare, we think of the two separate dimensions in considerations 1 and 2, "the greatest good of the greatest number," as in Bentham's slogan (even though, operationally, only the first clause really mattered for Bentham).[8] Alternatively, distribution raises two fundamental and separable issues: equality, which can be thought of as the *relative* standing of the less well off strata, and maximin, which can be thought of as the *absolute* standing of the *least* well off stratum. In the examples that follow, I will measure equality simply by taking the mean of the differences from the mean; Amartya Sen has demonstrated some subtle and important differences in measures of equality, but these do not affect the basic argument developed here.[9]

Each of these four basic criteria has its proponents. The first point I want to develop is that the inadequacy of each can be dramatized by the fact that it will support choices which violate all three of the other basic criteria. Despite the enthusiasm of Rawlsians, on the one hand, and of utilitarians, on the other, single-minded reliance on any one of these basic criteria, even for the pure problem of justice, leads to disaster.

The more basic difficulty is that any complete principle which attempted to avoid these disasters would violate transitivity. Another way of saying this is that *any* principle which always sides with three of these basic criteria will take public policy in a cycle (under some possible conditions)—a result that raises basic questions about the kind of connection commonly assumed between ideal theory and public policy.

Let me demonstrate the first difficulty with a series of simple numerical illustrations. I am assuming that all of the issues about what we are distributing and about how we measure it have already been resolved. Suppose we solved these issues to a degree beyond anyone's wildest optimism. We have an index for, say, Rawlsian primary goods or Ackermanian manna that we can represent, for these purposes, with cardinal, interpersonal shares to ranked positions.[10] Even with such a solution, the pure problem of justice is far more difficult than has been imagined.

The point can be made as a sequence of abstract horror stories. Each horror story can be thought of as a minimum test for an adequate theory of justice. When three of our basic criteria prefer one alternative, it is the one that should be chosen. Each horror story consists in siding with one of the four against the other three. I will later show, however, that these four minimum tests, in combination, violate transitivity. Hence, any principle that satisfied all four would not define a unified and coherent direction for public policy. In that sense, we have to choose between morally adequate choices in particular cases (avoiding the four horror stories) and coherent progress in our sequence of policy choices over time. In either case, the notion that we can gradually realize an ideal with morally adequate principles is undermined. The true complexity of justice does not, by itself, imply relativism or subjectivism,[11] but it does disappoint common expectations about the kind of solution our principles ought to provide.

Scenario 1: Equality violates maximin, numbers, and the total. This scenario is just an extension of Rawls's argument against equality. The leveling approach to equality can be ruinous to all— lowering the total in a way that makes most people worse off, including those at the bottom. This possibility is illustrated by the choice between A and B below:

A	B
10	2
20	2
30	2
40	2
50	2
60	2
70	2

Scenario 2: The total welfare violates maximin, equality, and the numbers criterion. This case simply expands on the distribu-

tive objection to utilitarianism that has become a commonplace of recent theories of justice emphasizing the separateness of persons and the great sacrifices which maximizing the total can sometimes require. In this case, most people are made worse off, equality is decreased, and the minimum is devastated:

A	B
10	1
20	1
30	1
40	1
50	1
60	1
70	1,000

Scenario 3: Maximin violates equality, the total, and the numbers criterion. This case is an extension of Douglas Rae's critique of maximin. Rae showed how maximin can distribute less in total, less equally.[12] Particularly in cases where the middle classes are devastated, the welfare state may, nevertheless, improve the lot of those at the bottom while the rich continue to get richer. In that case, the total may decrease while inequality increases along with the minimum share. The example is not fanciful. Some may regard it as a good description of the "British disease," a syndrome that has, at times, been thought to affect many of the aging welfare states of the West. In this scenario, I have simply added a factor—the numbers affected. If distributing less in total, less equally was a serious objection to maximin, an even more serious objection is distributing less in total, less equally, while at the same time making most people (or most strata) worse off. Here is an example:

A	B
10	11
20	15
30	15

40	20
50	30
60	30
70	100

In the move from A to B, the total is lowered from 280 to 221, five out of seven strata are worsened, and inequality is increased. Only a fanatical advocate of maximin would support such changes because of the small increase of the minimum share (from 10 to 11).

Scenario 4: The numbers criterion violates the total, maximin, and equality. Serving the majority here distributes less in total, less equally, to the detriment of the least favored. This case may be thought of as a tyranny of the majority that violates both utilitarian and distributive justice considerations at the same time:

A	B
10	0
20	5
30	5
40	45
50	55
60	65
70	95

The move to B serves the most advantaged four strata, but in a way that increases inequality (the mean of the differences from the mean increases from 17.14 to about 30), lowers the total (from 280 to 270), and devastates the minimum (from 10 to 0).

Each of these four scenarios can be thought of as a minimum test which the other criteria, taken in isolation, fail. If I am correct that these basic criteria should be followed when *three* agree, then we have four separate minimum tests for any principle of distributive justice. The power of each test is that it combines both of the members of either the aggregative or distributive family with a member of the rival family. When aggregative interests are so clearly served along with a central element of distribution, or when distributive interests are so clearly served along with a central element of the general welfare, the result is very difficult to argue against. Let us label these four tests in the order of our four scenarios:

Test 1: Prefer alternatives prescribed simultaneously by maximin, the total, and the numbers criterion. In other words, prefer more in total when it helps most people, including the least well off.

Test 2: Prefer alternatives prescribed simultaneously by maximin, equality, and the numbers criterion. In other words, prefer equality when it is to most people's advantage, including the least favored.

Test 3: Prefer alternatives prescribed simultaneously by the total, equality, and the numbers criterion. In other words, prefer alternatives that distribute more in total, more equally to the advantage of most people (or strata).

Test 4: Prefer alternatives prescribed simultaneously by the total, maximin, and equality. In other words, prefer alternatives that distribute more in total, more equally, when it is to the advantage of the least favored.

When viewed in isolation, each of these tests seems overwhelmingly compelling. However, if they are taken together as constituting necessary conditions for an adequate principle of distributive justice, then no adequate principle of distributive justice can avoid violating transitivity. A simple illustration demonstrates this result. In the table on the following page, test 1 would force us to choose B over A, test 2 would force us to choose C over B, test 3 would force us to choose D over C, test 4 would force us to choose E over D, but then test 1 would lead us from E in a cycle back to A.

The move from A to B is required by test 1, because the total is increased from 250 to 270, the minimum is increased from 10 to 11, and three of the five strata are better off. The move from B to C is required by test 2 because the minimum is increased from 11

A	B	C	D	E
10	11	12	8	9
30	30	31	42	50
50	50	51	52	50
70	80	52	54	51
90	100	53	55	52

to 12, equality is increased (the mean of the differences from the mean is lowered from 28.24 to 14.64), and three of the five strata are better off. The move from C to D is required by test 3 because the total increases from 199 to 211, equality increases (the mean of the differences from the mean decreases from 14.64 to 13.7), and four of the five strata are made better off. The move from D to E is required by test 4 because the total increases from 211 to 212, the minimum increases from 8 to 9, and equality increases (the mean of the differences from the mean decreases from 13.7 to 13.36).

The cycle is completed with the move from E back to A. This would be required by test 1 because the minimum increases from 9 to 10, the total increases from 212 to 250, and three of the five strata are clearly made better off. Hence, if an adequate principle of distributive justice must pass our four tests, such a principle, however it is formulated, must violate transitivity.[13]

Why should this be disturbing? Recent theories of justice have given us a picture of ideal theory whose task is to offer a systematic solution that holds without exception (which solves the priority problem in Rawls's language), and which we are to attempt, perhaps only asymptotically, to approach so far as circumstances permit. We are given a unified and coherent picture of an ideal solution, in which all the elements of moral conflict have been put in their appropriate priority relations. The task of public policy is to get us *as close* as possible, even if the best we can possibly do is an approximation.

The violation of transitivity, however, supports a quite different picture of the relations between ideal theory and public policy.[14] It undermines the notion of a unidirectional approach to the ideal, where it is both possible and desirable for each state of affairs to be "more just" than the last. Such a ranking may no longer be possible because "more just" is no longer a transitive relation. This new picture is the one I have termed "ideals without an ideal" conflicting principles, *without* a single unified vision to be gradually approached.[15] Each element of moral conflict, if taken seriously, would lead public policy in a quite different direction. This may force an intuitionistic balancing of particular cases to take policy, over time, in a cycle. Because progress in one direction may force us to retrace our steps along another valued dimension, patterns of moral conflict can eventually take us back to where we started.

If we do justice to the true complexities of the pure-distribution problem, we must take account of all four of the basic criteria I have proposed. But once we take this step, it seems difficult not to accept the four minimum tests. Either one or more of these tests must be abandoned, or the notion that "more just" is necessarily a transitive relation must be. On substantive grounds, the former option seems clearly indefensible, for it would expose us to condoning one or more of our four horror stories as an embodiment of justice. The alternative, which I accept, is that there are crucial impediments to any systematic theory of justice.

1.5 Assignment: Conflicting Visions of Equal Opportunity

Regardless of how we handle the problem of structure, we face a separate set of issues in the problem of assignment: *who gets what position* in the structure. The life histories of individuals can be affected as decisively by assignment as by structure. No viable theory of distributive justice could afford to ignore the issue of assignment. Imagine one that did so. Then imagine that it ranked some sequence of situations A, B, C, D as successive improvements in terms of structure (as judged, for example, by the percentage of the stated value held by each tenth of the society). If no criteria are offered for assignment, but only for structure, then the sequence A, B, C, D could, in theory, be compatible with *any* objectionable set of limitations in terms of assignment. We might, for example, imagine the introduction of a caste system, or of an underclass, or of an apartheid system of racial segregation. In principle, nothing prevents objectionable forms of assignment from coexisting with an improved structure—say, greater equality in income distribution, greater totals, or whatever your favorite structural principle may be.[1]

Suppose we are committed to the proposition that the sequence of situations A, B, C, D represents consistent improvement on structural grounds. Then let us imagine that we also have a sequence of structurally identical situations A', B', C', D' that involve the introduction of a caste system. The second group of situations is *structurally* identical in that the payoffs to positions under A', B', C', D' are precisely the same as under A, B, C, D. If we have no criteria for assignment, then the structural criteria that would commit us to the proposition that A, B, C, D is an improvement would equally commit us to the proposition that A', B', C', D' must be an improvement. But within liberal theory, it is hard to imagine that, whatever the structural improvements, they would insulate the overall result in the second sequence from decisive objections. The point of such examples is that no defensible, substantive theory of justice can afford to ignore the assignment problem. Otherwise, such theories are vulnerable to representing as justice the introduction of apartheid, the creation of a caste system, or the creation of a permanent underclass.

In order to deal with the assignment problem, we need a viable theory of equal opportunity.[2] We need some fair system for *rationing* the chance to be unequal whenever there are going to be inequalities. Of course, if we had perfect equality of outcomes, then there would be little need to develop a theory of assignment. But there are substantial inequalities in every modern developed society, capitalist or socialist. Furthermore, if a theory were to be systematic, it would have to rank outcomes as they *approached* whatever ideal was posited. Even advocates of perfect equality of outcomes would have to evaluate many differing *degrees* of inequality (in addition to the many other difficulties such advocates would face).

However, the difficulty in developing a viable theory of assignment is that the values that are implicated by the equal opportunity problem do not fit together into a unified picture of an ideal solution—even under the best conditions that might realistically be imagined for a modern, large-scale society. The issue can be posed as a "trilemma," a kind of dilemma with three corners.[3]

A first principle at issue in the trilemma is *merit:* that is, that there should be widespread procedural fairness in the evaluation of qualifications for positions. By "qualifications," I mean criteria that are job-related in that they fairly can be interpreted as indicators of competence or motivation for performance. Whether we are talking about scholastic aptitude tests, civil service exams, or the evaluation of publications for academic tenure decisions, we are all familiar with the culture of meritocracy. It is deeply embedded in the rationales and practices of most of our institutions.

But merit, by itself, is not enough. Arguments for this conclusion are dramatized by an example that I will borrow from Bernard Williams. Imagine a society dominated by a warrior class.[4] From generation to generation, the children of the present warriors become the new warrior class and rule in turn. At some point, critics achieve a major reform. "From now on," they announce, "there shall be equal opportunity, because we shall select the best warriors through a suitable competition." They then design an elaborate warrior-Olympics that selects the most competent warriors. The competition is held, but it makes virtually no difference to the outcome. The competition is won, overwhelmingly or perhaps entirely, by the children of the present warriors.

At first, to make it simple, let us imagine that the causal mechanism is quite obvious. The children of the present warrior class are both well trained and well nourished. The rest of the population, we might imagine, is on the verge of starvation. This fact turns the equal opportunity competition into a series of wrestling and boxing matches between three-hundred-pound sumo wrestlers and ninety-pound weaklings. Clearly, such a competition would not adequately realize equal opportunity. Note, however, that its results would be supported by the principle of merit. The sumo wrestlers, we can assume, really are better warriors than the weaklings. They are better warriors because they have had a lifetime of favorable conditions to develop the desired characteristics, while their rivals have had a lifetime of grossly unfavorable conditions to prepare for the same competition.

Real equal opportunity, it might be argued, must get at those conditions, for they determine the real terms of competition. The difficulty, of course, is that those conditions are protected by the liberty to confer benefits within the private sphere of family relations.

A more ambitious account of equal opportunity would add to merit the second requirement that there should be *equality of life chances*. By this I mean that we should not be able to predict the eventual places in society of new-born infants about whom we know certain arbitrary native characteristics such as family background, race, sex, religion, and ethnicity. This criterion captures what was objectionable about the warrior society.[5] We could (but should not be able to) predict the winners and losers in the competition merely by knowing the class into which they were born. Of course, this principle is widely violated in our own society, as various sociological studies demonstrate. If we know father's income or education, we can make good statistical predictions of the life chances among any cohort of new-born infants.[6]

The causal mechanism operating here is, to a large extent, simply a more discreet version of what was blatant in the warrior society example. Advantaged families differentially influence the development of qualifications, talents, motivations, and so forth in their children compared to less advantaged families. Those favorable causal conditions prepare such children to do compara-

Table 2. The Trilemma of Equal Opportunity

	Option 1	Option 2	Option 3
Merit	+	+	−
Equal life chances	−	+	+
Liberty in family	+	−	+

tively well in meritocratic competition. The principle of merit then becomes a mechanism for generating unequal life chances.

It is worth mentioning that in real life we do not fully realize any of these principles. But we attempt to approach each of them and, to one degree or another, we are successful (even though each principle might take public policy in a different direction). The point is that these criteria do not combine to make a unified and coherent scenario for the appropriate relations between liberty and equality, even under the best conditions that might realistically be imagined. Consider the three options pictured in table 2. Option 1 is exemplified clearly by the warrior society. Liberty within the family (the liberty to confer benefits) protects the process whereby advantaged families differentially benefit their children in the developmental competition so that, as a statistical matter, those children will achieve unequal life chances. Suppose we attempted to achieve both merit and equal life chances. Then, as pictured in option 2, we would have to somehow insulate children from the advantages their parents would wish to confer upon them. Perhaps some system of collectivized child rearing would do the job. Or perhaps a school system could be designed that would even out advantages and disadvantages from class background and block the exit options of private schools, tutoring in the home, and so on.[7] Whatever the precise details, any such scenario would require a significant sacrifice in liberty within the family. A third possibility would be to preserve liberty within the family, but to attempt to realize equal life chances independently of the principle of merit. This third option might be termed the "reverse discrimination" scenario because it would require that people be assigned to positions according to some pattern that departed systematically from merit. One strategy would be simply to hire less-qualified people from comparatively disadvantaged backgrounds. An alternative version of this scenario would assign all positions randomly, perhaps through a job lottery. Regardless of the details, any version of option 3 would require a significant sacrifice in merit (and in the values promoted by meritocracy—that is, procedural fairness and efficiency).

Clearly, each of our three scenarios is a horror story. Achieving any two of our principles precludes achieving the third—under any realistic scenario of favorable conditions.[8] It is as if we had a three-cornered stool, but only two legs available to hold it up. Even after we prop up any two sides, lack of the third leg is enough to undermine or destabilize the whole structure.

One reasonable response to this pattern of conflict would be to trade off these three principles in particular cases, but to avoid any systematic attempt to fully realize any of them, given the cost in competing principles. Such a position would, of course, be an example of what now is commonly termed "intuitionism"—the trading off of competing principles in particular cases without any systematic solution that can be fully realized.[9]

The intuitionist position is unpopular and dissatisfying, in part, because it is widely seen as vague in its prescriptions. However, such a charge is not entirely appropriate. Clearly, when there are strong gains to be made without a corresponding loss in competing principles,[10] or significant losses without a corresponding gain,[11] then there will be a case for choice of a policy option within the intuitionist framework. There will also be cases under other conditions, but the two possibilities just mentioned are the most obvious ones.

Whether or not we adopt an intuitionist response, the trilemma poses a significant obstacle to the ambitions of systematic theory.[12] Either we give up one of the pieces or we have to admit that the three components of the trilemma do not fit together, even under the best conditions that might realistically be imagined. If we are left with principles in intractable conflict, even under favorable conditions, then we do not have the kind of ideal solution—defined without moral conflict—aspired to by systematic theory. We do not have a solution to the priority problem. Instead, we have "ideals without an ideal."

1.6 Democracy and Progress

From the perspective of many theorists of justice, democracy is a narrower topic than distributive justice, because many theories would include the right to participate in political institutions as part of the more general distribution of primary goods or of fundamental rights and liberties in a just society.

Other theorists, however, would regard the conundrums of distribution just discussed as providing an argument for focusing on democratic *procedures* rather than on outcomes. Perhaps, if we cannot settle substantive questions on the merits, we can at least determine procedures in which each person's conscientious views get an appropriate hearing and an appropriate chance to influence a fair process of collective decision making.

The difficulty is that the democratic tradition has bequeathed to us a variety of fundamental values at stake in democratic procedures, a variety of ideal images of what an appropriate collective procedure might be. Because these ideal images cannot all be simultaneously realized, they require some hard choices. I believe that figure 1 provides a useful way of picturing the dimensions along which this democratic debate tends to range. I have labeled the north-south dimension "Madisonian" versus "majoritarian."[1] By Madisonian, I simply mean the degree to which the system includes impediments of one sort or another to popular majorities. These impediments are usually justified, at least in theory, by a desire to prevent tyranny of the majority.[2] Theoretically, the construction of impediments could go far beyond anything envisioned by Madison, so that, strictly speaking, he would not have advocated a perfectly "Madisonian" system. The term, however, provides a useful label for a basic motivation underlying checks and balances, the territorial, federal, and bicameral character of many American representative arrangements, and the operation of judicial review and other institutions that serve as impediments to majorities. Alternatively, movement south along the same dimension simply means that there are no effective impediments to popular majorities, so that the latter tend to get their way. As Dahl noted in a classic study, the American system is not very majoritarian. With a system of "minorities rule," it is somewhere in the upper-right-hand quadrant of figure 1.[3]

The east-west dimension is familiar in that it depicts the degree to which the system is indirect (representative) or direct (relying on the participation of members without the intermediary of representatives). For both the north-south and east-west dimensions, many difficult judgments of degree would be required to make any precise comparisons. The main usefulness of the diagram is that it captures a wide range of debate and a variety of conflicting images within a single space, so as to clarify how gains in one value can be expected to require costs in another.

The American system would fit somewhere in the upper-right-hand quadrant of figure 1. To varying degrees, most parliamentary systems would fit somewhere to the south of the American system. Depending on the impediments they offered to popular majorities, they might fit in the lower portion of the northeast quadrant or the upper portion of the southeast one.

The western positions in figure 1 are most usefully exemplified by certain extreme ideal images. Suppose, for example, that the Warner-Amex Qube system in Canton, Ohio, were used for actual government policy making. Each resident could respond immediately on any question posed on the two-way cable television system. Constant referendums would thus be feasible on all public questions. Some would regard instantaneous, majoritarian direct democracy as the perfect embodiment of a certain influential, ideal image. Others would regard it as a reductio ad

Figure 1. The Forms of Democracy

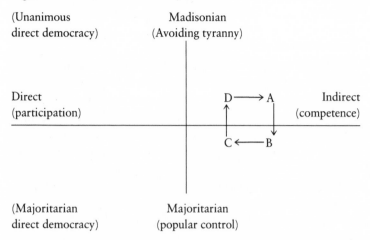

(Unanimous
direct democracy)

Madisonian
(Avoiding tyranny)

Direct
(participation)

Indirect
(competence)

(Majoritarian
direct democracy)

Majoritarian
(popular control)

absurdum. In any case, any extreme version would fit the lower-left-hand corner of the diagram.

By contrast, Robert Paul Wolff's proposal for unanimous direct democracy fits the extreme upper-left position.[4] The unanimity rule gives everyone a veto, providing the greatest possible protection against tyranny of the majority from new policies. It would not provide protection from omissions, but that is not an issue we need to pursue here.[5] The placement of unanimous direct democracy in the upper-left corner and the placement of majoritarian direct democracy in the lower-left corner illustrate how extreme direct systems (both implementable through a two-way cable system) can be crucially different on our north-south dimension.

In applying the limited liberalism model to my discussion of justice, I argued that there were not only fundamental conflicts in our ideal images, but also fundamental conflicts in our notions of moral progress intended to realize those ideal images. We can get the same cycles in applying democratic principles that we encountered in applying principles of justice. I do not have in mind here the cycles familiar to students of the classic voting paradox.

Cycles in *applying* particular democratic arrangements (say, majority rule) to policy or candidate choice can be distinguished from cycles in the design of the democratic arrangement itself. How a cycle of democratic reforms might arise can be charted in figure 1.

Imagine an American-style status quo somewhere in the upper-right-hand quadrant, at point A. Within the family of arguments loosely counted as democratic, a variety of reforms might be supported that would increase majority control over policy outcomes (proportional representation, reform of the electoral college, a less activist or independent judiciary, political control over the Federal Reserve, and so on). I am not advocating these reforms, but only pointing out that were they to come about they could move the entire system south, from A to B in the diagram.

From B we could imagine a second line of reform based on the argument that real democracy requires far greater direct participation. Even within the confines of a generally representative system, a number of reforms could be designed to move the system westward to a point such as C. Referendum and recall provisions and proliferation of direct primaries, town meetings, and other direct-governing arrangements within specific jurisdictions are some of the reforms that could be employed to move the system in this direction.[6]

From point C, the greater power in the hands of an aroused populace might well produce calls for protection against tyranny of the majority. Reinvigoration of the separation of powers, checks and balances, and an activist judiciary determined to protect various constitutional rights could move the system from C to a point such as D, directly north.

However, from point D arguments about the greater competence of representatives could be employed to undermine the earlier proliferation of referendums, primaries, town meetings, and other direct institutions, so as to return the system to our original status quo, point A. Each step in this scenario relies on values that are deeply rooted within the general family of democratic arguments.[7] Movement south depends on the emphasis of popular control, movement west on participation as a value in itself, movement north on the prevention of tyranny of the majority, and movement east on the greater competence of representatives. Depending on which of these partial images is given greater emphasis, one can go round and round. Each direction for reform has plausibility because of its emphasis on a distinctive value. However, the end result is the same kind of cycle that we encountered with distributive justice. Conflicting values in the identification of the ideal yield conflicting directions for moral progress—directions which, step by step, can take us back to where we started.

Focusing on democracy rather than on the full range of issues in the theory of justice does not provide a basis for avoiding either of the two basic problems we encountered earlier with systematic theory. We get neither a unified and coherent picture of the ideal nor an unambiguous route to moral progress. Rather than a systematic solution, the limited liberalism model is a more plausible interpretation of the moral complexities at stake in democratic theory, just as it is in the theory of justice.

Despite these limitations, the move to proceduralism as a response to substantive difficulties has merit, as we will see in part 3. However, more is required than a formal proceduralism based merely on the character of democratic institutions. Consideration of procedures in the context of all the background conditions for liberty of political culture will provide the basis for more ambitious conclusions.

Part Two

■■■■■■■■■■■■■■■■■■■■■■■■■■■■■■■■■■►

Strategies of Reconstruction

2.1 Criteria for an Acceptable Theory

If I am correct about the impediments to systematic versions of liberalism, where does that leave efforts to reconstruct liberal theory? Perhaps the aspirations of systematic theory demand too much. It may be possible to define criteria for an acceptable theory, criteria which it is possible for some versions of liberal theory to fulfill, but which are, nevertheless, far less ambitious than the requirements for systematic theory.

I propose that we consider four criteria for an acceptable theory of the first principles of a liberal state. Such a theory, at the least, should provide explicit grounds for satisfying these criteria:

1. It should *differentiate* among alternatives: it should provide an explicit basis for determining, if only incompletely, which states are better than other states, *selecting one or a few most preferred states* from a plausible construction of the feasible set. There are two crucial ways in which the theories considered here fail this criterion. They can be distinguished as:

 (a) *vacuousness:* a theory can fail to differentiate by legitimating all (or virtually all) the realistic possibilities;
 (b) *blind alleys:* a theory can fail to differentiate by ruling out all the realistic possibilities.

Vacuous theories legitimate too much; blind-alley theories legitimate too little. We will find that some forms of consent theory turn out to be vacuous. And if we assume, as I do, that we live in a world of states, one obvious way a theory could produce blind alleys is through philosophical anarchism (ruling out all the realistic possibilities).

These are not the only possible ways of failing criterion 1. A theory might, for example, offer no prescriptions whatsoever. However, these are the two ways that will play a role in our argument, so they are worth distinguishing.

Political philosophy *fails to be prescriptive* if it tells us either that all the possibilities are absolutely unacceptable or that they are all equally acceptable. In failing either criterion 1(a) or 1(b), political philosophy basically would be telling us that there was nothing to choose from among the alternatives. Theories failing these criteria would hold that, even as a matter of aspiration, no distinctions need to be made and no guidance needs to be offered about the most basic differences among political systems. If these minimal criteria cannot be satisfied, then in an important sense the subject would have nothing to offer. I am assuming that an adequate theory must, at the least, make some distinctions among states and, in that sense, be prescriptive.

2. An acceptable theory should be *individually binding*. For each person subject to its authority, the state should have an explanation for why *that* person is obligated to uphold the regime. This criterion can be broken down into two parts:

(a) The scope of the individually binding requirement must be *universal* for those subject to its authority.

(b) The manner must be particular or satisfy the particularity requirement; that is, the citizen must not be equally obligated to uphold regimes other than his own as part of his political obligation.[1]

Legitimate states hold that individuals are obligated to uphold and obey their authority. The basic idea of criterion 2 is merely that the explanation for that obligation should apply to all those who must comply with the obligation. Since part of the very notion of having a state is that the state apply its authority universally within a given territory, the individually binding character of its obligations must apply universally throughout its territory.

The last part of criterion 2, the particularity requirement, is based on the notion that states have a claim on the loyalty of their citizens—a claim that is not equally satisfied for those citizens by any number of other states with similar characteristics. Of course, those other states, if they are legitimate, may make similar claims on *their* citizens. Just as I have obligations to my mother that I do not have to total strangers, no matter how similar to my mother those strangers may be, I have obligations to my state, if it is a legitimate state, that I do not have to any number of other states, no matter how similar to my state those states may be. If I am a citizen of state X, it is *my* state in the sense that I owe special obligations to it. I am assuming that if a theory of the first principles of a liberal state purports to explain the obligations of citizens to support it, then the special character of those political obligations needs to be accounted for.

3. An acceptable theory should solve or deal successfully with the *jurisdiction problem*. By this I mean that the fundamental basis a theory offers for its prescriptions should not provide rival theories (offering rival prescriptions) with grounds for claiming jurisdiction over the result—grounds for claiming that their prescriptions have the same justification. Such jurisdiction problems undermine the sense in which a theory can be taken to solve anything. If, for example, rival courts claim jurisdiction over the same issue, the mere fact that each might give us a kind of impartial decision does not help us to resolve the issue until we find some way to resolve, in turn, the jurisdictional conflicts among the courts' claims to decide. We will see that the rivalries among theoretical "decision procedures" pose a similar problem, leaving us with no court or decision procedure for choosing among them.

4. An acceptable theory should satisfy criteria 1–3 without

falling into *indoctrination problems*. The manner of establishing obligations and their acceptance should not be subject to a de-legitimating charge that people were brainwashed or coercively molded so as to support the regime in the required way. We need, of course, a more detailed, constructive account of what would constitute not being brainwashed or coercively molded. This problem will detain us later at some length.

These are criteria which a liberal theory of the state must satisfy if it is to offer authoritative prescriptions—at the levels of both social and individual choice. The key social-choice question is: Which states are better than others? The key individual-choice question is: Why are individuals within a state bound to support the answer to the social-choice question? To deal with the social-choice question, an acceptable theory should differentiate among alternatives so as to satisfy criterion 1. To deal with the individual-choice question, members should be bound to uphold the social-choice response so as to satisfy criterion 2. To deal adequately with both of these questions, a theory must also confront criterion 3: if a theory's implications are to be authoritative, they must avoid jurisdiction problems; that is, they must avoid providing a fundamental basis for rival theories to provide incompatible prescriptions. Theories bedeviled by jurisdiction problems undermine their own authority. Finally, indoctrination problems must also be avoided if the theory's prescriptions are to be authoritative; if their apparent authoritativeness rests on collective brainwashing, then they are subject to obvious, delegitimating arguments. Hence, a theory needs to satisfy all four of our criteria if it is to provide an authoritative basis for choice at both the social- and individual-choice levels.

Most of part 2 will juxtapose these criteria with a scheme for classifying the basic strategies available to liberal theory for establishing its first principles. I will argue that all but one of the strategies can be expected to fail one or more of the criteria just proposed. This argument will set the stage for part 3, which proposes a constructive strategy that does purport to satisfy all of these criteria.

2.2 Beyond Intuitionism

Our first criterion challenges us to decide whether a theory can distinguish among the range of relevant alternatives. It requires that an acceptable version of liberal theory provide an explicit basis for distinguishing the morally preferred political arrangement (or a limited class of such arrangements) from most of its serious rivals. By "serious rivals" I mean political alternatives within some plausible construction of the feasible set, and for which significant philosophical claims have been advanced.

Of course, what is meant by "liberalism" or "liberal theory" is itself a matter of considerable dispute. We can generally distinguish two approaches to this problem. One approach would classify normative theories or ideologies as "liberal" in terms of *what* they prescribe, while another approach would classify them in terms of *how* they prescribe it. The first approach relies on the substantive prescriptions resulting from a theory, while the second relies on the kinds of arguments employed by a theory to support its substantive prescriptions.

The first strategy is exemplified by Maurice Cranston's quip: "A liberal, I suppose one could say, is a person who believes in liberty, as a nudist is a person who believes in nudity."[1] As liberals are those who believe in liberty, liberal theories, on this view, are those which offer systematic justification or support for liberty. By contrast, the second strategy would identify as "liberal" those theories which employ a certain mode of argument. An example is Ronald Dworkin's claim that "a certain conception of equality, which I shall call the liberal conception of equality, is the nerve of liberalism."[2] Dworkin means by equality a certain limitation on the arguments which it is appropriate for the state to employ in justifying its policies.[3] Whatever their other differences, Rawls's theory of justice, Ackerman's notion of "neutral dialogue," and the recent attempts to reconstruct utilitarianism all rely on a foundational conception of impartiality or equal consideration as a strategy for deriving the first principles of a liberal state.[4]

We need not decide the question here whether liberalism is best defined in terms of its substantive conclusions or in terms of its modes of argument for those conclusions. The position I will develop can plausibly be classified as "liberal" on either account. On the one hand, its centerpiece will be an attempt to justify the political liberties of thought, belief, and association—prescriptions that have long been at the core of whatever substantive consensus liberalism has achieved. On the other hand, my argument for liberty will depend on recognizably liberal methodological assumptions. It will, in fact, be based on a claim about the conditions under which certain forms of moral evaluation would be possible in a liberal state.

Why do our criteria require an "explicit" basis? By this I mean that criteria must be offered spelling out the proposed priorities. Relying solely on "intuitionism" is not enough. The intuitionist is committed to a plurality of principles without any clear weights or priority rules and without any method for resolving conflicts among them. The label "intuitionist" indicates that a person has no further explication of the trade-offs to which he is committed in particular cases. Intuitionism is, in an important sense, the absence of a theory.[5]

However, suppose there were a very decisive intuitionist who could always select his preferred alternative from a list within the feasible set. Would this ability to determine preferred alternatives satisfy our criteria? It would still fall short because the basis for selection—if it were truly intuitionist—would defy further explanation. In this connection, we should distinguish what might be called *systematic intuitionism* from the *unsystematic* variety that fails criterion 1 (see section 2.1 above). Some writers, most notably Brian Barry, have experimented with indifference curves for the trade-offs between fundamental principles such as liberty and equality.[6] If the trade-offs between all competing principles can be fully captured by a series of clearly ranked indifference curves, let us call the position that results systematic intuitionism. This position does not represent the absence of a theory providing priority rules. Rather, it embodies a complex statement of a single clear priority rule: Prefer alternatives on the most highly ranked indifference curve achievable. Provided that all of the moral considerations are adequately captured by the indifference-curve analysis, there is no indeterminacy about how to evaluate any alternatives that may present themselves. Systematic intuitionism of this kind is not really intuitionism, precisely because it is systematic. It is simply the use of a distinctive device for stating a complex principle that is supposed to have clear priority over all competing considerations.

It is the unsystematic variety of intuitionism—where the moral complexity of possible trade-offs has not been reduced to a series of ranked indifference curves—that represents a basic challenge to the theoretical aspirations of liberal political philosophy. Unsystematic intuitionism leaves us without guidance. We are stuck with incommensurable, conflicting factors whose relations to one another are regarded as a matter of unsettlable dispute. At most we may know which factors to weigh. However, even the metaphor of "weighing," standard though it is, is misleading. The absence of any common metric for comparing incommensurable considerations is itself a central part of the problem.[7] It is the mysteriousness of intuitionism, leaving each of us to confront conflicting ultimate principles without further guidance, that violates the "explicitness" requirement of our criteria.

Yet the main thrust of my argument thus far has been that unsystematic intuitionism is unavoidable. Liberal theory, in particular, must inevitably assign a primary role to intuitionism; it is beyond any reasonable construction of its capacities to produce a full-fledged systematic alternative.[8] Such a conclusion will not only be disappointing to many, but it will also appear to foreclose completely the prospects that any construction of liberalism will satisfy our criteria for an acceptable theory. However, this pessimistic conclusion is mistaken. As we will see in part 3, other strategies hold promise for satisfying our criteria despite all the negative and limiting conclusions developed here.

Why should we be concerned with these criteria? Why, for example, should we require an explicit basis for selecting a morally preferred state from the feasible set (criterion 1)? Without passing even this minimal test, liberal theory seems to be nothing more than a bundle of conflicting principles offering us no definite direction, even for our aspirations. As Bruce Ackerman has argued, a successful case for the morally preferred state would dispatch, at a stroke, the charge that liberalism, philosophically, is nothing more than "a pitiful blob of self-contradiction."[9] It is for this reason that his theory, along with the other main attempts to revive liberal theory, adopts a version of this criterion as its main order of business.

If a theory's prescriptions are so easy to fulfill that most states already satisfy them, then it fails our first criterion because it is vacuous. On the other hand, if its prescriptions are impossibly difficult to fulfill, so that all the serious possibilities are ruled out, then it fails our first criterion by landing us in a blind alley— by limiting its prescriptions to possibilities that fall outside the feasible set. What we require is some basis for distinguishing the morally preferred state from most or all of the rival alternatives that deserve to be taken seriously.

Of course, we can only consider the range of alternatives informally. There are always new possibilities to be imagined or invented, new objections to be weighed, new implications of familiar principles in new situations. Given these complexities, it seems quixotic to expect to narrow the range of possibilities to one preferred alternative.

Furthermore, the alternatives for which serious philosophical claims have been advanced will vary from one period to another. There will be similar variation in our understanding of the range of feasible alternatives and of the probable collective and individual responses to various empirical conditions. I need to assume only that the state of debate is *robust:* that a wide variety of alternatives is advanced with sophistication from a wide variety of moral and ideological perspectives. These criteria are really a short-hand device for assessing what one proposal or another contributes to the current state of theoretical debate.[10] They are merely a way of formulating the problem: What does any given proposal contribute to the state of debate about the fundamental alternatives available to liberal theory?

Our question is: Can liberalism produce any definite conclusions about its moral priorities, at least when favorable conditions are assumed? If these definite conclusions do not narrow the alternatives to one, they should eliminate everything but a limited subclass whose members are essentially equal in their realization of significant prescribed values. We should be able to characterize why and how the members of this subclass are equivalent and how they are, together, distinctive compared to the full range of rival possibilities.

What are the ground rules for determining the feasible set of alternatives? I will follow Rawls and assume the favorable conditions of what he calls "ideal theory."[11] I will assume good-faith efforts at strict compliance with the principles proposed, both in the present and in the relevant recent past.[12] Furthermore, I will assume only "moderate scarcity" and not the extreme scarcity of resources that blights many countries today in the third (and fourth) world.[13]

The first task for liberal theory is to prescribe a preferred solution under an optimistic scenario of conditions. Unresolvable dilemmas or troubling indeterminacies would not be surprising under situations of tragic conflict or of extreme scarcity. But acceptable versions of liberal theory should be able to differentiate the most preferred alternative (or a subclass of equivalents) under favorable conditions when they are insulated from these complications.

2.3 Political Thought Experiments

Recent liberal theory has been distinctive for its thought experiments: transporting us to an imaginary situation or transforming our motivation so that we choose political principles under conditions in which only the morally relevant factors bear on the decision. Two kinds of imaginary devices have been employed—changes in the situation of choice and changes in the motivation (within which I include filtering requirements by which only certain motivations are selected, while the rest are prevented from bearing on the decision).[1] When the motivation for choosing principles has been altered or filtered in the interests of impartiality, I will classify it as "refined"; when people choose, or are imagined to choose, with unaltered motivation (as, realistically, we would expect them to do in actual life), I will classify those motivations as "brute." When the situation for choosing principles is the one in which those who must abide by the principles live together as an ongoing enterprise, I will classify it as an "actual-" choice situation. When the situation for choice is an imaginary one, held to be morally relevant, but not the situation in which those who must abide by the principles must live together as an ongoing enterprise, I will term it "hypothetical."[2] These distinctions are represented in figure 2.

An example of category 1 is offered by actual-consent theory. According to this approach, if people consent in real life, they are obligated to uphold the state; if enough (whatever that means) do actually consent, then the state is held to be legitimate and, somehow, everyone is obligated.[3] Motivation and situation are as we find them. Neither is subjected to some transformation in the name of impartiality or moral relevance.

Figure 2. Decision Procedures

Motivations	Situations	
	Actual	Hypothetical
Brute	1	2
Refined	4	3

Category 2 transforms the situation for choice but not the motivation. The state of nature in Robert Nozick's *Anarchy, State and Utopia* is a good example. We are to take the question whether there should be a state at all to the "best anarchic situation one reasonably could hope for."[4] The motivations of people in this state of nature are not altered; they must be given a realistic construction. We are to assume that some would join protection associations voluntarily; others would choose to be independent. As we will see later, a major problem facing Nozick's argument is whether his scenario for the minimal state is compatible with a realistic construction of people's preferences—whether, in particular, independents would be fully "compensated" in being forced to join the state.[5]

Category 3 transforms not only the situation, as in category 2, but also the motivations for choice in that situation. For example, in Rawls's original position, agents are to choose principles of justice so as to maximize their shares of primary goods without knowing who in particular they will turn out to be once the veil of ignorance is lifted. They are endowed with an abstract preference for primary goods regardless of the details of their actual life plans; they will know the latter only after the principles of justice have been chosen.[6] In Ackerman's spaceship dialogues, entrants to a new world argue over the distribution of "manna" through a filtering device for relevant arguments (the "neutrality" assumption). The perfectly sympathetic spectator of the classical utilitarians has both an imaginary vantage point (omniscience) and a postulated motivation (he reproduces in himself every pain and pleasure in the world and, hence, will prefer states of the world that maximize the net balance of pleasure over pain).

Of the possibilities presented in figure 2, the basic difficulty with the top-row categories (1 and 2) is that they are subject to indoctrination problems, while the basic difficulty with the right-column categories (2 and 3) is that they are subject to jurisdiction problems. The only possibility offering a prospect for avoiding both is category 4 (the left-bottom quadrant). My proposal is an instance of that approach.

A similar point can be made about our other criteria. Consider the varieties of actual-consent theory that fit in category 1. The problem with universal express-consent will turn out to be that it violates criterion 1(b) in section 2.1. As Wolff shows, to re-quire that everyone expressly agree to the state is to require the blind alley of philosophical anarchism. Alternatively, the problem with universal tacit consent will turn out to be that it violates criterion 1(a). In order to get everyone committed to support-ing the state, the criteria for consent are loosened to the point that virtually any state can claim universal consent. Such an ap-proach produces vacuous results by legitimating virtually every-thing. Furthermore, the problem with nonuniversal tacit consent will turn out to be that it violates criterion 2(a). Within the con-fines of actual-consent theory, those who don't consent have no reason to believe themselves obligated to uphold the law. The individually-binding criterion is not satisfied because the obliga-tion is not universal. By contrast, the problem with *hypothetical* contract theories will turn out to be that while they may satisfy cri-teria 1 and 2, they violate criterion 3. They are inherently subject to jurisdictional challenge.

But in hinting at how some main strategies violate one or another of our criteria, we are jumping ahead of ourselves. Let us turn to each category in greater detail. The rest of this book is largely organized around the possibilities presented in figure 2. The difficulties in categories 1 and 2 will be our subject in sections

2.4 and 2.5. The difficulties in category 3, the main focus of recent theoretical activity in liberalism, will be our subject in sections 2.6 and 2.7. Last, the opportunity represented by category 4 will be our subject in part 3.

2.4 Category 1: The Quest for Consent

In the simplest of our four categories (box 1 in figure 2), we are dealing with brute preferences and an actual, rather than a hypothetical, situation. My basic claim about the "brute" categories (whether actual as in box 1 or hypothetical as in box 2) will be that they are rendered vulnerable to indoctrination problems by their lack of a refinement mechanism for purging motivations of bias. Their vulnerability takes the form of a dilemma: nothing in the strategy rules out extreme efforts at indoctrination, but without such indoctrination, the strategy cannot plausibly be interpreted as leading to determinate results that satisfy our other criteria, in particular, criteria 1 and 2—the requirements that our theory be nonvacuous, that it avoid blind alleys, and that it produce obligations that are individually binding. Together, these criteria require some differentiated solutions and bind us to them.

The basic problem with category 1 is that it is vulnerable, generically, to indoctrination problems. Furthermore, each version of category 1 will fail one aspect or another of our first two criteria.

Recall that all four categories concern decision situations (real or imagined) for justifying a state, either by choosing the state (or its basic character) explicitly or by choosing the principles that justify it. For theories in each of our four categories, it is important to ask whether the choice in question must be unanimous, and what kind of agreement or consent is required of each participant (whether or not the notion of agreement is interpreted strictly, an issue I will attempt to refine further below).

With these distinctions in mind, my basic point about category 1 theories will be that they are, as a general matter, subject

Figure 3. Options in Category 1

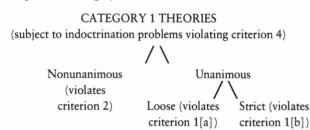

CATEGORY 1 THEORIES
(subject to indoctrination problems violating criterion 4)

Nonunanimous   Unanimous
(violates
criterion 2)   Loose (violates   Strict (violates
criterion 1[a])   criterion 1[b])

to indoctrination problems. In addition, they are vulnerable to violations of one or another of our other criteria, as shown in figure 3.

Theories fitting category 1 either require unanimous agreement or support, or they do not. If they do not, then they are vulnerable to criterion 2 because they lose their individually binding character. If they do require unanimous agreement, then if that agreement is loose, my claim will be that it leads to violations of criterion 1(a), by producing vacuous results. It legitimates too much to differentiate among states. On the other hand, if the notion of agreement required is strict, then it leads to violations of criterion 1(b) by, in effect, ruling out all the possibilities and creating a blind alley.

I will attempt to illustrate these difficulties by briefly examining some particular theories exemplifying each alternative. A good example of a theory requiring actual unanimous agreement in the strict sense is Robert Paul Wolff's argument for a system of "unanimous direct democracy" where "every member of the society wills freely every law which is actually passed." The result is that "he is only confronted as a citizen with laws to which he has consented."[1]

However, as Wolff rightly admits, this solution "requires the imposition of impossibly restrictive conditions which make it applicable only to a rather bizarre variety of actual situations." The reason is that we must imagine continuing perfect agreement on all issues of public decision: "Since by the rule of unanimity a single negative vote defeats any motion, the slightest disagreement over significant questions will bring the operations of the society to a halt. It will cease to function as a political community and fall into a condition of anarchy (or at least into a condition of non-legitimacy; a de facto government may of course emerge and take control)." [2]

Given a realistic construction of the variety of preferences in a modern large-scale society, it is implausible to suppose that unanimous voluntary agreement will maintain itself. Once it breaks down, the prescription that results—namely, anarchism—is irrelevant to our problem of differentiating among states. For this reason, the requirement for unanimous consent in the strict sense can be taken as a violation of criterion 1(b), the no-blind-alleys requirement.

Of course, we might imagine a coercive system of collective brainwashing that produced near-perfect homogeneity of preferences, perhaps on the order approaching what would be required to support continuing unanimity in the large-scale nation-state. But such a system, even if it were successful, would not produce unanimous voluntary agreement. It could realistically be maintained only through systematic manipulation and coercion, issues to which we will return in part 3. In any case, a choice situation that requires coercive collective thought control to support its conclusions exemplifies the other horn of our dilemma: its results are delegitimated because they rest on indoctrination, thereby violating criterion 4.

Suppose, however, that the no-agreement point were interpreted not as the breakdown or cessation of the legitimate state (as in the passage quoted above), but simply as the continuation of the status quo combined with nonpassage of whatever policy produced disagreement. This possibility brings into relief some important differences between hypothetical- and actual-choice situations. We can plausibly interpret an appropriately designed hypothetical situation as a one-time-only event with moral relevance for whatever population the situation is invoked. All of those who are born or enter the society at whatever time can participate in the very same thought experiment: they can all imagine themselves in Rawls's original position, or in Ackerman's neutral dialogues, or they can all delegate the choice of principles to the same imaginary utilitarian spectator. There is no problem of past actual participation not applying to new members (including newly born ones) as compared to old ones; no one actually participated in any of these imaginary scenarios, in any case.

By contrast, actual-choice theories face the problem that new members are born, old ones die; new members arrive, old ones leave. What has unanimous support at one time may not have it at another. Even if, somehow, the laws on the books were passed unanimously, there is no guarantee, as time goes on, that each person will be "only confronted as a citizen with laws to which he has consented." What relevance does the unanimous consent of past generations have to him? He is "subject to the will of another" just as much as if he were an outvoted minority in a decision taken in the present.[3]

A related point is that policy omissions (failures to adopt new policies) can be just as salient and burdensome as policy commissions (the adoption of new policies). There may be unexpected emergencies, new issues, new requirements for action. The most important issues of the moment may never have been previously decided, or even formulated as matters for public debate. The unanimity rule, by giving everyone a veto, holds each of us hostage to the will of any other person who might block the required action.[4]

As Wolff makes clear, the special attraction of the unanimity rule is that it defines a system where "every member . . . wills freely every law which is actually passed." As a result, he has "consented" to every law with which he is "confronted." However, once both new issues and new members are taken into account, it becomes implausible to claim that continuing whatever policies were previously passed preserves unanimous support, at least for those policies. New generations were not party to those earlier decisions, and the consequences of policy omissions are not consequences to which they have consented.[5] The breakdown of unanimous consent confronts such a theory with violations of criterion 2. If I have not actually consented to such a law, how, within the confines of this kind of actual consent theory, am I supposed to be bound to uphold it? Wolff abandons this option because it is not truly compatible with individual autonomy. Because his assumptions lead him to take strict unanimous choice seriously, he is led to anarchism and, hence, in our scheme, to violations of criterion 1(b) (the blind-alley criterion).

The basic point is that if we interpret the unanimity rule strictly, for an actual, ongoing society rather than for a one-time-only hypothetical situation, it does not provide the basis for differentiating choices among nation-states. Rather, Wolff is correct to conclude that the rule, when taken seriously, implies anarchism. Alternatively, if unanimous agreement is given a looser interpretation, it is possible to escape anarchism and provide a basis for morally acceptable states. The difficulty is that to get continuing unanimous agreement under realistic conditions, agreement or consent has to be defined so loosely that it provides no basis for differentiating conclusions. Rather, agreement defined so loosely would legitimate a host of states indiscriminately. Relying on loose unanimous agreement will lead, if taken seriously, to violations of criterion 1(a), the nonvacuousness requirement.

The difficulties that lie down this road are suggested by Locke's loosening of what we have been calling strict agreement in the definition of tacit consent, as eventually developed in the *Second Treatise:*

> The difficulty is, what ought to be look'd upon as a tacit Consent. . . . And to this I say that every Man that hath any Possession or Enjoyment of any part of the Dominions of any Government doth thereby give his tacit Consent, and is as far forth obliged to Obedience to the laws of that Government, during such Enjoyment, as any one under it; whether this his Possession be of Land to him and his Heirs for ever, or a Lodging only for a Week; or whether it be barely travelling freely

on the Highway; and, in Effect, it reaches as far as the very being of anyone within the Territories of that Government.[6]

Once tacit consent is defined so broadly that receiving any benefit—simply using the king's highways, or even "the very being of anyone within the Territories of that Government"—counts as consent, it does become plausible to claim that the conditions for unanimous tacit consent can be continually fulfilled under realistic conditions in a modern large-scale nation-state. So long as someone has not explicitly rejected the state's legitimacy—and attempted to leave the country so as to relieve himself of all obligations to it—he can be counted within the framework of tacit consent defined so loosely. As Hanna Pitkin concludes in her critique of this doctrine of tacit consent, few states would be ruled out by this strategy: "Being within the territory of the worst tyranny in the world seems to constitute tacit consent to it and create an obligation to obey it. Only physical withdrawal—emigration—and the abandoning of all property frees you from that obligation; there is no such thing as tacit *dissent*" (emphasis in original).[7]

The basic difficulty is that when agreement is interpreted loosely, it is plausible to include everyone in the state in the agreement, but virtually no state is ruled out; by contrast, when agreement is interpreted strictly, it becomes implausible to include everyone in the agreement, so virtually every state is ruled out (by the requirement for unanimity). Unanimous actual agreement is far too demanding a condition to provide the basis for conclusions *differentiating* among modern nation-states under realistic conditions. At the very least, realistic conditions will require that there be numerous complex questions affecting large numbers of people who have conflicting interests at stake, and conflicting conscientious opinions about the result. Under such conditions, we cannot expect perfect unanimity to maintain itself voluntarily over time. Inevitably, disagreements will arise, both about what decisions ought to be made and about how people ought to make them.

To require continuing unanimity in the strict sense would effectively rule out the modern nation-state; to require continuing unanimity in a sense loose enough to legitimate some modern nation-states would legitimate too many to be useful for our purposes. Within the confines of unanimous-actual-choice theory, we are faced with violating either criterion 1(a) or criterion 1(b)— in effect, the choice of legitimating too much or of legitimating too little. One alternative, of course, would be to abandon the unanimity requirement entirely.

However, *nonunanimous* versions of category 1 only seem to encounter additional difficulties. Unanimous agreements, at least when undertaken voluntarily, appear to bind everyone who is party to them and, in that sense, provide a certain immunity from further controversy. If acts of consent produce obligations in the way that promises do, then if everyone has consented, everyone is obligated. We have at least some grounds for committing everyone to whatever policies and/or system was consented to—regardless of whatever else they might advocate.[8]

This basis for countering rival prescriptions seems to vanish once unanimity breaks down (or if it is never achieved). Why should *I* be obligated because *you* consented, any more than I would be obligated because you promised? Even if my view is a minority one, until we get some justification for submitting the matter to majority rule (or to some other nonunanimous decision rule), my view cannot be dispatched by citing the greater numbers who support a rival view.[9] The numerically predominant view has often been morally suspect and may well be in the future.[10]

Consider what happens to actual-consent theory once the inevitability of nonconsent on the part of many is acknowledged —once, in other words, the quest for unanimity is abandoned. Joseph Tussman's position offers a good illustration. He argues that obligations to the state must derive from the model of a "voluntary organization"; his argument builds on the view "that obligations are, or even must be, voluntarily assumed." However, he is forced to confront the fact that

> any description of a body politic, like the United States, would have to recognize that there are some, or many, "citizens" who could not be

described as having consented. There is no point to resorting to fiction to conceal this fact. It makes more sense to speak of the social compact as an ideal which is never completely realized. Non-consenting adult citizens are, in effect, like minors who are governed without their own consent. The period of tutelage and dependence is unduly prolonged. And this . . . is a failure of political education.[11]

Tussman has simply attempted to work through the implications of the primacy that "consent of the governed" (conceived as actual, voluntary agreement) has in American political culture. But the result is an incoherent theory of political obligation because of what he calls the "shrinkage" of the body politic to a subgroup of the politically self-conscious. Their agreement cannot obligate the others any more than my promise could obligate you.

If there were some magic percentage beyond which support was widely, and justifiably, acknowledged to be binding on everyone, then the shrinkage problem would not undermine nonunanimous actual agreements as a fundamental basis for political principles. But there is no such magic percentage. It is certainly not 50 percent plus 1 (majority rule). Majorities, like other winning coalitions, can sanction or support unjustified and drastic actions whose consequences are felt by losing coalitions. From Madison, Tocqueville, and Mill to the present, avoiding the possibilities for tyranny of the majority has been one of the central tasks of modern democratic theory.[12] Increasing the percentage required for approval does not solve the problem; it only makes passage of new policies or legislation more difficult—which means more people may be frustrated by having to experience the consequences of an unwanted status quo.[13] Of course, once a system has been established, those who are already bound to it for whatever reason may then find that they are also bound to uphold majoritarian-approved results from which they dissent. But we are probing arguments about the fundamental issue of what binds them to the system in the first place. What these points amount to, at bottom, is that nonunanimous-actual-consent theory, in avoiding the problems with criteria 1(a) and 1(b), faces a fundamental challenge in criterion 2. If only some people consent, then it seems exceedingly problematical that those who do not consent would be individually bound to uphold the result.

It is arguable that actual-consent theory encounters these difficulties because it is being employed to solve too much. Consent is deeply rooted in Western, especially American, political ideology. In the Declaration of Independence we are told about "Governments . . . deriving their just powers from the consent of the governed." By being employed to solve "too much," I mean that consent theory is being employed to address two separate questions simultaneously: Which states are more legitimate or morally appropriate than others? and Why am I (or any other member) obligated to obey or uphold the authority of my state? In other words, consent theory is commonly applied (a) to the social-choice problem of evaluating and comparing states and (b) to the individual-choice problem of establishing one's linkage to the state through political obligation. There is, as we will see in part 3, a natural connection between these two questions. But actual-consent theory provides too slim a basis for resolving both simultaneously.

The difficulty is that if consent is to serve as a self-sufficient response to the individual-choice problem of political obligation, it is rendered virtually useless as a self-sufficient response to the social-choice problem of comparing states. The reason for this conundrum is, basically, that if actual consent is to provide a basis for everyone's political obligations to the state, then everyone must have consented. Something approaching unanimous or universal consent is required. But if unanimous consent is given a strict interpretation, then, as Wolff illustrates, virtually all states are ruled out. On the other hand, if unanimous consent is given a loose interpretation—loose enough to apply to everyone, say, within the territory (so as to get them all obligated to obey the state)—then meaningful differentiations among states are lost (as we saw with Locke's loosening of tacit consent). It is always, of course, possible to abandon the unanimity requirement, but that would produce an incoherent theory of political obligation (one in which I am obligated because you consented). What this shows is that the aspiration overreaches to employ actual-consent theory simultaneously as the basis for both the social choice-problem of evaluating states and the individual-choice problem of his political obligation. Actual-consent theory certainly may have a role, but it cannot be employed to provide the sufficient conditions for the solution of both problems at the same time.[14]

By contrast, theories of hypothetical—as opposed to actual—consent may be employed for both problems. They can, in a sense, apply universally to everyone within a territory, while at the same time yielding differentiating conclusions. Rawls's theory of justice is a prime example. It purports to provide distinctive, significant conclusions and it ties those conclusions to a kind of consent— they are the conclusions we ourselves would supposedly reach, to the extent that we were rational and to the extent that we judged the problem under ideally fair conditions.

But Rawls's theory does not affect the conclusions just reached about actual-consent theory. In Rawls's theory, universal consent within the territory is achieved only through a scenario that departs from the limits of realism. The purely imaginary character of the scenario renders it vulnerable to jurisdiction problems from rival scenarios that also purport to tell us what we would, rationally, choose under fair or impartial conditions—but with slight variations in the notions of rationality or impartiality. As we will see below, any differentiating conclusions that result can easily be evaded by rival constructions of the hypothetical story. What we are terming category 3 theories such as Rawls's have the merit that they may satisfy criteria 1 and 2 but they are generically vulnerable to criterion 3, jurisdiction problems.

Returning to category 1 and variations on actual-consent theory, the nonunanimous-choice strategies ran into trouble because they employed consent as the basis for political obligation as well as for a theory of the legitimate state. Because they proposed that we regard everyone within the state's territory as obligated to it while, at the same time, admitting that not everyone had consented, an incoherent account of political obligation resulted, leading to violations of criterion 2.

But perhaps the basis for moral prescriptions in a given society is not every *individual's* consent but the collective, shared understandings of the society. While every single individual has not consented to those understandings, they are widely acknowledged and their status as shared conventions might arguably support their application to the society in question. In this way, some variation of nonunanimous-actual-consent theory might be employed for social-choice judgments about the legitimacy of the state without also being required for individual-choice judgments of political obligation. In a way, this option can be thought of as an attempt to employ nonunanimous-consent theory for the evaluation of the state, while relinquishing the previous ambition to provide a theory of political obligation as well (or at least one that relies on the analogy between acts of consent and promises).

Michael Walzer's argument in *Spheres of Justice* exemplifies this strategy.[15] Because it is the most sophisticated recent effort of this kind, it can usefully illustrate the difficulties in this general approach—brute actual-choice theories that are nonunanimous in their requirements.[16] Walzer's central claim is that there are qualitatively distinct "social goods" and that "internal" to our "shared understanding" of each good are criteria for its distribution within its own sphere. "Tyranny" occurs when a given good is distributed for reasons irrelevant to those criteria, typically through command over other goods (from another sphere) which are "dominant," such as capital. Thus, medieval Christians condemned the sin of simony, for example, because "the meaning of a particular social good, ecclesiastical office, excluded its sale and purchase."[17] Similar objections apply to prostitution and bribery; given certain "shared understandings" about how sexual gratification and political power are supposed to be distributed, the intrusion of money is a morally irrelevant determinant, one that perverts those shared understandings.

Walzer believes that a distinctive theory of justice can be developed from the mere fact of shared understandings about the appropriate spheres of each social good, combined with the requirement that these spheres be respected. "Justice is *relative* to social meanings" and, indeed, "in matters of morality, *argument simply is the appeal to common meanings*."[18] Obviously, everything depends on the "shared understandings" about each good and its respective sphere in a given culture. Walzer's book is organized around his list of goods: membership, security and welfare, money and commodities, office, hard work, free time, education, kinship and love, divine grace, recognition, and political power. Is this an exhaustive list? Would we all interpret our shared understandings about the spheres of justice this way? Others have proposed quite different lists of the primary social goods whose distribution defines the problem of justice. For the design of institutions, Rawls's list reduces to liberty, equal opportunity, and income and wealth.[19] Harold Lasswell, in a famous analysis, proposed power, enlightenment, wealth, well-being, skill, affection, rectitude, and deference.[20]

There are two main difficulties with this general strategy of appealing to shared (but not unanimously shared) understandings. The first is: how are we to decide between rival lists and rival understandings of their appropriate spheres? For Walzer, this issue seems relatively straightforward. It comes down to a problem of social anthropology—an investigation and interpretation of shared understandings about social goods and their boundaries in a particular culture. He treats the whole issue of choosing among rival notions in the same culture parenthetically: "(When people disagree about the meaning of social goods, when understandings are controversial, then justice requires that the society be faithful to the disagreements, providing institutional channels for their expression, adjudicative mechanisms, and alternative distributions.)"[21]

Yet there will also be good-faith disagreements about how (if at all) to resolve disagreements in good faith, how to design channels for political expression, and how to adjudicate disputes. We lack shared understandings of a methodological kind about how to interpret and choose among whatever shared understandings may actually exist in our culture. Except where there is complete agreement, rival notions each will have a foothold. For the theory to yield any determinate content, we would require criteria for choosing among rival accounts of our shared moral notions. Without such criteria, the theory is threatened with silence in the face of serious moral controversy. But such criteria cannot be developed without abandoning the reliance on relativism, on nothing more than the sheer fact of shared understandings.

Once the possibility of a manipulated or indoctrinated consensus is acknowledged, any claims that this kind of theory could satisfy criterion 2 are exploded. Unanimity about shared understandings is unrealistic and is not claimed by the theory. But then the issue arises: why should those who disagree be bound by the consensus? If there were machinery in the theory to give us confidence about how the consensus was arrived at, then perhaps there could be some basis for resolving this issue. But such machinery would, by definition, take us outside the confines of category 1 (the actual-brute category) because preferences would no longer be merely brute. There is no such machinery in Walzer's theory, nor could there be without some radical change in its basic character. But without such machinery, there are no grounds for binding dissenters to a consensus that is open to delegitimating charges of manipulation. Why should such dissenters defer to the consensus unless there are grounds for being confident in the greater rationality of its collective process? With such grounds, we would have a different kind of theory.[22] Without such grounds, we have no basis for responding to criterion 2.

What Walzer's relativism does to his attack on totalitarianism reveals a second major difficulty with the general strategy. Within this relativistic framework, there can be no criteria, except shared understandings within the culture, for the alteration and manipulation of that culture. It is for this reason that it is appropriate for us to treat Walzer's theory as a prime example of category 1, the reliance on brute-actual preferences ("brute" because there are no criteria for protecting or refining the formation of preferences; "actual" because it is the existing consensus which must provide the basis for argument).

The central political implication of the book is supposed to be the condemnation of totalitarianism. However, imagine a totalitarian regime that happens to succeed in the task that many have attempted—brainwashing its citizens into accepting a set of shared understandings about the proper sphere of its political power. Once such shared understandings are accepted, there are no grounds within the confines of relativism to condemn the regime. The expansion of political power onto virtually every other sphere of life (as the boundaries were previously drawn) cannot now constitute "tyranny," by definition, once that expansion is supported by the culture's shared understandings.[23] Thus, once an Orwellian regime operates perfectly, once it succeeds in totally manipulating its own political culture, its totalitarianism is transmuted into justice by the relativistic strategy of relying entirely on shared understandings. Rather than providing us with the ultimate grounds for condemning totalitarianism, this relativistic theory of justice has laid the groundwork for its defense—provided only that thought control and propaganda are sufficiently effective.

Many of the most disturbing cases of injustice and exploitation involve acceptance by the victims of the ideology rationalizing their victimhood. Provided that those ideologies are accepted within a given culture, a consistent relativism provides no grounds for contrary evaluation. The same argument that Barrington Moore applied to Untouchables, ascetics, and even some concentration camp victims can then be applied to entire regimes.[24] If an entire society is victimized by a totalitarian regime—but its members have been thoroughly brainwashed to accept these abuses of power as legitimate—then there are no grounds for condemnation within a consistent relativism. For such a theory, "tyranny" would have become "justice."

We require transcultural criteria for the alteration and permissible manipulation of moral cultures. But such criteria must do more than simply reflect whatever understandings happen to be shared within those cultures at a given time. The strategy I will propose in part 3 is, in part, a response to this problem because it focuses on the conditions under which values and preferences develop. Without criteria directed at this latter problem, actual-choice theories are vulnerable to the basic dilemma: either they fail to yield determinate implications or they yield determinate implications only by the kind of manufactured consensus that renders them vulnerable to indoctrination problems.

2.5 Category 2: Realistic Hypotheticals

In category 2 of figure 2, there is a morally relevant hypothetical story about the choice of the state or the choice of the first principles by which the state should be evaluated. The story is imaginary, but the people are realistic in a special sense: they are as we would find them in actual life under conditions where no refinement mechanisms have been employed to purge their motivations of bias or indoctrination. In this respect, the people are no different than they were in category 1. Brute preferences are combined with an imaginary story which, for some reason contended by the theorist, is morally relevant to us in that it bears on our evaluation of the state. As in category 1, my basic line of argument for category 2 will be that without indoctrination, brute preferences produce sufficient disagreements and indeterminacies that they lead to failures to differentiate (violating criterion 1), but that with indoctrination, they violate criterion 4.

I will focus on interpretations of category 2 that strive for unanimity or unanimous acceptability, at least in some sense. The agreement or consent of people might well vary in the extent to which it is strict or loose, but in constructing hypothetical stories with moral relevance, we need some basis for tying the authority of the result to everyone. Hypothetical, nonunanimous-brute theories would fail the individually-binding criterion (2), just as did the actual-choice versions of nonunanimous-brute theory. When unanimous acceptability is not achieved, we have the same problem of justifying the decision rule by which those who disagree can justifiably be overruled or ignored. If there is no further step at which unanimous acceptability is achieved, or if no refinement mechanism exists to establish the greater rationality or objectivity of the consensus (as compared to the minority view), then criterion 2 must be violated. There is no reason to believe the result to be individually binding.

I will take Robert Nozick's argument for the minimal state as offering a good specimen of category 2, that is, of a hypothetical-choice theory employing a realistic construction of unrefined or brute preferences. As we will see, it aspires to unanimous acceptability through a compensation argument.

As in the discussion of actual-consent theory, it is worth distinguishing between strict and loose interpretations of consent or agreement. By the strict interpretation of agreement, we mean consent or satisfaction with the result that is explicit and unambiguous to the agent as an account of his actual preferences at some identifiable point in time. It is not a matter of what *we* think a person would agree to if she were rational or if she really thought about the issue; nor is it a matter of our interpreting certain acts—which the agent clearly thought she was performing for other reasons—as appropriate tokens of consent according to our conventions. Rather, by strict agreement, we mean that she actually did agree (or consent or indicate, in terms of her actual preferences, satisfaction with the result) at some point and that she knew precisely what she was doing when she did so. Of course, this kind of strict agreement may play a role in a hypothetical scenario, in which case, as part of the story, we must imagine that the people involved actually do agree. We can also leave open the possibility of applying strict agreement retroactively (as Nozick does in the doctrine of full compensation),[1] or of requiring that the unanimity be prospective (rather than merely retroactive). But if the agreement is retroactive, then there must actually come a point in the story when the person's actual preferences explicitly and unambiguously support the result.

Nozick's theory strives for unanimity with an extremely weak form of strict agreement. If this form is unavailable, given a realistic construction of brute preferences, then so will more demanding forms. This case will help support a more general claim: that strict (voluntary) unanimous agreement is too demanding a requirement, whether for actual or for hypothetical constructions of brute preferences. We have already seen that loose interpretations of agreement (such as Locke's doctrine of tacit consent) fail to yield differentiating conclusions, because they can be invoked by an enormous variety of states. If using the king's highways or finding yourself within the territory is taken as tacit consent, then maintaining consent of the people in such a loose sense does not do much to distinguish among states. Whether we are dealing with actual or hypothetical constructions of brute preferences, strict agreement rules out too much, while loose agreement legitimates too much to be of any use in satisfying our first criterion.

According to Nozick, we are to take the question of whether there should be a state at all to the "best anarchic situation one reasonably could hope for."[2] The state of nature is offered as a morally relevant hypothetical situation for determining whether or not there should be a state. The test for whether we should have a state is to imagine our not having one—under conditions that are both realistic and optimistic—and then we shall see whether a state would have to be introduced or invented. The imagined alternatives must be realistic, for otherwise they would not be alternatives bearing on our range of choice; they would not constitute, even remotely, alternatives for us. The construction of the state of nature must be optimistic because a pessimistic or Hobbesian account of the state of nature could justify almost any state (even a Leviathan). The idea is that if we can justify the state in preference to the best nonstate alternative, then we would have convincingly justified the state and, indeed, a particular kind of state.

We are given a hypothetical history. The state could have arisen by the scenario Nozick describes; and, the argument goes, this scenario would have required no morally impermissible steps: "If one could show that the state would be superior even to this most favored situation of anarchy, the best that realistically can be hoped for, or would arise by a process involving no morally impermissible steps, or would be an improvement if it arose, this would provide a rationale for the state's existence; it would justify the state." [3]

But there are innumerable possible scenarios under which states far more extensive than Nozick's "minimal state" (limited in its functions to protection against force, theft, fraud, and interference with contracts) might also have come about without violating rights (in his sense). Within Nozick's strictly nonpaternalistic position, people even have the right, voluntarily, to sell themselves into slavery or to arrange for their own murders. [4] If they were to do so, no rights would be violated. A state whose subjects were mostly slaves (or whose rights were comparable only to those in modern totalitarian societies) *could have come about* through no morally impermissible steps. Clearly, if slavery could conceivably come about through no morally impermissible steps, then so could less drastic states more extensive than the minimal state, a prime example being the modern welfare state. What Nozick requires to sort through these counterfactuals is not merely the claim that the minimal state (and only the minimal state) could come about through no morally impermissible steps, but that this hypothetical scenario—and only this hypothetical scenario—is compatible with a plausible, realistic construction of what we could reasonably expect to happen in the state of nature he describes. In particular, it must be uniquely compatible with a plausible, realistic construction of the preferences we can attribute to these imaginary people in his choice scenario. We are not impressed by the hypothetical story that if everyone were to wish, voluntarily, to become slaves, then a totalitarian society could come about through no "morally impermissible steps." The force of this hypothetical is completely blunted by the implausibility of attributing such preferences to the people under any realistic construction.

Let us explore the precise scenario by which Nozick proposes to justify the minimal state. It illustrates the difficulty of preserving unanimous acceptability with brute preferences, realistically construed. We can simplify Nozick's story into the following four steps:

1. Individuals (with rights) live in the state of nature.
2. The individuals in step 1 form voluntary associations to protect themselves.
3. The associations in step 2 sort themselves out territorially (so that each is dominant in its own territory), forming an "ultraminimal state" (where those who join and pay get protected and those who do not, do not).
4. The ultraminimal state in step 3 compensates the independents in its territory so as to incorporate everyone and form a minimal state.

The "rights" assumed in step 1 are "side-constraints" upon action. It is not permissible to violate even one person's rights, regardless of whether the motive is to protect a greater number of others. Numbers of rights violations are not to be compared or balanced; part of the appeal of the theory is the simplicity of the basic position that one never violates rights.[5] Because even one rights violation would delegitimate the outcome, and because the independents have the right to remain independent unless they voluntarily cede that right to the minimal state, the theory ends up requiring unanimous acceptability for the transition to the minimal state. As noted in step 4 above, Nozick attempts to accomplish this through a "compensation" argument. However, in order to remain compatible with the theory's fundamental assumptions, compensation has to be interpreted in a sense that makes it a proxy for unanimous agreement or consent from those who apparently disagree. And once compensation is interpreted in this way, it becomes impossible to get significant substantive conclusions from the theory. So long as a choice scenario is both realistic in its construction of brute preferences and unanimous in its requirements, it will simply not produce them.

For our purposes, we do not need to dispute steps 1–3 in Nozick's four-step scenario. These transformations depend on empirical assumptions about the market for protection services (assumptions that we can grant for purposes of argument). But if the scenario reached only so far as step 3, it would not have accomplished its purpose, since the so-called ultra-minimal state is not a state at all. It does not satisfy a state's minimum defining feature: it cannot rightfully claim a monopoly over the legitimate use of force in its territory.[6] The independents, those who have not voluntarily joined the protection association, have the same right to employ legitimate force as does the association (the "ultra-minimal state"). The independents cannot be incorporated without losing a crucial right, the right to interpret and defend their own rights as they see fit—a right that Nozick calls "self-help enforcement."[7]

If the association takes away this right without consent, then the resulting state is illegitimate, because even one rights violation is enough to delegitimate the outcome (it is this characteristic of Nozick's theory that brings it within the category of theories requiring unanimous acceptability). But if the independents retain this right, then no state has been produced. If the scenario reached only this far, then the whole point of the story would have been lost. We would have imagined an alternative to the state—namely, anarchy—only to see it eventually yield anarchy.

Of course, Nozick might have argued that all the independents simply decide, voluntarily, to buy protection contracts and join the state. These people are imaginary, so actual history does not limit the endings that might be devised for the story. But this reduces the scenario to our imagining that there was anarchy but that somehow, miraculously, absolutely everyone agreed to form a state. It strains credulity to imagine unanimity on such a question.[8] But anything less than unanimity either prevents a state from resulting or violates rights so as to delegitimate the resulting state.

Note that, for our purposes, the aspiration for unanimity should not be viewed as a peculiarity of the theory, but rather as a way of satisfying our criterion 2—as a way of making the obligations to support the state *individually binding*. Hence, while the details of this problem may be special to Nozick, the general issue applies to any theory in this category that might aspire to satisfy our conditions.

Nozick's scenario has not produced the unique legitimacy of the minimal state. Instead, up to step 3, it has produced only a forced choice between a legitimate nonstate (anarchy) and an illegitimate state (through forced incorporation of the independents).

The move from step 3 to step 4—a move that Nozick requires if there is to be any point to the argument—seems, at first glance, to be doubly objectionable. Not only does it appear to violate the rights of the independents, by taking away their right to self-help enforcement, but it also appears to violate the rights of the members by forcing redistribution—forcing the members to pay for protection services to be given to the independents, after they are incorporated.[9] Nozick believes, roughly, that these two (apparent) wrongs make the next step right. The idea is that forced incorporation can be justified through compensation. On the one hand, the members have not had their rights violated through redistribution to the independents (giving the independents services they have not paid for), because they owe compensation to the independents for taking away the right to self-help enforcement. On the other hand, the independents have not had their rights violated through forced incorporation, because they are fully compensated. And if one interprets compensation strictly, as Nozick does, and if it is actually paid, then it becomes a proxy for a kind of consent, applied ex post facto.[10] This aspect of compensation becomes explicit from his borrowing of the "indifference curve" terminology from economics: "Full compensation keeps the victim on as high an indifference curve as he would occupy if the other person hadn't crossed."[11]

X's indifference curves are a representation of X's actual preferences. Once he has been fully compensated in his own estimation, there is a sense in which he has consented to the change: he regards the new situation (with compensation) as at least as good as the old situation (without compensation). Just as voluntary consent opens the "border" for crossing, full compensation after the fact legitimizes apparent border crossings through a kind of subsequent consent. In fact, the only objection Nozick offers to the extreme case of an eccentric who goes around breaking arms and writing fat checks to fully compensate the victims is that not all the victims could possibly be fully compensated—because a general climate of fear would be created throughout the community.[12]

However, once compensation is taken seriously (and Nozick must take it perfectly seriously if he is to preserve the simple side-constraint view of rights that boundary crossings are never to be permitted without consent), then the options resulting from the argument reduce to those pictured in figure 4. For our purposes, Nozick must take compensation perfectly seriously or else he loses his basis for satisfying criterion 2 and making the result individually binding.

The possibilities in figure 4 depict the options available after step 3 in the hypothetical history. Obviously, either the independents are incorporated into the state (option A) or they are not (option B). If they are not, then, by the criteria stated earlier, the protection association does not qualify as a state. It does not have the requisite monopoly over the legitimate use of force in the territory because the independents retain the same right to use force as does the dominant association. Since the thought experiment for the possibility of justifying the state would then have failed, anarchism would have won the argument and the theory would then violate our criterion 1(b).

If the independents are incorporated (option A in fig. 4), a necessary part of that incorporation is the loss of the right to self-help enforcement. It is precisely the right to use vigilante justice, to interpret and enforce one's rights entirely as one sees fit, that distinguishes anarchy from the state. Hence, if the transition to a state is to be accomplished, there are two possibilities: either

Figure 4. Nozick's Scenario

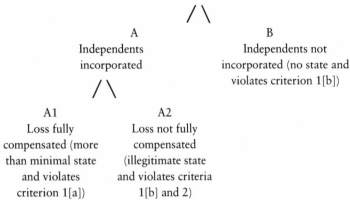

OPTIONS FOR THE RESOLUTION OF NOZICK'S SCENARIO

A
Independents
incorporated

B
Independents not
incorporated (no state and
violates criterion 1[b])

A1
Loss fully
compensated (more
than minimal state
and violates
criterion 1[a])

A2
Loss not fully
compensated
(illegitimate state
and violates criteria
1[b] and 2)

the loss of this right to self-help enforcement is fully compensated
(option A1) or it is not (option A2). If the loss of the right to self-
help enforcement is not fully compensated, then the resulting state
is not legitimate. For Nozick, even one rights violation is enough
to invalidate the process. Hence option A2, while providing a
state, does not provide a morally acceptable one. For our purposes,
option A2 can be interpreted as violating both criteria 1(b) and 2.
It violates criterion 1(b) because we are still without a justification
for state authority. It violates criterion 2 because less than full
compensation cannot be considered a proxy for consent. Hence,
with inadequate compensation, the case for the theory satisfying
the individually binding criterion breaks down. Clearly, prospects
for a successful completion to the argument turn on option A1.

What does it take to fully compensate the independents for
losing the right to self-help enforcement? Recall that they are independents precisely because they previously turned down the
option of joining the protection association. Now Nozick proposes to take away the very independence they wished to preserve
and, in compensation, to give them merely the protection services

they had previously refused! It strains credulity to imagine that they feel fully compensated, in their own estimation by this forced bargain.

To be fully compensated, they must be on as high an "indifference curve" without the right but with the compensating services and/or goods as they were previously with their rights but without the compensation. The case can only be made plausible if many more services and/or goods are provided than would be compatible with the meager offerings built into the definition of the minimal state (the minimal services provided are what make the minimal state "minimal").

When we begin to imagine what other goods and services might be provided in order to make the resulting compensation sufficiently attractive to place the independents on as high an indifference curve as they would have been on otherwise, the resulting structure of the state begins to look quite different. We might imagine the new state providing money, food, medical care, education, and a host of other human services.[13] In order to render plausible the claim that the independents are fully compensated, the apparent redistribution would have to be substantial. I say "apparent redistribution" because, as Nozick rightly notes, if transfers are paid as compensation, they should not be considered redistribution (even though they will have this appearance because goods or services are moved from one group to another).[14]

Whatever the details, the resulting state will be more than minimal if full compensation must be paid. In fact, since many of the independents may have failed to join earlier because they could not afford to, the particular character of the more-than-minimal state that results might turn out to be precisely the one Nozick is most concerned to argue against, namely, that of the modern welfare state.

It is, of course, possible that none of these offerings will turn out to be sufficient. From the standpoint of the independents, perhaps no compensation will be enough to make up for loss of their rights. We might imagine hardy individualists, who do not wish to be subservient to any government, objecting to their forced incorporation into the state.[15] In that case, however, the scenario simply ends up in the A2 category and the state that results is illegitimate because rights have been seized without full compensation. Criterion 2 is then violated because there is no basis in the people's own preferences for binding them to the state (from which they would prefer to remain independent). Criterion 1(b) is also violated because we end up with the blind alley of anarchism once again.

On the other hand, once we assume that it *is* possible, at least in principle, to compensate for the loss of the independents' rights, the required goods and services clearly surpass those offered by the minimal state—provided that full compensation must be provided. And as we saw earlier, anything less than full compensation should be construed as a rights violation because it would not constitute any sort of consent or permission (even if retroactive) for border crossings. Once border crossings without permission are tolerated, the entire theory begins to disintegrate.[16]

The possibilities in figure 4 reduce to: (A1) legitimate but more extensive states than the minimal state; (A2) an illegitimate state; and (B) no state. Nozick's proposed conclusion, the unique legitimacy of the minimal state, is not one of the possibilities. The argument clearly does not produce differentiating conclusions. Option B, anarchism, rules out all the possibilities that involve having a state. Option A1 fails to differentiate among states. From it, we only know that some indeterminate range of more extensive states may be legitimate. We cannot know more from the argument because the issue turns on an empirical question about a hypothetical history: it depends on the preferences of imaginary people. Within the ground rules of realism, there is wide latitude in how much compensation might be required and in how much these people might turn out to value their independence. What we can conclude is that if the argument legitimates any state at all, it legitimates an indeterminate range of states that engage in at least some redistribution. That is virtually the full range of states in the modern world today. Clearly, option A1 fails criterion 1(a), the nonvacuous requirement.

We reached this dead end by assuming a realistic construction of brute preferences without any explicit efforts to transform those preferences through indoctrination. Nozick, like Walzer and the actual-choice theorists of category 1, does not provide protection from indoctrination for the process of preference formation. We should see what happens when this assumption is relaxed. Suppose, for example, that everyone in the territory belonged to a religious cult which raised its children to defer entirely to the judgment of a particular leader on all questions of public policy. Its members were indoctrinated in the sense that no rival views were ever discussed, even in private, and heavy social sanctions were applied to anyone offering the merest hint of doubt or of free-thinking. In the territory of this homogeneous and coercive cult (a territory we might call Cult-land), once the leader approves joining the minimal state, everyone unanimously and sincerely follows. In other words, Cult-land achieves the transition to the minimal state without having to confront the compensation problem, simply because there are no independents to be compensated. It achieves the transition to the minimal state without having to confront the problem of disagreement, simply because there is none.

While such a hypothetical story would lead, unanimously, to the minimal state, there is no reason for that story to hold any moral relevance for us. It is delegitimated as a moral example for us because it depends on preferences and choices that are determined by indoctrination. For a merely hypothetical story to maintain moral relevance, the choice needs to be voluntary; it needs to be free of coercive manipulation. Without indoctrination, we can see from figure 4 that Nozick's scenario leads to indeterminate results. With indoctrination, on the other hand, it leads to results that lack any moral relevance as an example for us. Without indoctrination, the scenario violates either criterion 1a or criteria 1b or 2; with indoctrination, the scenario obviously violates criterion 4.

The indoctrination example also hints at another major problem. Hypothetical histories have a different claim on us than do real histories. Once we get into the business of creating hypothetical stories, their relevance for us must rest on some other claim than that they actually happened. The indoctrinated-hypothetical scenario has clearly lost all moral relevance for us. This is a crucial objection to brute-hypothetical scenarios. However, even if one constructed a scenario that had a greater claim of moral relevance, it would still face the problem of satisfying criterion 3, the jurisdiction problem.[17] It would still have to establish that its claim to moral relevance could not be matched by rival theories making the same fundamental claim to constitute an appropriate basis for moral choice. Because this jurisdiction problem is the central issue in category 3 theories, I will put it off until the next section. It is worth noting, however, that the same issue arises for category 2—only the latter category's responses are complicated by the additional, delegitimating hurdle of indoctrination problems.

2.6 *Category 3: Impartial Decision Procedures*

Theories in category 3 of figure 2 combine a hypothetical situation with an explicit effort to refine the preferences or motivations that bear on the choice of principles—to refine them so as to eliminate the biases that might otherwise deflect the choice through morally irrelevant factors. Such refinement mechanisms clearly provide a response to the indoctrination problems that bedevil categories 1 and 2.

Category 3 has provided the basis for the resuscitation of systematic liberal theory over the last two decades. One basic idea is at the core of this strategy: the definition of an appropriately unbiased moral perspective or decision situation for the selection of first principles that are to have priority in a liberal state (at least under ideal conditions). Rawls's "original position," Ackerman's notion of "neutral dialogue," Dworkin's "equal concern and respect," and Peter Singer's reconstruction of the perfectly sympathetic spectator of the classical utilitarians all have this character.[1] Each defines a perspective of *impartiality* for the equal consideration of relevant claims or interests.

Moral decision procedures such as the Golden Rule or Kant's Categorical Imperative have long played a role in ethical debate. The obvious difficulty has been that these procedures have been specified loosely enough that it is easy for proponents of rival substantive conclusions to cite their preferred outcomes as the result of the same procedure.[2]

By contrast, the procedures in category 3 attempt to control the factors that may be brought to bear on the decision by making the deliberations hypothetical. The opportunities for contaminating the argument with irrelevant factors are controlled by taking the deliberations to a hypothetical situation in which the factors at play are fully specified and sealed off from real-life biases and contingencies. At first glance, this strategy seems to have a great deal of merit. If each step in the procedure is specified sufficiently, then it should be possible to bring proponents of rival principles employing the same procedure to the same ultimate conclusions.

Yet from this general idea, we can conclude virtually nothing about *which* particular fully specified strategy should have supremacy. Even slight variations in the account of impartiality or of interests in a fully specified moral decision procedure can produce radically different first principles—a fact dramatized by the dispute between Rawls and Harsanyi over interpretations of the original position that yield principles as different as maximin and average utility.[3] Many procedural devices seem to embody a kind of impartiality or equal consideration. "Equal counting," the "veil of ignorance," and "moral musical chairs" are a few of the recent contenders.[4] Similarly, many rival conceptions of interests might be considered impartially by such a procedure. Rawlsian primary goods, Ackermanian "manna," and utility in one sense or another are the proposals most prominent in recent debates.[5]

The difficulty is that proponents of each procedure (specifying a notion of impartiality and a notion of interests) can make precisely symmetrical claims: each can derive first principles from his own preferred account of the moral point of view. The basis for any particular principle supported in this way is open to reasonable disagreement precisely because the rival procedures embody slightly different rival conceptions of moral reasonableness, each making the same fundamental claim.

Fully specifying the procedure does not evade the jurisdiction problem. Rather, it dramatizes and clarifies it. Once we specify a variety of these procedures, the conclusions from any particular version of the strategy are too easy to evade—even for liberal theorists committed to the same general strategy of arguing from the impartial consideration of interests. We need some basis for differentiating conclusions (for criteria that select a subclass of most-preferred alternatives) which it would be difficult for *any* recognizable version of liberal theory to evade. Because even slight variations in the account of impartiality or of interests yield radically different political conclusions, any proposed response to criterion 1 is subject to jurisdictional challenge—when supported in this way.

Any viable version of category 3 must specify how relevant claims or interests are going to be considered in an impartial or appropriately unbiased way in the hypothetical situation. As I noted earlier, the initial problem with hypothetical situations is that we can see that proponents of rival principles can devise rival stories designed, in turn, to support their respective principles. The central question about the strategy is: Can some characterization of the factors in such a hypothetical situation be *immune* from jurisdictional challenge by other theories advocating other factors? Unless there is some such characterization, the jurisdiction problem is inescapable for any version of this kind of theory.

The quest is for a characterization of factors in the decision situation that is so neutral about the controversies in question that it is above reasonable challenge. Can a theory achieve strict neutrality and at the same time offer substantive conclusions?

To illustrate the general problem, let us turn to the two most ambitious versions of a category 3 theory in recent years, Rawls's *A Theory of Justice* and Ackerman's *Social Justice in the Liberal State.* In discussing Rawls, Thomas Nagel cogently states the strategy at the core of both theories: "A theory of the good is presupposed, *but it is ostensibly neutral between divergent particular conceptions.* . . . It is a fundamental feature of Rawls's conception of the fairness of the original position that it should not permit the choice of principles of justice to depend on a particular conception of the good over which the parties may differ." [6]

Is it possible to develop a viable but *neutral* theory of relevant claims or interests that might immunize substantive conclusions from jurisdictional challenge? A neutral theory would dramatically reduce the room for reasonable disagreement; it holds out the promise of a firm basis for whatever principles result from the impartial consideration of everyone's relevant claims or interests. If a theory is beyond reasonable challenge in its claim to neutrality, it trumps the conclusions of rival, less neutral theories.

However, to the extent that this promise is directed toward satisfying our criteria, it is, I will argue, chimerical. To situate the argument, both Rawls and Ackerman offer us imaginary-choice theories: the moral point of view is formalized by a hypothetical but morally relevant decision situation which is constructed so as to perfectly insulate its results from contamination by irrelevant factors. [7] In constructing these imaginary situations, we are not limited by practical constraints. It is not an argument against one of these decision situations that its defining conditions would be impossible to realize. The moral relevance of the imaginary thought experiment lies in the claim that if we could realize those conditions, then our conclusions would be completely uncontaminated by morally irrelevant factors. Provided that we can coherently and plausibly work through what would be arrived at under the appropriate imaginary conditions, we have a strategy for supporting the resulting principle: it is the one that would be chosen under the admittedly imaginary but allegedly perfect conditions for making such a choice.

Figure 5. Options for Hypothetical-Choice Theories

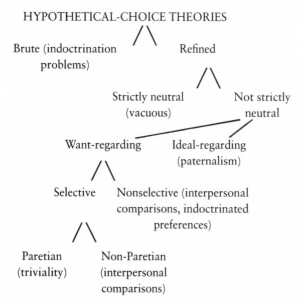

Of course, any particular version of such an imaginary-choice theory must offer its own account of what factors are morally relevant or irrelevant and of *what* gets impartially considered. It is in confronting the latter task that the neutrality issue arises.

As figure 5 shows, some versions aspire to strict neutrality in their consideration of relevant claims or interests, while others do not. My basic line of argument will be that strict neutrality, if taken seriously, blocks the road to any differentiating conclusions (prescriptions that might satisfy criterion 1). But once neutrality is loosened, then the basis for differentiating conclusions has been lost and the controversies applying to either want-regarding or ideal-regarding theories of interests (or other relevant claims) provide ample room for reasonable disagreement and ample grounds for jurisdictional challenges among competing thought experiments (violating criterion 3).

Let us begin with the aspiration for strict neutrality. In Rawls's case, this aspiration is expressed by his use of the "thin theory of the good." We are told that "the theory of the good used in arguing for the principles of justice is restricted to the bare essentials." We must use the thin theory because we cannot do without a theory of the good altogether: "To establish these principles it is necessary to rely on some notion of goodness, for we need assumptions about the parties' motives in the original position."[8] But these motives cannot be influenced by the particular conceptions of the good we happen to have acquired in actual life. As Rawls notes in a later article, "That we have one conception of the good rather than another is not relevant from a moral standpoint. In acquiring it we are influenced by the same sort of contingencies that lead us to rule out a knowledge of our sex and class."[9] Rawls might have added that if we were each to import our own particular conceptions of the good into the original position, the basis for any unanimous agreement would have been lost. No single result would rest on a firm basis because conscientious proponents of rival principles could each take their case to a version of the original position employing their own notions of the good. Jurisdiction problems would then bedevil these rival interpretations of the original position—each challenged by other versions that employ their favorite conceptions of interests to yield different conclusions.

Rawls, of course, does not take this route. His proposal is that, regardless of our actual notions of our interests, we should all rely on the same "thin theory." But how can we judge the self-interest of individuals without knowing anything in particular about them—anything that does not apply equally to everyone else? The thin theory leads from the "doctrine of rational plans of life" to the "doctrine of primary goods"; the latter is to guide the choice of principles of justice.

Rawls argues that an agent in the original position may further his own particular rational plan of life (whatever that may turn out to be once the veil of ignorance is removed) by maximizing his share of "primary goods"—goods that it is rational for him to want regardless of whatever else he turns out to want. In this way, he may supposedly choose moral principles out of self-interest while knowing nothing about himself that does not apply equally to everyone else.

Note that this account of a person's true interests based on his "rational plan" does not depend in the slightest on any tendency of persons in real life (or in the ideal just society) to "plan" their lives with any coherence or even in any consciously formulated way. Rather, "a rational plan is one that would be selected if certain conditions were fulfilled. The criterion of the good is hypothetical in a way similar to the criterion of justice." [10]

These rational plans are distinguished from other plans of life, first, in that they conform to certain "principles of rational choice," and second, in that they would be chosen by the person with "full deliberative rationality." The principles of rational choice are neutral with respect to particular substantive aims. They "define rationality as preferring, other things equal, the greater means for realizing our aims, and the development of wider and more varied interests assuming that these aspirations can be carried through." The concept of deliberative rationality is similarly noncommittal with respect to particular substantive aims. It specifies as "rational" whatever plan we would choose "with full awareness of the relevant facts and after a careful consideration of the consequences." [11] Plans are thus rational to the degree that they involve an effective consideration of means for realizing our aims and a choice of aims made with full knowledge of conditions and consequences.

It should be evident that a wide variety of plans requiring a wide variety of conditions for their fulfillment might well satisfy these conditions. Any plan that anyone would choose for himself with full awareness in the "deliberative" sense and according to these principles of rational choice thus qualifies as rational. In principle, there are few limits on the variety that rational plans may assume. As Rawls admits, "From the definition alone very little can be said about the content of a rational plan, or the particular activities that comprise it." Consider Rawls's example of the grass-counter: "Imagine someone whose only pleasure is to count blades of grass in various geometrically shaped areas such as park squares and well-trimmed lawns. He is otherwise intelligent and actually possesses unusual skills, since he manages to survive by solving difficult mathematical problems for a fee. The definition of the good forces us to admit that the good for this man is indeed counting blades of grass, or more accurately, his good is determined by a plan that gives an especially prominent place to this activity." [12] Despite the dizzying variety of life plans that might qualify as rational once the veil of ignorance is removed, Rawls believes that there is a sufficient basis for the choice of substantive principles in the original position. Guided by self-interest even though we know nothing in particular about ourselves, we would choose, Rawls believes, to maximize the minimum share of primary goods (the "maximin" notion of the "general conception" of justice).[13] Furthermore, once we take account of the comparative worth of the various primary goods, we would also specify the priority rankings of the "special conception" (liberty, then fair equality of opportunity, and then the maximin distribution of income and wealth).[14]

The key point for our purposes is that Rawls cannot get such ambitious substantive conclusions from the thin theory of the good and at the same time maintain its "thinness"—its neutrality between particular, controversial "fuller" theories. The thinness of the thin theory derives from the purely procedural and instrumental account of its component parts. The necessary and sufficient conditions for a rational life plan are defined in procedural and instrumental terms: "A person's plan of life is rational if, and only if, (1) it is one of the plans that is consistent with the principles of rational choice when these are applied to all the relevant features of his situation, and (2) it is that plan among those meeting this condition which would be chosen by him with full deliberative rationality, that is, with full awareness of the relevant facts and after a careful consideration of the consequences." [15]

The counting principles in condition 1 are purely instrumental; condition 2 is purely formal. It specifies only that the plan is the one that the person himself would choose under conditions of full awareness. How is this thin theory supposed to support the calculations of self-interest (behind the veil of ignorance) that yield the general and special conceptions of justice?[16] Without pursuing the issue in great detail, the basic point is that the thin theory is supposed to provide "the qualitative structure of the possible gains and losses in relation to one's conception of the good."[17]

This qualitative structure is supposed to yield the "three chief features" that make maximin (maximizing the minimum share) the rational choice for the general conception of justice (and for the distribution of income and wealth in the special conception). The first feature is that "the situation is one in which a knowledge of likelihoods is impossible, or at best extremely insecure." The argument turns on the second and third features:

> The person choosing has a conception of the good such that he cares very little, if anything, for what he might gain above the minimum stipend that he can, in fact, be sure of by following the maximin rule [second feature]. It is not worthwhile for him to take a chance for the sake of a further advantage, especially when it may turn out that he loses much that is important to him. This last provision brings in the third feature, namely, that the rejected alternatives have outcomes that one can hardly accept. The situation involves grave risks.[18]

These assumptions are not sufficient to support so strong a conclusion as maximin. To illustrate the slippage, consider the distribution problem for a society of two persons. In figures 6–8, the shares of primary goods to persons A and B are pictured on the vertical and horizontal axes, respectively.[19] Let us suppose that there is some amount of primary goods that satisfies the second and third features assumed by Rawls in the above passage. Let us call that amount "Z" primary goods. Anything less than Z is a disaster; and compared to the prospect of getting less than Z, we care "little if anything" to gamble for more. Rawls's pro-

Figure 6. Maximin with a Guaranteed Minimum

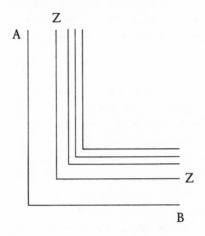

posed "maximin" solution is represented by the series of L-shaped indifference curves in figure 6. However, *any* distribution in the quadrants northeast of Z in any of the three charts satisfies the three features fully as much as does maximin. After we provide everyone with Z primary goods, we could maximize the total, as in figure 7, or we could maximize equality, as indicated by the 45-degree line in figure 8, or we could fill out the quadrant northeast of Z in any other conceivable way. All of these options satisfy the three features as much as does maximin. To require that the quadrant northeast of Z be filled out as in figure 6 is too strong a conclusion to draw from the assumptions available in the original position. Furthermore, it is a conclusion that would force us to continually prefer increases in the minimum over other competing claims—even when those other competing claims were very significant and the increases in the minimum were very small indeed.[20]

So long as we give at least Z primary goods to everyone, we have satisfied the security level assumed in the three features. It is an open question what we should do after that. The three features imply only a guaranteed minimum, not a minimum that continues to rise so far as possible.

Figure 7. Utilitarianism with a Guaranteed Minimum

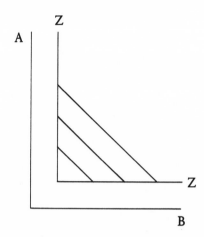

A guaranteed minimum is a far weaker and less controversial conclusion than a minimum that must be maximized. The latter principle can require great sacrifice from all other strata for the sake of tiny increases at the bottom—increases that might be above an already acceptable threshold. Suppose four Rawlsian primary goods is our definition of such a threshold. Nevertheless, maximin would tell us that distribution Y is preferable to distribution X:

X	Y
4	4.01
15	4.01
20	4.01
50	4.01

Given the meager information about his self-interest available to an agent in the original position, would it be rational to decide on maximin when another choice strategy that is conservative in its attitude toward risk—the guaranteed minimum—ensures all that was claimed for maximin (it satisfies the second and third

Figure 8. Equality with a Guaranteed Minimum

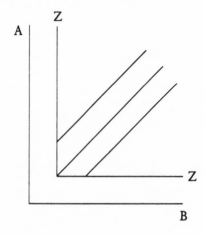

features), without committing itself to a host of additional and disturbing implications? After all, once the veil of ignorance is removed, *we* might be in one of the higher strata decimated by the choice of Y rather than X. And if we are at the the bottom, the tiny increment we get under Y counts for nothing, by hypothesis, since we are already above the threshold.

Suppose we are right in claiming that it is possible to get a *partial* substantive conclusion out of Rawls's three features in the original position. Does this partial conclusion offer any hope of satisfying our criteria? I believe Rawls faces the following dilemma: On the one hand, if the threshold defined by the three features is interpreted minimally, a plausible case can be made for neutrality, but at the cost of such radical incompleteness that the resulting principle is nearly trivial in its implications. It is so minimal in its demands that virtually any modern state satisfies it (or could easily satisfy it). Hence the theory, on this interpretation, would violate our nonvacuousness requirement (criterion 1[a]).

On the other hand, if the threshold is interpreted ambitiously, then its pretensions to neutrality can no longer be supported.[21] It then rests on a particular controversial theory of the good and the door has been opened to other controversial theories that can provide an equivalent basis for rival principles. It is then open to jurisdictional challenge by the full range of rival theories because it no longer has a plausible claim of strict neutrality with which to defend itself against charges of bias. The dilemma, in other words, amounts to a hard choice between the violation of criterion 1(a) and the violation of criterion 3.

The minimal interpretation of the threshold maintains a claim to neutrality (but at the cost of radical incompleteness) because it might seem reasonable, if we have no idea of our particular rational life plan to calculate that the brute "necessaries" (to use Adam Smith's phrase) required for survival and bare membership in the society conform to the security level stated in the three features.[22] Compared to the risk of falling below such a subsistence minimum, we might indeed "care very little, if anything" for increments above it. Why gamble on winning the jackpot introduced by great inequality if the possibility of such payoffs introduced the risk of starvation or other comparable disasters? In this way, Rawls's second and third features can be given a plausible interpretation that seems to be neutral between particular life plans and substantive aims. Not knowing what my life plan will turn out to be, I must, nevertheless, secure certain subsistence conditions necessary for pursuing any rational life plan at all.

But such a minimal safety net would be endorsed by virtually every developed country, capitalist or socialist. Giving everyone at least subsistence leaves almost everything after that an open question. For example, should we strive to increase equality, total output, or the minimum level after everyone has been given at least subsistence? What should our priorities be *within* the quadrant defined by Z in figures 6–8? Rawls's assumptions are sufficient to get us *into* the quadrant, but they are insufficient to direct us after that. The difficulty is that this is where serious debate begins, not where it ends.

The basic point is that when the security level is set so low that it plausibly corresponds to the three features, it leaves almost everything unsettled. Most important for our purposes, the requirement that such a minimal safety net be satisfied would be virtually useless in satisfying criterion 1(a) (nonvacuousness). However, it is only the minimal interpretation of Z, the security level, that can maintain a plausible claim to neutrality.

On the other hand, if we were to set Z ambitiously—say, two cars and a home of one's own—we would be positing a controversial theory of the good for everyone. The third feature requires that we regard anything less than the threshold as an unacceptable disaster, while the second feature requires that we not be interested in gambling for anything more—at least *relative* to the risk of falling below it.[23] Having (at the time of this writing) one car but not two, I can, personally, quite easily imagine a plan of life where I would prefer (a) the *chance* of becoming a millionaire introduced by tolerating inequalities to (b) strict equality but with the guarantee of a second car. The point is that an ambitious interpretation of the threshold will depend on a controversial theory of the good—one that conforms to some rational life plans but clearly not to others, particularly in its attitude toward risk. For such a theory of the good, anything less than the second car (or whatever else is demanded of the ambitious threshold) must be absolutely unacceptable. And compared to the risk of not getting the second car, the prospect of gambling to get Howard Hughes's fortune must mean nothing. Because the ambitious threshold clearly violates neutrality, it opens the door to other controversial theories of the good as the basis for competing principles.

A similar difficulty arises with the priority rankings embodied in the special conception. Once we take account of the qualitative differences among the various primary goods, we are supposed to value liberty, fair equality of opportunity, and income and wealth in lexical order (meaning that no amount, however great, of a lower-ranked value is worth any sacrifice, however small, in a higher-ranked value). Without going into all the details of this well-known controversy, it is worth noting that the same basic difficulty arises with the special conception: a neutral interpretation, a really "thin" theory, does not support these significant substantive results; to get the latter, a particular, controversial theory of the good must be assumed.[24]

Recall that the doctrine of rational life plans could maintain its claim to neutrality only by being purely procedural and instrumental. My rational plan of life is supposed to be the one I would choose for myself with full knowledge of conditions and consequences and in accordance with the rational means/ends relations determined by the various counting principles.[25] Knowing only this much in the original position, there is no basis for the strong priority relations expressed by lexical order. I might be an aspiring capitalist whose life plan is not furthered in the least by the civil liberties to which Rawls gives first priority. As such a capitalist, I might prefer to give first priority to the income and wealth Rawls places last. Or my rational plan of life might be more directly furthered by placing fair equality of opportunity first. Perhaps I am a member of a racial or sexual minority whose members place highest priority on equal opportunity—even above liberty of conscience and political expression (although we might value these highly as well). My rational plan of life, in Rawls's precise sense, might be far more effectively furthered by inverting one or another of these priority rankings. From the original position, I simply cannot know whether or not this is the case.

The point is that the "thin theory of the good"—if it remains truly thin—provides no basis for determining these rankings, one way or the other. So long as we consider life plans in a purely procedural and instrumental way, a plausible claim to neutrality can be maintained, but only at the cost of leaving the comparative value of the various "primary goods" indeterminate.

On the other hand, if we import into the original position a more full-bodied conception of the good—one that includes particular substantive aims—then the claim to neutrality among substantive aims is lost. Rawls has suggested this last possible line of revision in more recent articles, where he proposes that a particular "model conception of a moral person" should be assumed in order to obtain his proposed conclusions.[26]

According to this model conception, "we take moral persons to be characterized by two moral powers and by two corresponding highest-order interests in realizing and exercising these powers." The two moral powers are "the capacity for an effective sense of justice" and the "capacity to form, to revise, and rationally to pursue a conception of the good." The key point is that in the original position the agents are to assume that they have "highest-order interests" in securing the conditions necessary for the exercise of these two moral powers: "Corresponding to the moral powers, moral persons are said to be moved by two highest order interests to realize and exercise these powers. By calling these interests 'highest order' interests, I mean that, as the model-conception of a moral person is specified, these interests are supremely regulative as well as effective. This implies that, whenever circumstances are relevant to their fulfillment, these interests govern deliberation and conduct." [27]

With these moral powers and their corresponding interests in mind, Rawls believes that we can get the priority relations in the special conception. He summarizes this construction of the argument as follows:

(i) The basic liberties (freedom of thought and liberty of conscience, etc.) are the background institutions necessary for the development and exercise of the capacity to decide upon and revise, and rationally to pursue, a conception of the good. Similarly, these liberties allow for the development and exercise of the sense of right and justice under social conditions that are free.

(ii) Freedom of movement and free choice of occupation against a background of diverse opportunities are required for the pursuit of final ends, as well as to give effect to a decision to revise and change them, if one so desires.

(iii) Powers and prerogatives of offices and positions of responsibility are needed to give scope to various self-governing and social capacities of the self.

(iv) Income and wealth, understood broadly as they must be, are all-purpose means (having an exchange value) for achieving directly or indirectly almost any of our ends, whatever they happen to be.

(v) The social bases of self-respect are those aspects of basic institutions which are normally essential if individuals are to have a lively sense of their own worth as moral persons and to be able to realize their higher-order interests and advance their ends with zest and self-confidence.[28]

Because of our "highest-order" interests in securing the conditions for the exercise of the two moral powers, we are, supposedly, to adopt the principles of the special conception. Once again, the same issue arises. Why is it rational to accept these very strong priority rankings? Why are we to accept the primary goods in the order enumerated, where the slightest sacrifice in liberty is not worth the greatest possible increase in equal opportunity, and where the slightest sacrifice in equal opportunity is not worth the greatest possible increase in income and wealth? Rawls makes clear that he still adheres to the priority rankings.[29] In any case, without the priority rankings, the theory would fall into intuitionism.

To preserve the priority rankings, Rawls would have us assume that our interest in liberty comes first, because the highest-order interests in our moral powers are served first by liberty; equal opportunity is second because our next-highest-order interests in our moral powers are served by equal opportunity, and so on.

Clearly, the claim to neutrality has been greatly weakened by the introduction of these assumptions. We are being asked to base principles of justice on a particular controversial theory of the good or, if you will, a particular model conception of a moral person, when other variations would clearly lead to different priority rankings and different principles. Once these moves are made, the strictly neutral strategy for avoiding jurisdiction problems has been abandoned. When we employ such a controversial theory of the good, we can get substantive results, but they can be matched point by point by rival thought experiments employing rival theories of the good whose neutrality is similarly at issue.

To clarify the general issue, it is worth considering a second example of a theory aspiring to strict neutrality.[30] Neutrality plays an even more explicit role in Ackerman's *Social Justice in the Liberal State*—probably the one contemporary effort to reconstruct liberal theory that rivals Rawls's in its ambition and systematic character. Neutrality is one of three assumptions that are meant, together, to constrain legitimating conversations about distributive justice. However, the other two assumptions, rationality and consistency, will permit an enormous range of possible distributions to survive elimination.[31] But once neutrality is introduced, Ackerman argues, only his own proposal survives. He defines it as follows:"Neutrality: No reason is a good reason if it requires the powerholder to assert: (a) that his conception of the good is better than that asserted by any of his fellow citizens, or (b) that, regardless of his conception of the good, he is intrinsically superior to one or more of his fellow citizens."[32]

For our purposes, the difficulty with this innovative and appealing proposal is that if it is interpreted strictly, the resulting conclusions are emptied of substantive content. On the other hand, if it were to be interpreted more loosely, then no particular principle resulting from it would rest on firm ground. Rival positions could then invoke rival legitimating dialogues and the same pluralism would result as that which followed when Rawls suggested weakening neutrality.[33] In our terms, the options boil down to a hard choice between violations of criterion 1 (the emptiness of strict neutrality prevents any selection of a few most preferred states) and violations of criterion 3, the jurisdiction problem.

Let us focus on the strict interpretation of neutrality. The argument that passes neutrality is supposed to sanction equality.[34] The one successful move in the dialogues is "I'm at least as good as you are, therefore, I should get at least as much." The difficulty is that neutrality, on the strict interpretation, does not permit any definite answer to the further question, At least as much what? A particular, inevitably controversial theory of the good is required to answer that question; but that is precisely what is barred by neutrality.

The strict interpretation is clearest in Ackerman's attempt to rule out utilitarianism. We are presented with a dialogue between "Manic" (who likes mountaineering) and "Depressive" (who likes philosophizing). The former claims he should get more "manna" because he will derive more utility from it:

DEPRESSIVE: How, then, is the utility number relevant to our discussion?

MANIC: It translates the value of philosophizing and mountaineering into a common yardstick: subjective satisfaction.

DEPRESSIVE: But surely there are other possible yardsticks. Why can't I, for example, construct a calculus that ranks all conceptions of the good in terms of the amount of philosophic wisdom they produce and instruct the computer to tell us how much of that good each of us will produce with the manna. (He does so.)

COMPUTER: Depressive scores one hundred units on the wisdom index; Manic scores 10 units.

DEPRESSIVE: Why, then, is your yardstick better than mine?

MANIC: Do I have to answer that? [35]

Manic cannot answer the question without violating neutrality —when interpreted strictly. As the Commander in Ackerman's dialogue concludes: "We are reaching a dead-end, my friends. We search in vain for a neutral yardstick for measuring the 'real' value of different conceptions of the good. To justify one yardstick over all the other possible ways of ranking values will require utterances that are inconsistent with at least some of the ideals affirmed by some of your fellow citizens." Hence the objection to utilitarianism: "The problem with utilitarianism is its teleological character, its effort to evaluate distribution rules by how much 'good' they produce. *Any* such effort requires a specification of the good that will be contested by *some* citizens who insist on measuring their good by a different yardstick, one that gives them more manna than their competitors."[36]

While successful in ruling out utilitarianism, this conception of neutrality is so strict that it can be employed, with equally devastating results, against the yardsticks Ackerman eventually uses himself to settle the distribution problem. He later permits Depressive to argue, supposedly consistent with neutrality, "If I'm at least as good as Manic, I should get at least as much of this stuff that both of us desire."[37] This simple argument yields the conclusion of equal initial shares of manna—an argument that is later broadened to include birthrights, education, rights to free exchange, and obligations to future generations.

Yet any particular yardstick for determining "as much" in this dialogue can be subjected to the same basic critique that Ackerman levels against utilitarianism. Even for the simplified distribution problem employing the imaginary substance manna, a variety of yardsticks might be devised under which some persons would do far better and others far worse, depending upon their particular conceptions of the good. Some obvious possibilities include equal opportunities (or time shares) for employing as much of the manna as one might like at a given time or equal chances at lottery tickets for rich payoffs, or equal life-support payments doled out in increments for as long as one might live. There is no reason to regard identical physical chunks of manna as a yardstick immune from controversy, while every other possible specification of content for equality is regarded as nonneutral.

Furthermore, why should equal physical quantities of manna be compatible with neutrality when equal satisfaction is ruled out as a neutral solution? If I claim only that I should be as satisfied with my share as you are with yours, it is hard to see how that amounts to claiming that my "conception of the good is better"—for I am proposing, in a sense, to treat our differing conceptions *equally*. Similarly, I may propose such equal treatment without claiming "unconditional superiority," without claiming

that I am "intrinsically superior" to my competitors.[38] Only if
equal amounts of manna were assumed at the outset to be the appropriate criterion for judging that persons are equally well-off,
would it follow that differing distributions yielding equal utilities
were a slight to some conceptions of the good. Yet this would be
to assume, arbitrarily, a particular and contested solution to the
fundamental issue: what allotments are to be regarded as superior
or inferior?

The case against equal satisfaction would appear to rest on the
passages quoted above objecting to utility as a yardstick. But it is
successful, I believe, only if interpreted so strictly that any substantive content to a yardstick can be ruled out because it "will be
contested by *some* citizens who insist on measuring their good by
a different yardstick."[39] Some citizens, in other words, can always
be expected to disagree about a yardstick for distributional questions because they will do better according to some other possible
yardstick for evaluating everyone's shares. If any yardstick contested in this way by some citizen is ruled out by neutrality, then
no yardstick with substantive implications can ever be arrived
at—consistent with this demanding conception of neutrality.

The door is opened even more widely to such controversies
once the debate moves beyond the simplified manna problem to
the full question of distribution under ideal conditions. Here it is
not manna but income and wealth that count as material equality.
Furthermore, the argument ranges over genetics, education, and
obligations to future generations. In each of these cases, any choice
of a particular yardstick is open to controversy. Any answer to
the question An equal share of what? would appear open to the
same argument Ackerman employs against utilitarianism: why
one yardstick for measuring shares rather than another?[40]

Even the division of the general distribution problem into a
series of discrete power dimensions (genetics, education, property
rights, political power) is itself a step toward certain distributional
metrics compared with a diversity of possible alternatives. Some
theories might lump these all together and permit inequalities

in one to compensate for inequalities in another. Other theories might add different dimensions. Degrees of liberty, social esteem, interpersonal power, job satisfaction, health—the list of possible elements of value in a distributional theory is open-ended and controversial.[41] Since the root notion of Ackerman's strategy is that all exercises of "power" are to be subjected to the equalizing rule of neutral dialogue, it seems too much to expect that any particular conceptualization of these power relations, any particular distributional yardstick, can plausibly be claimed as the uniquely uncontroversial solution, the uniquely neutral content for equal power relations.[42]

Even if the case for equality were granted for purposes of argument, each of these conceptualizations of power relations could be employed to fill out a notion of equal distribution with dramatically different substantive implications.[43] The dilemma should be clear: on the one hand, without a yardstick or metric, the theory is empty; but on the other hand, we cannot provide it with a metric or yardstick and at the same time remain neutral among substantive theories of the good. Once the proposed differentiating conclusions depend on a particular substantive theory of the good, they can be avoided by rival theorists employing rival theories of the good in support of their own preferred ultimate principles. Once neutrality is loosened, the basis for jurisdictional challenges arises, violating our criterion 3.

Returning to the typology in figure 5, the difficulty with the first option—interpreting interests and other relevant claims with strict neutrality—is that it robs the resulting principle of significant substantive content. In Rawls's case, when the thin theory of the good is interpreted neutrally, when it is interpreted in a purely procedural and instrumental way so as not to be biased toward any particular conception of the good, no support can be found for any significant priority rankings among the so-called primary goods. Similarly, when we interpreted Rawls's proposed threshold in a manner that might seem compatible with neutrality, we could only get a guaranteed minimum interpreted so minimally that it was virtually useless as a basis for differentiating conclusions.

A parallel difficulty emerges for Ackerman. His book has a "mantra" that goes: "I'm at least as good as you are, therefore, I should get at least as much." But this formula cannot be filled out without an answer to the next question, At least as much what?—without an argument for one particular distributional yardstick compared to the competing alternatives. This is precisely the move forbidden by strict neutrality (as we saw in the dialogue ruling out utilitarianism). Since, as Ackerman's Commander concluded, "we search in vain for a neutral yardstick," neutrality interpreted this strictly leads to an empty formalism. Without some particular *content* specified for what is distributed equally, the resulting principle offers no hope of providing the differentiating conclusions required for criterion 1.

2.7 More on Category 3: Preference, Utility, and the Good

To give further content to the kinds of controversies that arise once the quest for strict neutrality is abandoned, let us turn to the remaining classifications in figure 5. We are concerned here with conceptions for assessing interests in a theory that purports to assess everyone's interests impartially. I will adapt some terminology from Brian Barry by dividing these theories into "want-regarding" and "ideal-regarding" theories of the good.[1] The want-regarding versions conform to citizen sovereignty, while the ideal-regarding ones do not. I will say that a principle adheres to *citizen sovereignty* if it judges a person X to be better off if, and only if, at least some of X's *actual preferences* are satisfied. The citizen is sovereign in the sense that it is his or her preferences which must be satisfied if the theory is to assess that person as better off.

Want-regarding and ideal-regarding theories each introduce

distinctive sources of controversy. The first issue for want-regarding theories is *which* preferences of an individual ought to count as defining his good. Recent efforts within utilitarianism to wrestle with this problem can be used to illustrate the difficulty.

First, some theories do not discriminate at all among preferences; they count all of them. Consider, for example, Hare's attempt to reconstruct utilitarianism. Hare's theory, like other utilitarian theories in the tradition of the impartial spectator, is a hypothetical-choice version of the impartiality argument: "What the principle of utility requires of me is to do for each man affected by my actions what I wish were done for me in the hypothetical circumstance that I were in precisely his situation; and, if my actions affect more than one man (as they nearly always will) to do what I wish, all in all, to be done for me in the hypothetical circumstances that I occupied all their situations (not of course at the same time but, shall we say?, in random order)."[2]

Hare moves from this equal consideration of everyone's interests to maximizing aggregate utility by conceptualizing equal consideration as equal weighing in an overall sum, and by defining individual interests according to the satisfaction of desire or utility—without introducing any distinctions among the preferences whose satisfaction is to count as desire or utility. This failure to discriminate among preferences confronts him with the problem of "fanatical" desires whose fulfillment requires harm to others: "For example, if the Nazi's desire not to have Jews around is intense enough to outweigh all the sufferings caused to Jews by arranging not to have them around, then, on this version of utilitarianism, as on any theory with the same formal structure, it ought to be satisfied."[3]

Incorporating such fanatical preferences thus appears to produce devastating consequences. It is worth pausing to consider Hare's defense to such an obvious objection: "The problem is to be overcome by, first, pointing out that fanatics of this heroic stature are never likely to be encountered (that no actual Nazis had such intense desires is, I think, obvious); secondly, by remembering that . . . cases that are never likely to be actually encountered do not have to be squared with the thinking of the ordinary man, whose principles are not designed to cope with such cases."[4]

Are such cases of fanaticism as fantastic and hypothetical as Hare claims? Perhaps he is right that it is difficult to imagine an *individual* Nazi whose preferences are so intense in favor of the Holocaust that they outweigh, in a strict utilitarian calculation, all the misery they would require. But the problem cannot be dispatched so easily. For one thing, it does not require such a horrendous individual utility monster. The desires of numerous individuals must be taken into account. If there are enough Nazis with hatred of even moderate intensity, a strict utilitarian calculation about total preference satisfaction in the society may conceivably support horrendous policies directed against Jews or other minority groups—once the numbers and intensities on both sides are summed up throughout the society.[5]

Perhaps Hare's mistake, and that of many other utilitarians, is to admit that satisfaction of preferences such as that of the Nazis toward the Jews ought to count as a form of utility in the first place. An alternative strategy, advocated by Ronald Dworkin, is to count only "personal" preferences (about one's own situation) and not "external" or "public-regarding" preferences (about the situation of others).[6] However, such a strategy would not only rule out nasty external preferences such as the Nazi's, but it would also rule out noble external preferences such as altruism and devotion to the good of mankind. Are we to count wants that support selfishness but not those that support self-sacrifice? We end up with a severely truncated view of the human good if we limit it to "personal" preferences (applying only to ourselves) and rule out all "external" preferences (applying to others).

Why does Dworkin propose to rule out consideration of "external" preferences, such as the Nazi's? The difficulty is that "political preferences, like the Nazi's, are on the same level—purport to occupy the same space—as the utilitarian theory itself." A suitably "restricted," defensible utilitarianism "cannot, without contradiction, be neutral between itself and Nazism. It cannot accept at once a duty to defeat the false theory that some peoples' preferences should count for more than other peoples' and a duty to strive as to fulfill the political preferences of those who passionately accept that false theory, as energetically as it strives for any other preferences. . . . If utilitarianism counts the fact of these preferences it has denied what it cannot deny, which is that justice requires it to oppose them."[7]

While Dworkin has an easy target here—few would deny that justice and Nazism are absolutely incompatible—we need to probe further the grounds within liberal theory for not counting Nazi preferences equally with all others. We might distinguish the Nazi Dworkin imagines—who argues for the persecution of Jews on the grounds that Jewish preferences should count for less—from the consistent utilitarian Nazi who bedeviled Hare by counting all preferences equally. Such a consistent Nazi cannot be dismissed as advocating unequal counting. Rather, he just offers a different conception of what should count equally—but in an environment in which enough people have intense, nasty preferences that unconscionable results would follow from counting them equally.

Furthermore, note that Dworkin's explanation for why we should rule out the Nazi's external preferences—that Nazism and utilitarianism occupy the same theoretical "space"—would also rule out preferences for more plausible theories of justice which also occupy the same space in that they are full-fledged rivals to utilitarianism. Dworkin can, of course, respond that these other full-fledged rivals are incorrect. But the difficulty is in determining, in the first place, which is the correct theory of justice.

It is far from clear that a "restricted utilitarianism" (one which counts only personal preferences) will consistently yield plausible results in terms of distributive justice. Suppose a prosperous majority is faced with demands for redistribution on behalf of a dispossessed underclass. There will be varying results as to how a strict utilitarian calculation involving purely personal preferences will come out. It is a complex empirical question depending on incentive effects, declining marginal utility of income, the numbers affected on each side, and the intensity with which an ideology of property entitlements is held in the population. Setting aside the interpersonal-comparisons difficulties facing Dworkin's postulated "utilitarian computer," a utilitarian calculation will sometimes favor redistribution, but it will also sometimes oppose it.[8] Even if strong altruistic sentiments among the prosperous majority favor redistribution, those sentiments cannot be counted in determining what justice is, if we follow Dworkin's argument, because those sentiments would be based on a theory that rivals restricted utilitarianism in occupying the same theoretical "space."

Most important, in some cases the utility from altruism would tip the balance toward redistribution, but purely selfish "personal" preferences would support starvation among the underclass (in a calculation based on selfishness but not on malice). Dworkin would have us avoid counting the altruistic sentiments in determining what justice is because they are based, as the Nazi preferences were, on a rival theory of justice—a rival to restricted utilitarianism (which counts only personal preferences). But this argument depends, crucially, on restricted utilitarianism itself being a reliable guide to distributive justice. In this case, it does not appear to be. The sentiments Dworkin would have us discount support feeding the underclass, while selfish calculations will, at least sometimes, support the opposite conclusion.

We can make the problem even worse by imagining a clever Nazi who has read Dworkin's theory and supports redistribution of Jewish property to Aryans by plugging only personal utility calculations into the "utilitarian computer." If the society has a concentration of prosperous Jews and a lot of poor Aryans who receive great utility from getting even a chance (or a lottery ticket) for the confiscated properties and businesses, it is quite possible that utilitarian calculations based purely on selfishness will support confiscation and persecution. Furthermore, if such a society also has a lot of altruistic sentiment, it could well be the case that counting external preferences would protect the Jews from persecution, but counting only selfish preferences would not. Dworkin's strategy of ruling out all external preferences depends absolutely on the prior claim that utilitarianism restricted to personal utility is a completely reliable guide to distributive justice. It is this crucial claim which seems dubious in these examples.

A different strategy is offered by John C. Harsanyi, who derives average utility from a variant of Rawls's original position. He attempts, in effect, to rule out Nazi external preferences but not altruistic ones. He proposes to exclude "all clearly antisocial preferences, such as sadism, envy, resentment, and malice." Harsanyi bases this exclusion on a conception of the dimensions of personality that are relevant to membership in what he calls "a moral community": "Utilitarian ethics makes all of us members of the same moral community. A person displaying ill will toward others does remain a member of this community, but not with his whole personality. That part of his personality that harbours these hostile antisocial feelings must be excluded from membership, and has no claim for a hearing when it comes to defining our concept of social utility."[9]

If we are to pick and choose among the preferences to be satisfied, we need some justification for our selection apart from the assumption that our operative theory of the good is preference satisfaction. Whatever we think of Harsanyi's notion of moral community, it makes no pretense to being neutral among theories of the good. Rather, it is a particular, controversial moral ideal— only one among the many that could be inserted into a model of impartiality. This exclusion of some preferences based on our moral evaluation of their appropriateness represents a sharp departure from the utilitarian tradition, which has generally avoided specifying the substantive content of preferences.[10] That tradition has been preoccupied with measuring the quantity and sometimes the quality of preference satisfaction, but not its legitimacy or illegitimacy. If utility is ultimately what counts for a utilitarian, and if satisfaction of certain preferences is experienced by some persons as utility, then it is difficult to see how a utilitarian theory can exclude some preferences entirely from consideration and maintain the basic claim that all utility and disutility experienced by everyone have been counted equally. Not counting certain preferences brings into question the claim to equal consideration at the foundations of any version of systematic utilitarianism. On the other hand, counting all preferences, including "antisocial" ones, exposes the resulting theory to horrendous counterexamples, as in Hare's Nazi problem.

It is worth noting that Hare offers a second line of defense against the fanatic-Nazi problem—that "cases that are never likely to be actually encountered do not have to be squared with the thinking of the ordinary man." However, once numbers are taken into account, it is not unrealistic to imagine such fanatical preferences directed at minority groups being supported on utilitarian grounds. Continuing religious and political conflicts in Lebanon and Northern Ireland, as well as a case I applied earlier to utilitarian theory—Idi Amin's expulsion of the Asians from Uganda [11]—illustrate that intense preferences of large numbers can be directed at the imposition of severe deprivations on particular groups. The issue is not a purely imaginary one limited to philosophical discussion.

Hare argues, however, that in employing such counter-examples, we are confusing the "level 1" thinking of the ordinary reasoner with what he calls the "level 2" thinking of the abstract philosopher. It is only the level 2 thinking of the philosopher that need hold proof against every "fantastic" counterexample we might imagine. Yet how would Hare's level 2 theory deal with such a case? Hare tries to avoid the problem by focusing on the design of the appropriate level 1 principles to be "implanted" in the population through moral education. Yet the goal of this moral education is ultimately utilitarian and the point of these counter-examples is to show that such an ultimate aim is inappropriate when utility is defined so as to be entirely indiscriminate about which preferences must be satisfied.

Want-regarding theories all involve commitment to one or another controversial theory of the good. Ackerman's anti-utilitarian dialogue quoted in section 2.6 above incisively made the point that preference satisfaction is, itself, *not* neutral among theories of the good. Rather, it is a specification of one particular theory with special controversies attached to it. Clearly, the choice of which preferences are to be counted is a first major source of controversy. A second notorious set of issues facing want-regarding theories is the interpersonal comparison of want satisfaction. Let us briefly explore this second major controversy before tying the discussion back to our basic criteria for an acceptable theory.

Ever since Lord Robbins's influential article in 1938 expressing skepticism about the possibility of rigorous interpersonal comparisons,[12] proponents of want-regarding theories such as utilitarianism have faced the dilemma that they must either confine their judgments to strict Pareto improvements or they must face the quagmire of interpersonal comparisons. The former path leads to triviality; the latter inevitably produces controversy and indeterminacies. Once again, we are faced with a choice between theories which either do not significantly differentiate, or do so based on a controversial account of the good whose usage opens the theory to jurisdictional challenges by other theories using rival controversial accounts of the good. Once again, we are faced, at bottom, with a choice between vacuousness (violating criterion 1[a]) and jurisdiction problems (violating criterion 4).

In reacting to the story of an Indian Brahmin who regarded himself as "ten times" as capable of satisfaction as a lowly Untouchable, Robbins wrote: "I could not escape the conviction that, if I chose to regard men as equally capable of satisfaction and he to regard them as differing according to a hierarchical schedule, the difference between us was not one which could be resolved by the same methods of demonstration as were available in other fields of social judgment." Robbins concluded: "Every mind is inscrutable to every other mind and no common denominator of feeling is possible."[13]

If we take this "inscrutability" seriously, then want-regarding theories are limited to an extremely narrow range of judgment. We can, of course, follow Pareto in approving of changes that make some people better off and no one worse off. That inference requires only (ordinal) intrapersonal comparisons. But almost every political choice of any significance in the real world will make at least some people worse off, while perhaps making others better off.[14] Provided we assume that any defensible want-regarding theory cannot be entirely insensitive to the question of how at least some of these losses compare to at least some of the gains, the basis for significant evaluation of policy alternatives is blocked once the "inscrutability" claim is taken seriously. Significant policy choices will require some mixture of gains and losses, placing them in the realm of what the economists call the "Pareto noncomparable."

The notorious attempts at an end run around these difficulties (the Kaldor-Hicks and Scitovsky compensation tests) rest on what William J. Baumol called "a concealed interpersonal comparison on a money basis."[15] Using money as a place holder for utilities requires the assumption that a pound or a dollar "yields the same amount of satisfaction to whomever it is given, rich or poor." As Little concluded in his now-classic assessment of welfare economics, "Presumably, most people would agree that such an assumption is ridiculous."[16] Of course, the use of compensation tests to make evaluations beyond the limitations of the Pareto principle can be modified to take account of differences between groups such as declining marginal utility of income. Cost-benefit analysis is often applied so as to incorporate such weights, but they can only be developed in a rough fashion and there is wide room for reasonable disagreement about any particular application.[17]

Hence, we can see that the basic difficulty for want-regarding theories arising from interpersonal comparisons is that, on the one hand, sticking within the limits of the Pareto principle avoids the

problem but at the cost of silence on most issues of social importance; on the other hand, venturing beyond those limits commits
the resulting theory to interpersonal comparisons of want satisfaction—interpersonal comparisons that are inevitably controversial
and can only be accomplished in a rough fashion.

The remaining option in figure 5 raises difficulties of an entirely different kind. As we just saw, want-regarding theories must
face both (a) the problem of determining which preferences are
relevant to an individual's good and (b) the problem that might
be summarized as the Pareto dilemma: either stick to the limited
range of judgment sanctioned by the Pareto principle or commit the theory to controversial and inevitably inconclusive claims
about interpersonal comparisons of want satisfaction.

However, these difficulties can largely be avoided by the second main option, ideal-regarding theories. These latter theories
depart from "citizen sovereignty": they support the conclusion
that a person is better-off regardless of whether any of his actual
preferences have been satisfied. The most prominent contemporary illustration is Rawls's doctrine of primary goods. While it
was useful, earlier, for us to use Rawls's thin theory of the good
as an illustration of the attempt to achieve strict neutrality, the
set of inferences the thin theory is supposed to support—the doctrine of primary goods—can be used to illustrate the problems of
ideal-regarding theory.

The point is that in the original position we make assumptions
about our interests which are supposed to hold *regardless* of what
our actual preferences turn out to be, once the veil of ignorance
is lifted. For purposes of distributive justice, we are supposed
to value liberty first, equal opportunity second, and income and
wealth third. These conclusions are based on a conception of our
interests, regardless of whether, in actual life, our preferences bear
any relation to these priorities.[18] For such ideal-regarding theories, there is no problem of picking and choosing among actual
preferences, accepting some while rejecting others. On this view,

the fact that a value or aim is among those actually accepted by an agent gives it no special status whatsoever in the determination of that agent's good. As a result, such ideal-regarding theories avoid the conundrums just mentioned about interpersonal comparisons of want satisfaction. Degrees of want satisfaction play no role in this kind of theory.

However, ideal-regarding theories avoid these two basic difficulties at a price. They are committed to what might be called *strong paternalistic inferences,* such that an agent X must be better off even if *none* of X's own preferences would support such a conclusion. The paternalism problem challenging ideal-regarding theories shifts the burden of proof; it demands of us a rationale for discounting X's own conceptions of his good in evaluating X's own good. This view would not, in the least, deny that there is room for some paternalistic judgments; only that, when we set aside X's own views, some justification is required.[19]

Few would deny that in at least some isolated cases, there are good grounds for paternalistic inferences. Even strongly paternalistic inferences—where we conclude that an agent is better off even if none of his own preferences support that conclusion—are undeniably appropriate in special cases. Consider the person who suffers from the delusion that he will fly upward if he jumps out the window.[20] If we restrain him so he never gets the chance to test his theory, our inferences about his welfare may, quite appropriately, be strongly paternalistic. More generally, Barrington Moore has documented cases of injustice whose most shocking aspect is the acceptance by the victims of the ideology rationalizing their oppression. Moore's analysis ranges across Untouchables, ascetics, and even some concentration camp victims.[21] But these dramatic cases apply to special circumstances. The problem facing ideal-regarding theories of the good is that they are not limited to such unusual and isolated cases. Rather, they apply generally to whole populations to provide criteria to support a theory of distributive justice or a solution to our differentiation criterion. This general range of application makes the burden of proof confronting a strongly paternalistic theory more difficult. We may have to neglect the actual preferences of whole populations in our evaluation of their own good. What is it that disqualifies their own views from having any weight in, or bearing upon, this evaluation?

I do not mean to argue that this question poses an insurmountable obstacle. My point is only that the special paternalistic burdens of ideal-regarding theories open up room for controversy and reasonable disagreement that are fully comparable to the difficulties we encountered earlier with want-regarding theories. In both cases, once the quest for a strictly *neutral* theory of the good has been given up, no single canonical solution can dispatch its rivals while resting immune from challenges by other controversial theories of the good for which symmetrical claims can be made. Any one of these non-neutral theories of the good can be combined with a notion of impartiality to support significant substantive conclusions. But such support is easily matched by rival theories that share the same basic strategy but apply it to support rival conclusions—by employing their own non-neutral theories of the good. As can be seen in figure 5, we face a choice between building a firm basis for largely empty conclusions (the strictly neutral strategy) and building an insecure basis for significant conclusions (the non-neutral strategies just discussed). By an insecure base, I mean one subject to jurisdictional challenge by rival procedures making symmetrical claims. The strictly neutral strategy survives the jurisdiction problem only by failing to offer differentiating conclusions. The non-strictly-neutral strategies will sometimes offer differentiating conclusions (satisfying criterion 1), only to fail the jurisdiction problem (criterion 3). These latter theories, by relying on some controversial theory of the good in order to get substantive conclusions, become vulnerable to jurisdictional challenge by rival theories that employ a rival controversial theory of the good to get comparably ambitious results. The basic dilemma for these hypothetical thought experiments is that strictly neutral theories lead to substantively empty conclusions, violating criterion 1, while less-than-strictly neutral theories are subject to jurisdiction problems, violating criterion 3. In neither case do we get a firm basis for significant conclusions—conclusions with strong enough substantive implications to satisfy our criteria for an acceptable theory.

Part Three

The Ideal of a Self-Reflective Society

3.1 Toward Reconstruction

As we saw in parts 1 and 2, systematic versions of liberalism seem to require too much. It may, nevertheless, be possible to develop an acceptable theory that satisfies the criteria specified in section 2.1. Such a theory would distinguish among states: it would not be vacuous (satisfying criterion 1[a]) and it would not produce blind alleys (satisfying criterion 1[b]). Furthermore, such a theory would provide a basis for its authority that binds each citizen to the state (satisfying criterion 2), that avoids jurisdiction problems from rival theories (satisfying criterion 3), and that avoids delegitimating arguments from indoctrination problems (satisfying criterion 4).

Our survey of rival strategies in part 2 shows how difficult it is to satisfy all of these criteria. If my claim is correct that at least one possibility plausibly does so, then the difficulties we have already encountered with rival strategies establish the distinctive merit of our proposal.

For a theory to be individually binding, it must justify the authority of the state and it must do so in a fairly demanding way. It must provide an account of the state's authority that is both

universal (applying to everyone subject to that authority) and particular (applying to the relation between *that* state and its citizens,
but not to other states and those same citizens). Thus, criterion 2
demands a great deal.

Besides being a demanding requirement, it is also a powerful
one if we can satisfy it. *If* we can explain why everyone subject
to the authority of the state is individually bound to support it,
then we have explained, in an important sense, why the state is
legitimate. A legitimate state, in other words, is one that everyone
(subject to its authority) is obligated to uphold. This notion of
legitimacy will play a key role in the argument as it unfolds.

Note how difficult it would be to satisfy criterion 2 in the
context of our other requirements—how difficult it is to establish an individually binding connection that is also universal. As
we saw with actual-consent theory, interpreting consent or agreement *strictly* does a plausible job of satisfying criterion 2(b) (the
individually binding character of the obligation), but at the cost
of violating criterion 2(a) (the universality requirement). Furthermore, attempts to satisfy 2(a) only lead to blind alleys (violating
criterion 1[b]) because the requirement for universal consent in
the strict sense leads, in effect, to anarchism.

On the other hand, interpreting consent or agreement *loosely*
may satisfy both parts of criterion 2, but at the cost of failing criterion 1a (the vacuousness test). Consent or agreement has to be
defined so loosely in order to get everyone in a modern nation-
state committed that consent in that loose sense could be claimed
by an enormous variety of states.

Suppose, however, that we consider consent in a hypothetical
rather than an actual form. With an imaginary thought experiment, as in strategy 3 (see fig. 2), it does seem possible to provide
differentiating conclusions. Various versions or reconstructions of
impartial thought experiments in the style of Rawls, Ackerman, or
the other cases of strategy 3 already discussed can be expected to
yield results that satisfy our first two criteria.[1] However, to do so,

they must open themselves up to jurisdiction problems (violating criterion 3). To get distinctive results, they cannot maintain strict neutrality. And if they do not maintain strict neutrality, then they are open to jurisdictional challenge by rival accounts of relevant claims or interests that support rival principles.

It would seem that our requirements for an acceptable theory, while less ambitious than the requirements for *systematic* theory discussed in part 1, are, nevertheless, too demanding. Such a negative conclusion would, however, be premature at this point.

3.2 The Legitimacy Problem

The first issue of political philosophy is the *legitimacy problem:* Are any states morally legitimate in that their authority is justified? I will interpret the authority of the state as being justified when all its members have a moral obligation to obey its commands. Hence, the problem of political obligation (applied to all the citizens of the state) is ultimately equivalent, on this view, to the problem of which states (if any) have solved the legitimacy problem. Of course, in some cases obligations to the state may conflict or have to be overridden by other obligations, but that is an issue about the comparative *strength* of political obligations, not about whether they apply in the first place.

This formulation of the legitimacy problem is rather demanding. To avoid complicating issues, I will say that (fully) solving the problem in this sense is *sufficient* for the state's legitimacy, but I will leave open the question of whether it is necessary. For some purposes, it may well be useful to ignore the question of individual obligation altogether and focus merely on which partially legitimate state is preferable to which other partially legitimate state. But my focus here is on ideal theory, on the question whether a theoretical solution satisfying all of our criteria is possible, at least under favorable conditions.[1] If we can answer this question affirmatively, then another stage in the development of liberal theory can focus on the assessment of options for less favorable conditions—conditions where the theoretical solution cannot be fully realized.

States that justifiably determine political obligations for all of their members will be regarded here as having solved the legitimacy problem. Hence, the legitimacy problem poses an ethical issue and not merely a sociological one. Legitimate states are not merely those that the people in them happen to regard as legitimate. Nevertheless, the actual support of the population will play a crucial role in my argument. Actual support—under certain favorable and demanding conditions—will determine solutions to the legitimacy problem.

It should not be surprising that the actual support of the members plays some role in determining whether a state is legitimate. If our criteria ignored this factor entirely, then there might be cases where we, as philosophers or theorists viewing the matter from outside, held some state to be fully legitimate despite the active and continuing dissent of most of the population. The purely sociological claim that the state lacked significant support would, by itself, block any claim that a full solution to the legitimacy problem had been achieved. Actual support seems to be necessary but not sufficient. Factors justifying that support are, of course, required as well. The legitimacy of the state poses a moral problem that requires that we take account of *both* subjective and objective factors. We need to consider both what people actually do think or believe and some normative criteria that apply independently of those beliefs.

Ideal theory pursues the question whether a solution to the legitimacy problem is possible at all, given favorable conditions. It does not directly prescribe what we should do when those favorable conditions are not achievable. Yet I believe it will be useful and clarifying to see whether we can develop a theory that satisfies our four basic criteria, even under favorable conditions. If we can, then we will have gotten a version of liberalism that coherently clarifies its moral priorities in a manner that is free of the decisive objections that apply to rival versions.

Why are category 3 theories (see fig. 2) subject to jurisdiction problems in a way that my proposal, in category 4, is not? There is a difference, as Ronald Dworkin pointed out in discussing Rawls, between a hypothetical bet and a real one.[2] If you really made a bet under appropriate conditions, then you are now obligated. To argue that you might have rationally and under fair circumstances made one bet or another, and that now you should receive the proceeds from this bet or that, seems irrelevant and unconvincing. Which imaginary bet should you collect on? There will be competing claims based on competing hypothetical constructions of what you rationally ought to have done. This is the jurisdiction problem facing theories in category 3.

By contrast, there are some conditions under which we can think of whole societies as, in a sense, *actually* placing a bet on a certain kind of shared understanding. It won't do to legitimate just any shared understanding, as Walzer does in his book *Spheres of Justice*. Some bets, some choices or commitments, are coerced. Some people have such defective knowledge or judgment that they should not be permitted to gamble. But if the clearly objectionable cases are ruled out, then the agreements that are actually made are not suspect. The difference between categories 3 and 4 is that theories in category 3 would hold a society to a particular, purely hypothetical bet. My proposal in category 4 would only hold a society to the one that has actually been placed under conditions where its collective ability to bet in the appropriate way has been guaranteed.

We have not now placed our bets. In that sense, my argument is as hypothetical as any of the others. But if we did, the actual collective commitments would trump any imaginary claims that under other conditions we might have done something else.

The fact of actually making the bet establishes a presumption that you are obligated to abide by the result—unless there is some basis for placing the action in the suspect category. In the same way, the fact of an actual consensus establishes a presumption that the consensus or shared understanding is authoritative—unless there is some basis for placing it in the suspect category.

The beginning point of our argument, the legitimacy problem, is unavoidable. Any satisfactory account of the fundamentals of liberal theory—or, indeed, any satisfactory account of political theory, whether within or outside the liberal tradition—would have to offer a response to the legitimacy problem. States, by their very nature, demand the right to command the obedience of *all* their members, at least on selected important matters. For an institution to qualify as a *state* in the first place, it must have a monopoly over the authoritative use of force in the territory. If there are "independents" (to use Nozick's term), then in an important sense the conditions for having a state will not have been fulfilled. Independents are persons in the territory who, because they are immune from the commands of the state, could claim the same right to use force as does the state. Independents have no obligations to uphold the state or its actions. In that sense, they represent a challenge to the state's legitimacy and an obstacle to solutions of the legitimacy problem.

What does it mean to say that the state's use of force is "authoritative"? By this I mean (a) that the uses of force are backed by sufficient power to overcome any expected internal opposition, and (b) that they are backed by norms of evaluation that are widely shared within the society. The mere fact that others—for instance, criminals—may use force successfully does not, by itself, mean that the monopoly claimed by the state no longer applies. Criminals do not exercise authoritative force; what they do is not backed by the widely shared norms of evaluation in the society. Or, if criminal action is widely accepted in this way, we should question whether the essential conditions for having a state have begun to break down.

Most states exercise authoritative force. Some may succeed in exercising *justified* authoritative force. To say that the authoritative force of the state is justified is to say that many or most citizens are obligated to uphold the actions of the state. A *minimal* solution to the legitimacy problem has been achieved when many or most members are obligated to obey. I will say, however, that a *full solution* has been achieved only when *everyone* (all the members) has an obligation to uphold the state and its authoritative actions.[3] Of course, most of the state's authoritative actions do not actually involve force. Nevertheless, the threat of authoritative force, if only implicit, distinguishes the state from most other institutions. And the ability to claim an authoritative monopoly over the use of force in a given territory may be taken as a distinguishing feature of the state.

Hence, a fully legitimate state does not merely command its members effectively. All its members also have a justified obligation to uphold its actions, including its authoritative commands. Of course, whether members do have such an obligation may depend on what is commanded. The basic character of the state may change if its policies change drastically enough. "Upholding" the actions of the state does not, of course, mean agreeing with those actions. Upholding means living up to the obligations of membership (whether or not they are backed by force).[4] Realistically, we can expect disagreement wherever there is meaningful freedom of thought. Since meaningful freedom of thought will turn out to be necessary for the ideal of the self-reflective society to be achieved, dissent and disagreement will have to be compatible with solutions to the legitimacy problem, if the argument is to be successful. As a result, we will have to grapple with the same basic issue we saw in our previous discussion of consent theory: How is the authority of the state to be justified over those who disagree or dissent, particularly when dissent or disagreement is virtually inevitable under any acceptable account of realistic conditions?[5]

How are we to get universal obligations to support the state in a manner that satisfies our four criteria? If we rely on actual consent so as to get everyone bound to the state, we either get vacuous conclusions (violating criterion 1[a]) or we get the blind alley of anarchism (violating criterion 1[b]). We could, of course, weaken the requirement that we get everyone bound to the state, but then we would not solve the legitimacy problem in the sense just proposed. Furthermore, we would violate criterion 2 (the individually-binding requirement). We might escape this problem by forcibly indoctrinating everyone so as to achieve unanimous consent, but this would hardly satisfy any plausible account of voluntary consent. Furthermore, it would satisfy these criteria only at the cost of obviously violating criterion 4—the nonindoctrination requirement.

Alternatively, if we were to take one of the strategies of hypothetical consent, we might satisfy our first two criteria (and perhaps the nonindoctrination criterion as well), but only at the cost of jurisdiction problems. As we saw earlier, hypothetical stories can indeed be constructed that will yield distinctive results so as to differentiate among states. Furthermore, these distinctive results can be linked to each member through scenarios of hypothetical choice: the result can be presented as the choice we ourselves would make, to the extent that we were rational and under the appropriate hypothetical conditions for making the choice. Furthermore, if the resulting principles were sufficiently demanding in their requirements for liberty of political culture, they might satisfy the nonindoctrination criterion as well. It is, in other words, conceivable that this sort of theory (category 3) might be developed so as to satisfy three of our four criteria for success.

The difficulty is that this strategy is inevitably vulnerable on our remaining criterion, jurisdiction problems. Rival imaginary thought experiments all presume to be the appropriate tribunal for determining the first principles of the liberal state. Each claims jurisdiction over the choice of ultimate principles. Slightly different constructions of the appropriate hypothetical conditions yield drastically different outcomes. As we saw in detail earlier, a *strictly neutral* construction of relevant claims or interests might plausibly presume to override such jurisdictional challenges. But such a strictly neutral account of claims or interests would make any ambitious, substantive theory of justice impossible. Hence, if we wish to get substantive results from a hypothetical thought experiment, we are left with less-than-strictly-neutral assumptions. As a result, each of the rival theories is rendered dependent on a controversial theory of the good—under conditions where adoption of one rival controversial theory rather than another would yield a significantly different outcome. Hence, rival hypothetical thought experiments do not settle moral controversies about political morality. Rather, they embody those controversies by making symmetrical claims, each purporting to have priority over its rivals.

Once strict neutrality is abandoned, the jurisdictional conflicts are interminable among rival hypothetical thought experiments. None of these hypothetical histories is our history. Each can be challenged by a rival imaginary story yielding different conclusions and claiming jurisdiction over the same issue—the first principles of the liberal state. Clearly, if all four of our criteria are to be satisfied, a different strategy will be necessary.

My strategy will be to fill out category 4 rather than category 3. I claim that the ideal of a self-reflective society provides grounds for its own legitimacy. It purges itself of indoctrination problems, so that its claims to authority cannot be trumped by rival, merely hypothetical scenarios. In filling out category 4, I propose to combine the refinement mechanisms of hypothetical history with the binding authority of a legitimate, actual consensus.

The political practices of any society, I assume, lay claim to legitimacy. The values and other assumptions according to which they support that claim I will refer to as *the norms of evaluation internal to that political practice*. It is, of course, theoretically possible that the political practices of some society might not even lay claim to legitimacy. For example, a state might attempt to support itself with nothing but sheer force. In that case, there would be no norms of evaluation internal to those practices. But that possibility does not offer a counterexample to my argument. My claim will be that there are certain conditions under which a full solution to the legitimacy problem would be possible. If a political system makes no effort even to claim legitimacy, that is no bar to the thesis that, under some conditions, those systems that *do* lay claim to legitimacy could be correct in that claim.

I propose that we consider four demanding conditions which, together, purport to be sufficient for political practices justifiably to claim obligations for support from all their members. If all members are obligated in this way, then the legitimacy problem has been solved and the practices justifiably define the appropriate norms of political evaluation for that society.

These four conditions are:

1. The practices must be *consensual,* that is, they must have wide support throughout the society.
2. The practices must be (at least minimally) *voluntary* in that exit should be unimpeded for anyone who might wish to leave.
3. The practices must supply *essential benefits.*
4. The practices must be *self-reflective.* By this I mean basically that they must be subjected to continuing critical examination through unmanipulated debate. As a result, I will assume that over the long term, the character of those practices (and the consensus about them) will be decisively influenced by the ongoing process of "self-reflective" political dialogue. A society which is self-reflective in this sense will have achieved what we will call a "self-reflective political culture."

These conditions are all *dialogic:* they reflect the strategy of founding legitimacy on a voluntary, self-reflective, collective understanding. They are the collective conditions for a political culture to freely impose its authoritative practices on itself. Essential benefits define the minimum conditions for full membership in the society. Hence, they are necessary for full participation in the collective dialogue. The exit condition is necessary if participation is to be at least minimally voluntary. The self-reflective condition provides for the dialogue's self-critical capacities; its nonmanipulation provisions are also necessary for the process to be voluntary. Last, the consensus condition defines the collective self-understanding that emerges from the dialogue. These four conditions, together, specify the ideal of a self-reflective society.

Each of these conditions will require elaboration. The first three will occupy us for the rest of this chapter. The self-reflective condition will require a chapter unto itself. First, however, it is worth outlining how the basic strategy aspires to satisfy our four criteria for success. Suppose a society's political practices satisfied these four conditions. I am arguing that the minimally voluntary provision of essential benefits through self-reflective practices produces obligations on the part of each member. If those conditions are satisfied for all the members, then they *all* have some obligation to support the result (we set aside questions about the *strength* of that obligation compared to other moral claims). Hence, such a system achieves a full solution to the legitimacy problem because all its members are obligated to support it.

I will interpret the ideal of a self-reflective society as claiming that when the political practices of a society have fully solved the legitimacy problem, then the norms of evaluation internal to those practices become the authoritative practices to apply to that society's political system. At that point we can plausibly claim that those norms of evaluation are immune from the jurisdictional challenges of rival theories precisely because it is those norms that everyone has an obligation to support. The special merit of filling out box 4 rather than box 3 in figure 2 is that the actual acceptance of certain practices—when they are accepted and evaluated in the required way—trumps jurisdictional challenges from the unending variety of claims from hypothetical thought experiments. When those practices survive the rigorous conditions we will define, they can presume to settle the basic questions about the political structure of that society—so long as the requisite conditions continue to be maintained.

It is *not* my position that actual practices always override or trump the claims of philosophers attempting to prescribe from outside the consensus. But we can distinguish between forms of consensus that are *suspect,* on the one hand, and those that have a justified claim to reasonableness and acceptability, on the other. The conditions proposed here are meant to clarify the latter possibility. When a consensus is suspect, there are good grounds for philosophical reform. But when it is both reasonable and acceptable, then it defines the appropriate grounds for evaluating the regime.

Of course, within such a consensus there is always continuing room for philosophical, moral, legal, and political criticism of the most vigorous sort. In fact, a continuing *openness* to such criticism will turn out to be a condition for our being confident that a consensus should not be placed in the suspect category. A justifiable consensus does not preclude further debate because it is always appropriate to advocate a new consensus—one that *would,* if generally accepted, satisfy the same conditions as did the previous one.

Note that for any individual, this position leaves open many appropriate possibilities for moral conflict. First, we have left open the question of the strength of the obligation to support the political practices of the legitimate state. Everyone is obligated to support them, but in particular cases, individuals or groups may well have conflicting obligations that are overriding.

Yet, it might be asked, why does the theory say nothing about the sources of these other possible obligations? The theory of legitimacy put forward here does not presume to settle every moral question. Like most contemporary liberal theory, it remains agnostic about ultimate moral and metaphysical questions outside of its chosen sphere (the political morality of the state).[6] Hence, there would remain many bases for moral conflicts, sometimes overriding ones, in the other moral claims left entirely open by whatever consensus happened to satisfy all of our conditions. In addition, there is plenty of room for disagreement and moral conflict in the advocacy of a change in the consensus, even if it is achieved.

Would a self-reflective political culture require that everyone in it be self-reflective or self-critical in some significant sense? My argument does not require anything approaching such a utopian aspiration. Effective voice could be given to interests across every significant cleavage without every individual choosing to exercise his or her self-reflective capacities. The formation of public opinion is a complex process involving many levels and interactions among competing elites. It has been usefully described as a "cascade" with many levels or pools that develop independently, but that also flow down from one to another, and sometimes bubble up as well.[7]

What we require for our argument is that the continuing political dialogue decisively influence the character of the overall consensus over the long term. Of course, this would happen were everyone to pay attention all the time. But it could also happen just as effectively if opinion leaders influential at each level pay attention to, and participate in, the dialogue. If those who are attentive to the ongoing self-reflective political culture are strategically placed in the formation of the consensus, then the consensus could easily be the product of the self-reflective political culture over the long term—even if many citizens choose, for some period, not to participate actively.

A related point which prevents the theory's requirements from becoming utopian is that whatever consensus is achieved need be only procedural. It may be a consensus merely specifying agreement on how to disagree—but also how, given those disagreements, each side must be given an appropriate hearing to resolve disputes. There is no need for substantive agreement on public policy or political philosophy. A purely procedural consensus would satisfy the demands of the argument. There is no need, in other words, that we settle the substantive issues confronting systematic theories that we confronted in the first two parts of this book.

If the ideal of a self-reflective society is fulfilled, there is a clear basis for satisfying all four of our criteria for an acceptable theory. First, given the demanding character of our proposed conditions, when taken together, it should be clear that criterion 1 is satisfied. The prescriptions of this theory are neither vacuous nor anarchic. They distinguish among most possible states so as to select a distinctive outcome. The conditions are demanding, but if a state satisfied them, the result would not be anarchism, but a state which simply maintained some demanding requirements for freedom of political culture. Furthermore, such a state should satisfy the individually binding requirement (criterion 2). My argument is that social practices determine obligations for each member under the proposed conditions. Even those who dissent must satisfy the obligations of membership so long as the various conditions apply— so long as they receive essential benefits, so long as exit is unimpeded, and so long as the practices are self-reflective and widely supported. Note further how the obligation resulting from benefits under these conditions satisfies what I referred to earlier as the particularity requirement: it is an obligation which the member has to the particular state in question. It is not an obligation which might hold, equally, between that citizen and other similar states. It is not, for example, an obligation to uphold just states in general. Rather, it is an obligation between that member and her state because it is that state which has supplied the benefits.

In addition, the ideal of a self-reflective society satisfies the jurisdiction problem because it requires adherence to an actual, ongoing consensus. This consensus is authoritative, first, because it is widely shared and, second, because it has survived the rigors of self-scrutiny required by a self-reflective political culture. There is a presumption in favor of actual commitments, provided they are not delegitimated by charges of manipulation or indoctrination.

Last, the ideal of a self-reflective society satisfies the nonindoctrination criterion precisely because its political practices are self-reflective. People are not indoctrinated to accept those practices. Rather, they are exposed to continuing, unmanipulated debate about them. Any shared understandings that survive such questioning take on the character of a continuing, rational consensus.

The basic idea is to take the self-purging aspirations of liberal-ism, not merely to the environments that citizens might imagine, but home to the environments in which they actually live. The appropriate decision procedure is not in some imaginary place; it is an ongoing society that is truly free and self-determining in the core components of its political culture.

3.3 Legitimacy and Obligation

The ideal of a self-reflective society offers an account of how social practices could produce universal obligations to support the state under favorable conditions. The argument is limited to ideal theory—to conditions where its demanding requirements could be fulfilled. However, it is worth noting that the range of conditions under which we commonly think social practices can produce obligations is far broader than the special conditions of ideal theory. In those cases as well, it is plausible to think of social practices as requiring a combination of subjective and objective conditions in order for them justifiably to determine obligations. In this sense, the tack we have taken here should not be surprising.

Consider the practice of promise-keeping. If I were to find myself in a society or culture in which the practice of promise-keeping was unknown, others would not understand what I was requesting were I to ask them to make, or abide by, a promise. Even if I explained the practice to them, unless it was widely ac-cepted, it would be hard to hold members of that culture to any apparent obligations they might seem to incur. Even if the practice was known, if it was not widely accepted—if, for example, it was generally understood that promises were made to be broken—then to hold someone to his or her explicit undertaking would simply be to misunderstand the relevant practice. For the practice of promise-keeping justifiably to produce obligations, the practice must, among other things, have widespread acceptance.

But developmental conditions also limit the application of a given practice. Consider *sati*, which was once widespread in India:

the practice of widows viewing themselves as morally required to sacrifice themselves on the burning funeral pyres of their husbands.[1] Sati persisted for centuries before being widely questioned. Women were indoctrinated to believe that their sacrifice was necessary.[2] No matter how widely accepted sati may have been, the fact that it lacked any claim to being self-reflective undermines any claim to legitimacy that might be mounted for it within our framework.[3] A similar point might be made even if women explicitly promised in the marriage ceremony that they would immolate themselves if their husbands were to die first. In the context of such developmental conditions, promise-keeping would provide only an equally suspect basis for such obligations.

While it is not surprising to think of practices as producing obligations, it is equally unsurprising to require a combination of subjective and objective conditions in order for those obligations to be justifiable. The obvious subjective condition is whether the practice actually has widespread acceptance. The obvious objective condition is whether that acceptance is suspect because of indoctrination problems. My proposal that a practice be self-reflective is, obviously, an attempt to respond to the latter issue.

The ideal of a self-reflective society requires a consensus on its defining political practices. By "consensus" I mean that there must be broad support *across* all the major cleavages in the society. By a *cleavage,* I mean a polarization among self-identified groups. Race, class, gender, and ethnicity are dimensions that commonly define such cleavages. There may, of course, be differences that do not define major cleavages. Eye color, for example, does not define self-identified groups that have perceived rivalries with other self-identified groups. Blue-eyed people do not commonly view themselves as members of the group of blue-eyed persons whose interests are in competition with members of, say, the brown-eyed group.[4] But members of a given race, class, or gender commonly do think of themselves in this way. If they do, then a consensus, in my sense, will require that there be substantial support for the political practices in question across any such major cleavage. We are, of course, talking about support, not for particular policies but for the defining political practices of the society, for the general rules of the game, not the details of any particular play.

Wide acceptance is not, by itself, sufficient to produce obligations. Authoritarian regimes that manage to achieve broad support for their political practices do not thereby produce obligations on the part of their citizens. For the claims of my argument to be triggered, several other conditions would also have to apply. The political practices would have to be self-reflective by instituting rather demanding requirements for freedom of political culture; essential benefits would have to be provided universally; exit would have to be unimpeded. Absent these other conditions, a consensus means nothing within our framework. Hence, the fact that Gorbachev claimed, in his first summit with Reagan, the same support from his people that Reagan had from his, would not (if the claim were true) yield any conclusion that the Soviet Union had solved the legitimacy problem in my sense. Within the ground rules of ideal theory, the U.S. has not achieved a full solution, either. But many of the principles we subscribe to are akin to principles that could provide the basis for a full solution.[5]

My claim is that the conditions of the self-reflective society are, jointly, *sufficient* for a full solution to the legitimacy problem. In other words, if the political practices of a society fulfill them for all members, then all members are obligated to support those political practices. Then, if a system lives up to the norms of evaluation internal to those practices, it has solved the legitimacy problem in our sense.

To take a simple example, imagine a political system that employed the familiar institutions of Western constitutional democracy so as to satisfy our conditions. Liberty of political culture would have to be encouraged in a rather demanding way to satisfy the self-reflective condition. Various scenarios for the universal provision of essential benefits might be devised. For the moment, let us assume that this is accomplished through a well-developed welfare state apparatus. Exit is unimpeded and the political system, despite significant dissent, continues to enjoy broad support. The political practices defining the state would then produce universal obligations for all members receiving the essential benefits. Because everyone would then be obligated to support those practices, the state, if it conformed to them, would be legitimate. What we have been calling a full solution to the legitimacy problem would have been achieved because all the members would be obligated to support the political system as it was then constituted.

More specifically, if the political practices in this constitutional democracy included elections, then there would be certain norms of evaluation attached to the conduct of those elections. It would not be enough for the regime to *claim* that it conformed to the accepted practices. For example, if it had secretly stolen the election and the election system continued to enjoy broad support (in part because no one realized it), then a full solution to the legitimacy problem would not have been achieved because the regime would fail to conform to the norms of evaluation internal to the practices that would, indeed, have legitimacy in that society—the practices of the election system the public would think it is employing.

Suppose, however, that voter fraud was well known to be common. I am assuming that where stealing elections is a well-known practice, it is not publicly accepted as a *justifiable* practice. Internal to the norms of evaluation that constitute election practices, at least in part, are norms condemning the stealing of elections.

But we might imagine another practice which was more or less like the elections we are familiar with, but in which it was publicly acknowledged that the ruling elites would steal the election whenever, in their great wisdom, they considered it to be in the national interest. To distinguish this practice from elections as we know them, let us call this the practice of Stealelections.

Could Stealelections maintain itself as one of the practices of a legitimate state in my sense? It is most unlikely that such a practice could withstand the glare of publicity, dissent, and criticism required in a self-reflective political culture. Stealelections has a norm that is self-delegitimating. It claims to count the votes in a fair and objective way, and then it will announce either true or false results, depending on which necessary for an outcome chosen in an entirely different way. We could reasonably expect such practices to lose their support when their true character is known—as would be required in a self-reflective political culture.

The example also raises the question of how varied will be the range of practices that satisfy our condition in various social contexts. Practices that are not self-delegitimating and that do survive self-reflective questioning may differ quite a lot in other respects. The difference between proportional representation and majority rule in single-member districts, for example, is not one that would be settled by any of the criteria developed here. If either system became the accepted practice in a state that fulfilled all of our conditions, then the norms of evaluation internal to *that* set of election practices would be the appropriate ones to apply in that political system. A similar point might be made about bicameral versus unicameral legislatures and, more broadly, about American-style presidential systems versus European-style parliamentary systems.

Within the position developed here, many questions must be settled *contextually:* they must be settled within the confines of ongoing practices. It is an illusion of systematic theory to think that an entire blueprint of the just society can be created from scratch, regardless of social context and regardless of the social norms widely shared in the society.

In considering the difference between proportional representation and single-member districts, I mentioned cases of relatively familiar democratic practice. Suppose, however, I had mentioned political practices outside our familiar democratic consensus, practices involving the systematic exclusion of some racial or ethnic group through discrimination or "white supremacy."[6] As an empirical matter, such practices are unlikely to satisfy our consensus condition (which would require a preponderance of support from those excluded as well as from those included).

But suppose that through a successful apparatus of repression, a consensus *throughout* the society were maintained. Obviously, the repression necessary to maintain such a consensus would violate the demanding requirements of liberty for a self-reflective political culture. Acts of repression often break a consensus because they become issues in themselves. Regardless of whether they have this additional effect, they would count, as we shall see, as crucial violations of one of our conditions.

Suppose, however, that the subordinate group, for reasons deeply buried in its history and distinctive culture, remains quiescent, without the dominant group having to exercise any overt acts of repression. For example, the great masses of legal ex-Untouchables in India are said to live in "psychological cages" that for a long time stifled effective expression of their interests.[7] As we will see later, for a political culture to be "self-reflective" it must give unimpeded and effective voice to the interests across every significant cleavage in the society. When voices are forcibly silenced through familiar forms of repression, it is obvious how this condition is violated. But when the problem is simply that a subordinate group has developed a distinctive culture of silence—so that it refuses to voice its interests—then can a consensus of racial and/or ethnic subordination maintain itself without violating our conditions?

White supremacy, or any similar practice of racial or ethnic subordination (as in a caste system), will, in itself, constitute a barrier to fulfilling the ideal of a self-reflective society. For such practices rob members of a relevant group (a group across one of the society's significant cleavages) of the ability to get an effective hearing for their interests. The fact that the practice might conceivably be so successful that it robs the subordinate group of any desire to voice its interests is only an indication of how dramatically our conditions are violated.

The remedies for such a situation are not obvious. The state cannot simply command people to give voice to their interests. However, the difficulty can be dealt with, indirectly, by specifying *background conditions*—social practices that would permit the ideal to be fulfilled. These background conditions will occupy us in section 3.5.

Of course, racially discriminatory systems are also likely to fail our condition of providing "essential benefits" to all members. Under realistic conditions, such systems can be expected to deny what Adam Smith called "the necessaries" to many members of the subordinate group. Smith's discussion offers a starting point for clarifying what we mean by "essential benefits." His proposal, however, does not go far enough for our purposes. In a classic discussion, Smith explained:

> By necessaries I understand, not only the commodities which are indispensably necessary for the support of life, but whatever the custom of the country renders it indecent for creditable people, even of the lowest order, to be without. A linen shirt, for example is, strictly speaking, not a necessary of life. The Greeks and Romans lived, I suppose, very comfortably, though they had no linen. But in the present times, through the greater part of Europe, a creditable day-labourer would be ashamed to appear in public without a linen shirt.

Smith went on to make the same point about leather shoes in his own time.[8]

Marx also included social and moral elements in his notion of the subsistence needs of the worker: "The number and extent of his so-called necessary requirements, as also the manner in which they are satisfied, are themselves products of history, and depend therefore to a great extent on the level of civilization attained by a country; in particular they depend on the conditions in which, and consequently on the habits and expectations with which, the class of free workers has been formed."[9]

These two famous discussions suggest that it is reasonable to include relativistic elements in a definition of essential benefits. Both Smith and Marx also grant that there is an obvious objective element, as well: that there are minimum physical requirements for survival. However, as in the other components of our argument, we will also specify an objective *developmental* condition. For the account of essential benefits to satisfy our argument, it will have to be the one that is both self-reflective and widely shared. In a self-reflective political culture, all the significant political practices will be the subject of continuing, unmanipulated debate. Obviously, the essential benefits provided for every member will count as one of the society's significant political practices. Hence, the character of those benefits must be part of the legitimating consensus and it must be open to continuing debate and criticism.

Even so, we cannot mean by "essential benefits" exactly what Smith meant by the "necessaries"—even when we add the requirements that the conventional element be both self-reflective and consensual. Or, if we were to limit the account in that way, it would be subject to disturbing objections. Recall Smith's formula: "whatever the custom of the country renders it indecent for creditable people, even of the lowest order, to be without." The examples of racial or ethnic subordination already mentioned make it obvious that the disparities between "orders" of people may be so great that to require only what is necessary for decent members of the lowest order may be too little for our purposes. If the lowest order is the lowest in a caste system or a system of racial domination, its essentials may be so meager that receiving such benefits would not serve our argument. For one thing, mere receipt of such benefits would not plausibly produce obligations. Most important, a group maintained in such subordination would be subjected to a continuing, coercive structure of domination—a kind of domination that would effectively shut them out of the political dialogue. As we shall see in our discussion of the background conditions for a self-reflective political culture, if a group is maintained in such conditions, one of the central requirements of the argument has been violated. Consider this description of the Untouchables:

> In earlier times Untouchables over many parts of India could not enter streets and lanes used by caste Hindus. If they did, they had to carry brooms to brush away their footprints in the dirt behind them. In

other places, Untouchables could not contaminate the earth with their spittle, but had to carry a box around their necks to keep pure the ground reserved for the spittle of caste Hindus. In still other parts of India an Untouchable had to shout warnings before entering a street so that the purer folk could get out of the way of his contaminating shadow.[10]

Of course, we have already specified the requirement that the account of essential benefits be both self-reflective and consensual. The caste system appears to have been widely accepted for long periods.[11] It is, however, doubtful that the consensus on these practices could have survived our self-reflective condition. However, suppose for a moment that I am mistaken in this empirical speculation. Imagine that the members of a subordinate group—whether Indian Untouchables, blacks in an apartheid system, or women in an extreme patriarchal society—accept the practices which keep them in their places, even when those practices are subject to continuing criticism in a self-reflective political culture. In the argument we are developing, receipt of essential benefits will constitute a basis for obligation. Is it plausible to regard such meager benefits as producing an obligation to support such an objectionable system?

Smith's formula required, roughly, whatever was necessary to be a "creditable" member of the lowest order. Our problem is that the gap between orders may be so great that creditable members of the lowest order may lack the self-esteem and mutual respect necessary for participation in a self-reflective political culture—where they have to voice their interests to members of other orders. Hence, I will amend Smith's formula to require the social conditions for what I will call "full membership" in a self-reflective society, even for persons of the lowest order. I will interpret the social conditions for full membership as including what is necessary for equal consideration of one's claims or interests in the public dialogue in such a culture. By equal consideration, I do not mean that your claims are considered by an equal number of people or that they are given an equal amount of television time. I mean only that they are treated as deserving equal consideration on their merits; they are not discounted because of the identities of the people involved (either in voicing the claim or in applying it). It is publicly accepted—by both speakers and listeners—that such claims deserve the same serious hearing given to the interests of other groups. The social conditions for full membership thus entail both self-esteem and mutual respect. In that sense, they include not only Smith's "necessaries" but additional requirements as well.[12]

Clearly, the Untouchables described above were denied those conditions. They would not voice their interests, nor would they be listened to if they tried. They lacked the social prerequisites for enough self-esteem even to claim equal consideration in the public dialogue. Systems of racial or ethnic subordination, if their practices are consensual, rob the subordinate group of the self-esteem necessary for full membership. Of course, if their practices are not consensual, such systems have no claim to legitimacy within my framework. But if they are consensual, even within the subordinate group, then their failure is in the provision of the essential benefit of full membership to all.

By specifying "social conditions for full membership," I mean to require what is *generally* necessary for self-esteem and mutual respect. There will always be members in a given group with special psychologies or idiosyncrasies that, despite every advantage, deprive them of self-esteem. Rodney Dangerfield may achieve enormous success and still lack self-esteem. In determining whether his receipt of the benefits of full membership produces any obligations on his part, we need only consider the social conditions that *generally* produce self-esteem and mutual respect. If obligations follow from the receipt of benefits, my position will be that the vagaries of his psychology do not relieve him of those obligations.

Suppose, however, that the Rodney Dangerfields of this world organize, claiming that if they are not provided with further luxury goods at public expense, then they will continue to lack self-esteem. Let us call this group the Unappreciated. Note that if the Unappreciated are claiming that they should get diamonds and BMWs as "essential benefits," then those benefits would have to be provided to everyone. Would they be willing to pay their share of such an enormous public expenditure? Could such a proposal ever achieve the required consensus?

Clearly, we can expect the answer to both questions to be negative. In addition, luxury goods are not plausible candidates for essential benefits in our sense because those benefits are defined with reference to members of the lowest order. They specify what would be necessary for members of the lowest order to achieve full membership in a self-reflective political culture. Upper-middle-class people feeling deprived without further luxury goods are not members of the lowest order. But suppose they claim to be. They present us with eloquent testimony of how oppressed they feel. To give such a claim plausibility, we can specify that they would have to be willing to trade places with members of the group generally recognized to be the lowest order—perhaps the ghetto underclass. The Unappreciated do not plausibly define a lowest order and therefore, pose no counterargument to our account of essential benefits.

But why focus on a lowest order? As in Smith's account, we are trying to specify what is truly essential for a kind of creditable membership in the society. Because the essentials must be provided to everyone, the focus must be on a minimum account that serves the purposes of the argument. Otherwise, the entire scheme would be patently impractical. Note that if, for some reason, there were no significant inequalities in the society, then any order or group could be picked at random. But every known developed society, capitalist or socialist, has substantial inequalities, as these might be judged along any plausible dimension proposed as an answer to our original problem of value (income and wealth, prestige, rights and liberties, primary goods, and so on). Hence, we can assume that there will be inequalities along significant dimensions and the theory must be designed to deal with that fact.

The general outlines of our strategy should now be clear. If a political system provides essential benefits—the social conditions for full membership—to all members, then all members acquire an obligation to support the system (provided that it also meets our other conditions). If all members are obligated to support a given political system, then its practices have become authoritative in that society. To the extent that the system lives up to its own authoritative practices, it then achieves a full solution to the legitimacy problem.

Clearly, a crucial move in the argument is the inference that from the receipt of essential benefits under these conditions, one can acquire an obligation. This issue has been a notable subject of debate and deserves extended discussion.

Readers familiar with H. L. A. Hart's argument from fairness will find nothing surprising in the notion that one can acquire an obligation through the receipt of benefits. Hart proposed: "When a number of persons conduct any joint enterprise according to rules and thus restrict their liberty, those who have submitted to these restrictions when required have a right to a similar submission from those who have benefited by their submission."[13] The right of those submitting to the rules yields a correlative duty of the others to obey, and this duty should be enforceable by public officials according to rules.

Rawls later proposed a similar principle, calling it the "principle of fair play," but added the proviso that the scheme of social cooperation had to be "just." In that way he left the obligation to uphold such schemes dependent on a more general theory of justice.[14]

The principle of fair play understood in the Hart/Rawls sense is far more general in its application than our proposal. The ideal of a self-reflective society requires that the benefits provided be essential, that exit be unimpeded, that the practices be self-reflective, and that a consensus about them be maintained.[15] Only when all of these conditions apply am I claiming that the individuals receiving the essential benefits incur obligations to uphold the practices. The Hart/Rawls principle of fairness would attribute obligations to individuals under the special conditions covered by my proposal, but it would also do so under a far wider range of conditions. These other cases are Nozick's target in his provocative assault on the principle. Nozick's argument is worth discussing in order to clarify the differences:

> Suppose some of the people in your neighborhood (there are 364 other adults) have found a public address system and decide to institute a system of public entertainment. They post a list of names, one for each day, yours among them. On his assigned day (one can easily switch days) a person is to run the public address system, play records over it, give news bulletins, tell amusing stories he has heard, and so on. After 138 days on which each person has done his part, your day arrives. Are you obligated to take your turn? You *have* benefited from it, occasionally opening your window to listen, enjoying some music or chuckling at someone's funny story. The other people *have* put themselves out. But must you answer the call when it is your turn to do so? As it stands, surely not. Though you benefit from the arrangement, you may know all along that 364 days of entertainment supplied by others will not be worth your giving up *one* day. You would rather not have any of it and not give up a day than have it all and spend one of your days at it.[16]

Nozick continues this line of argument with other examples: "If each day a different person on your street sweeps the entire street, must you do so when your time comes?" Or if you don't, then should you "imagine dirt as you traverse the street, so as not to benefit as a free rider?" He also asks us to imagine a book thruster, someone who tosses books into yards and then demands payment for them. These examples prompt his general conclusion that the principle of fairness is mistaken: "One cannot, whatever one's purposes, just act so as to give people benefits and then demand (or seize) payment."[17]

Nozick's attack, while compelling on its chosen ground, is overly broad if it is extended to our argument. These examples dramatize the difficulty of ascribing obligations when one or more of our conditions are absent. But they do not establish that obligations never follow from the receipt of benefits.[18]

Note that our conditions would not determine obligations for any of Nozick's cases. Not only are the practices in question not self-reflective, but the benefits provided are not essential. These practices offer entertainment or other minor benefits, rather than protection of some recognized, crucial interest. My claim is only that when all four of my proposed conditions are satisfied, it is plausible to attribute obligations to all those who receive the essential benefits. Nozick wishes to rebut the claim that obligations result from the receipt of benefits under a far broader range of conditions—conditions that do not affect my proposal one way or another.

To see the contrast posed by my proposal, consider this variation on Nozick's example suggested by one of my students who had recently returned from the Middle East.[19] Suppose you are in an isolated settlement under constant threat of attack. There are 364 other adults. Each person is expected, for one day, to man an early warning system to sound the alarm in case of real danger. After 138 days on which other persons have done their part, your day arrives. Are you obligated to take your turn?

Let us suppose further that the settlement meets our other conditions. Its practices are self-reflective. They are subject to continuing, unmanipulated critical examination. This is important, because if there were really no need for the early warning system, our evaluation might be quite different. If the enemies were entirely fictional or hallucinatory, then the case for each member being obligated would vanish. Also, let us assume that exit is unimpeded. If you don't want to man the system, you don't have to stay. The settlement has not made you a prisoner to its scheme of collective benefits. But if you do stay, you must either contribute what is expected of members or become a free-rider. And, in keeping with one of our remaining conditions, let us assume that there is a consensus on this practice and the obligation for members it defines. The debate about the practice has been self-reflective, but the consensus about its appropriateness or legitimacy survives, nevertheless.

In this case, it seems compelling to conclude that members who receive these crucial benefits are obligated, so long as they stay, to live up to the publicly accepted obligations of membership. The alternative would be to claim that they would be violating no moral requirements were they to choose to be free-riders. If the benefits provided were frivolous or trivial, then members could, in general, do without them. But if the benefits are among the essential conditions of full membership—and this conclusion is supported by a self-reflective consensus—then obtaining those benefits for each member is a matter of the most urgent priority. In this case, the benefit in question is survival, both individual and collective. If there are social practices that provide for your survival through other members living up to their acknowledged obligations (the obligations that are consensually and self-reflectively accepted as the obligations of membership), does it not seem plausible to attribute a similar obligation to you—so long as you continue, with the unimpeded option of exit, to be in the position of receiving the crucial benefits?

Practices that fulfill our conditions have the unique merit of being collectively self-imposed in a rational manner. The practices that survive self-reflective scrutiny with a consensus of support are collectively self-imposed in the sense that they have the requisite acceptance, and they are rational in the sense that they are self-reflective.

Note that, unlike some other efforts to reconstruct the fairness argument, our conditions do not require that the practices provide net benefits to each member (when compared with the costs of membership). Richard Arneson, for example, has proposed such a requirement.[20] If our other conditions are all satisfied, such a proviso would limit, unduly, the range of permissible practices. For example, suppose that a fully developed welfare state were to meet all of our provisions. Furthermore, suppose that to support the provision of essential benefits to all members, it turned out that the rich had to be taxed in such a way that it was plausible to conclude that they paid more than the essential benefits they received. They could survive nicely without welfare, food stamps, or subsidized medical care. Even law and order might be provided for them on competitive terms by private security forces. It might well be the case that their net costs of membership outweighed their net benefits. Still, I would argue that if such a welfare state satisfied all of our other conditions, it would then define the set of political practices that were collectively self-imposed in a self-critical manner. Wealthy members would then be obligated to pay taxes at the levels decided by the legitimate political institutions even if it could be argued that, for them, the burdens of membership outweighed the benefits. Of course, the wealthy have a built-in source of protection in our scheme in that, to maintain all of our legitimacy conditions, there must be continuing support for the system, on balance, across all the significant cleavages of the society. The cleavage between rich and poor would surely be such a significant cleavage, and if the tax rates become too burdensome, the requisite consensus on the overall political system could disappear. Despite this limitation, the possibility for significant redistribution remains—a possibility that Arneson's more restrictive proviso would rule out entirely.[21]

3.4 Liberty of Political Culture

The ideal of a self-reflective society is proposed here as a way of filling out box 4 in figure 2. It is meant to give substance to the notion of a refined-actual decision situation. Our previous objections applied to boxes 1–3, the brute-actual, brute-hypothetical, and refined-hypothetical alternatives. My strategy is to propose a particular way of filling out this remaining category that aspires to satisfy our four criteria for an acceptable theory.

To fit in box 4, a theory has to specify a refinement mechanism for preference development that is not merely imaginary, but is part of the actual ongoing lives of people in the system. On my proposal, this refinement mechanism consists in certain demanding conditions for liberty of political culture.

What form would liberty of political culture have to take in order to avoid indoctrination problems? First, note that our concern is with liberty of *political* culture. Under this heading I include liberty of political expression, belief, and association.[1] "Political" in this definition of political culture should be interpreted broadly to include:

1. evaluations of actual public policies and proposed alternatives;
2. evaluations of issues that one believes ought to be taken up by public policy;
3. evaluations of any possible alternative forms of governmental organization;
4. normative bases for any of the above in other realms of conscientious belief (such as religion);
5. factual findings (historical or current) sincerely believed to be crucial to any of the above.

In this kind of liberal state, members would be free to openly debate government policy, to advocate alternative policies or, indeed, alternative forms of government; they would also be free to join together in groups for these purposes without fear of persecution or reprisal. Liberty of political culture in this sense defines the least controversial and essential core of liberal theory.[2] At the outset, I have given this core a quite minimal interpretation. As we proceed, I will argue that taking these liberties seriously is more demanding than at first appears.

We have already seen some of the reasons why the basis for this principle is, at present, problematic. The most ambitious recent argument explicitly supporting liberty—Rawls's argument for its "priority"—requires a particular controversial theory of the good, one that is not sustainable by his own assumptions about the restrictions on choice in the original position. As we saw earlier, if the thin theory of the good is really thin, it cannot support such strong conclusions. But if thicker theories are admissible, then the door has been opened to a variety of controversial, substantive theories, no one of which, by itself, can be relied on to provide a firm basis for significant substantive principles. Scanlon's argument for freedom of expression was similarly based on a particular controversial ideal of individual development (autonomy), one that he later abandoned for a balancing-of-interests approach.[3] Isaiah Berlin's fallibilist argument for liberty requires, for its defense, an explanation of why our evaluation of liberty is not equally fallible itself.[4]

Most important, Mill's theory is susceptible to varying interpretations, each exemplifying one of the approaches just mentioned. "Individuality" is a particular, controversial ideal of human development, as is the "autonomy" that some commentators have found at the root of Mill's position.[5] Or is Mill's ultimate principle utilitarianism, in which case the basis for liberty would seem to be rendered insecure by the balancing of interests required for consequentialist calculations? Or, if the argument for liberty is the fallibilist one, as some passages suggest, why is it not self-referential?[6]

The issue can also be brought full circle. If the argument for liberty is that it serves truth, there is no reason offered for liberal states to value truth except that truth, in turn, serves utility. However, this connection is not only dubious in important cases, but it also presupposes a prior commitment to utilitarianism—which, especially in Mill's "ideal" version, is an eminently avoidable ultimate commitment for liberal theorists.[7]

My strategy will be to recast the problem in terms of a self-reflective political culture: one that is *significantly self-critical as a result of unmanipulated dialogue*. A political culture is "significantly self-critical" when the social practices defining its regulative institutions are consistently subjected to widespread and conscientious criticism. By "regulative institutions," I mean the state (its components and representatives) and other institutions that wield significant power in the society (such as corporations, unions, and even universities) under the authoritative protection of the state (hence, the Mafia, even if powerful, would not normally be one of the society's regulative institutions in this sense).

What do I mean by "unmanipulated dialogue"? Dialogue is reasoned debate designed to persuade on grounds conscientiously believed by the participants to be valid and appropriate. For an act of expression to contribute to political dialogue, its crucial normative and empirical premises must (a) be held with conviction by the actors and (b) be sufficiently exposed or open to analysis that they can be critically examined and debated by others. To merely defer to the judgment of Wise Man X does not contribute to political dialogue, but rather forecloses it. On the other hand, to argue that Wise Man X should be deferred to may be a contribution if its underlying premises are exposed for debate and held with conviction.

Contributions to political dialogue are not limited to discursive prose. Conscientious political views can also be expressed effectively in art, poetry, drama, and fictional works of various sorts. In fact, such works may have a far greater effect on their audiences than conventional political debate. Mark Twain's journalistic writings about racism were either censored or ignored, but his novel *Huckleberry Finn* employed irony to attack racism far more profoundly. Similarly, John Dos Passos's journalistic work on the Sacco and Vanzetti case had little impact compared to that of his novel *U.S.A.* (a far more searching argument that Sacco and Vanzetti could not have received a fair trial).[8] In these cases and countless others, a work of imagination can embody and express a political argument as fully developed as any we might see in conventional debate, but formulated so as to have a greater impact on the reader.[9]

In the sphere of culture, this argument only provides clear protection for literature and art that is formulated so as to contribute to political dialogue (in the broad sense of "political" defined earlier). This is, of course, a major limitation. However, this essay is designed to develop a distinctive basis within secular-liberal theory for freedom of political culture. It remains an open question how the state should treat other creations of culture that have no plausible political dimensions. However, because of the potential for abuse built into any form of censorship, once the case for freedom of *political* culture is granted, a basic presumption against other uses of censorship or prior restraint should follow. We should be skeptical of any institutional arrangements that would permit government officials to determine whether works of art or literature contain the redeeming social content characteristic of political dialogue.

However, it is undeniably the case that some inferior works which are clearly political will have a *fundamental* basis for protection within this argument, while some other works of "great" literature will not. Many aesthetic criteria have nothing to do with political culture, even when this notion is interpreted broadly. I acknowledge this limitation. My ambition here is to clarify a basis for the core of liberty; other issues, undoubtedly important, will have to await other efforts, perhaps employing different strategies.

Returning to the central argument, what do we mean by "unmanipulated" dialogue? I will approach this issue by defining two forms of *strong manipulation,* one *explicit,* the other *structural.* Political dialogue will be considered "unmanipulated" when it is not strongly manipulated in either the explicit or the structural sense. The idea is that dialogue should not be subjected to strong manipulation within the broad area of "political" culture defined earlier.

By explicit manipulation, I mean the imposition of penalties because of the content (actual or prescribed) of one's conscientious political views, whether held privately or expressed publicly (and whether the form of expression, or the manner of holding the belief, be individual or in association with others).[10] I am focusing on attempts to manipulate "conscientious political views" because it is one's conscientious views on public matters which contribute to political dialogue. Malicious statements, offered voluntarily when one knows (or has good reason to believe) that they are false, do not fall within this argument. It is an open question at this point whether or not the state might impose penalties (through, for example, the libel laws) to discourage such acts of expression—so long as they clearly fall outside the area of protection for conscientious political views.[11] Furthermore, by "conscientious views" I mean those formulated so that they contribute (or would contribute if expressed) to political dialogue.

What does it mean to say penalties are imposed "because of the content (actual or prescribed) of one's conscientious political views"? I mean "actual or prescribed" from the perspective of the state or of any other manipulator (as the manipulator attempts to determine what one's actual views are or ought to be). So if the state (or some other manipulator) concludes that my views are objectionable and subjects me to penalties as a result, I have suffered from explicit manipulation—even if its conclusions about what my views happen to be should turn out to be incorrect. The attempt at manipulation is not removed from the objectionable category merely because the state is incompetent in determining the true character of my beliefs. Similarly, I include "prescribed" views within "explicit manipulation" because there are cases where the state (or some other manipulator) might be satisfied if it succeeded in forcing insincere expressions of one's apparently conscientious political views (regardless of any further investigations into one's real views). If I face punishment unless I mislead others about my real views, then the expression of my political views has also been subjected to explicit manipulation. Whether or not the state succeeds in altering the real character of my conscientious beliefs, if it succeeds in forcing me to misrepresent them, it has distorted the character of public debate available to us all.

By the "imposition" of penalties, I mean that penalties are brought about (or are credibly threatened) involuntarily and/or coercively. They are brought about against one's will and, if necessary, through the use of force. By "penalties," I mean consequences clearly and significantly adverse to one's interests as these can be determined with respect to the status quo to which one is entitled according to the relevant legitimate practices. Practices can be considered legitimate either because they satisfy all the conditions of our argument or because they are held to be legitimate, in turn, by institutions or practices that do satisfy our conditions. So, for example, the practices determining relevant entitlements might be specified by the political system, and that system, in turn, might be legitimated by our argument; or the relevant entitlements might be legitimated by the market and the market might be legitimated by the political system.

Legitimate social practices define norms of evaluation for action in particular cases, according to which some factors are relevant and others are irrelevant. If one's conscientious views (including one's views about one's own actions) are considered irrelevant to the determination of outcomes according to a legitimate social practice, then the benchmark for determining penalties or damages to one's interests should also consider them irrelevant.

Let us begin with a simple case of explicit manipulation. If I am jailed because of the content of my political opinions (or for associating with others who hold similar opinions), then I have clearly been subjected to the kind of explicit manipulation that is unacceptable according to this argument. However, the issue of determining the appropriate status quo needs to be considered before we can know what counts as a "penalty." To take a trivial example, if I express myself badly in a debate tournament and for that reason do not win, I am worse off, but not worse off than I am entitled to be (under the familiar practices defining what we mean by a debate tournament). Not winning the debate tournament (or a prize or a fellowship) because of the way I express myself (orally or in writing) is not a "penalty" if it makes me no worse off than I am entitled to be (as determined by the relevant legitimate practices). However, if I were really entitled to win but did not because of a personal history of political views irrelevant to the debate, then I would have been exposed, involuntarily, to an unacceptable penalty resulting from political discrimination.[12] Of course, in particular, idiosyncratic cases, these factual issues are virtually impossible to investigate. This does not, however, undermine the general principle. If content-related penalties are imposed on conscientious opinions within the realm of political culture, then that realm has been explicitly manipulated.

I specified earlier that if one's conscientious views are considered irrelevant to the determination of outcomes according to a legitimate social practice, then the benchmark for determining harms should also consider them irrelevant. Consider a Jewish merchant in a largely Christian community faced with an organized effort, directed at his particular business, for citizens to patronize only "Christian" businesses. While we normally believe people can shop where they like, the practices defining market relations do not regard private convictions on religious or political matters as relevant to determining one's market entitlements or one's opportunities to compete in the market. The merchant's business is morally entitled to equal consideration in the marketplace regardless of his private, conscientious views. If the effort is sufficiently well organized that his business suffers substantially as a result, then his conscientious views have been subjected to the penalties of explicit manipulation.[13] But this result should not be surprising. On the argument proposed here, all conscientious views in the broad sphere of political culture are protected from explicit manipulation. The only question arises in determining what counts as a penalty. If we accept the interpretation of market entitlements suggested by these examples, then people and institutions, including corporations, are entitled to equal consideration in the market regardless of private convictions (of the individuals involved) which are irrelevant to their roles in the market. If that is the case, then boycotting them for those private convictions must count as explicit manipulation, regardless of how objectionable those convictions may be.

Of course, only an organized effort with an explicit target could be expected to have the significant effects we are attributing to market boycotts. Mere *advocacy* of the general benefits (whatever these might be presumed to be) of having only "Christians" as merchants would not count as explicit manipulation. When formulated as a contribution to political dialogue, such advocacy would, in fact, be protected by liberty of political culture. By contrast, the organized effort to punish the Jewish merchant for his private religious affiliation would not have this protection (because it would itself constitute explicit manipulation), despite the fact that speech would inevitably be a part of the behavior necessary to carry out such boycotts.

Note that this discussion applies to boycotts directed against individuals because of their private convictions. The idea is that the practices defining the market entitle merchants to equal consideration in the market regardless of their religious convictions. On the other hand, those practices would not entitle corporations (or individuals) to equal consideration *regardless of their activities in the market*. If people object to an individual's or a corporation's market activities, a boycott does not violate our criteria. Market activities, as opposed to private religious convictions, are not irrelevant to market activities. Hence, the Nestlé boycott was sparked by the health effects of that firm's marketing strategy for infant formula. On this analysis, a firm is not entitled to equal consideration of its products in the market, regardless of its market activities. A boycott that did not violate any other rights would be entirely compatible with our framework.

The limits of explicit manipulation are far from obvious. For example, the mere fact of speech, even when politically relevant, does not bring behavior within the realm of freedom of political culture as defined here. As Kent Greenawalt notes: "Blackmail, extortion, and criminal coercion . . . usually involve communication. Communication is a necessary or an almost inevitable element . . . in perjury, in larceny that depends on trick or fraud, and in solicitation; and it usually plays a part in armed robbery. Punishment for these activities has not been thought to raise serious constitutional difficulties. Yet, if anything constitutes speech, it is explicit verbal and written communications." [14]

It is not all forms of speech per se that we propose to protect under the banner of liberty of political culture. Rather, it is contributions—actual or potential—to political dialogue. Freedom of political culture protects conscientious views and sincere, reasoned efforts to persuade others about them so long as they fall within the sphere of the "political" defined earlier.[15] It also protects individuals joining together to express themselves—to add voices to the political dialogue that might never get a hearing if expressed by isolated individuals. But joining together to contribute to political dialogue—to reasoned, conscientious debate on matters of public policy—is quite different from joining together to impose penalties on identifiable individuals or groups merely because of *their* conscientious views. The freedom of the latter to remain free of explicit manipulation can be maintained without infringing on the freedom of the former to engage in political dialogue.

Blackmail, larceny, and bank robbery do not fall under the umbrella of protection for liberty of political culture, even though they may all require acts of communication. However, to say that various speech acts fall outside the area of required protection leaves it an open question whether the state should employ legal penalties (criminal or civil) to discourage them. I do not propose to develop a general theory of legal coercion and the criminal law. My argument in this essay is limited to the question of defining the sphere within which a self-reflective political culture might flourish.

One further complexity should be noted. I defined "explicit manipulation" as applying to the imposition of penalties for the content of one's conscientious political views "whether the form of expression or the manner of holding the belief be individual or in association with others." Thus far, we have focused primarily on isolated individuals. But the freedom to associate can be equally important. First, groups and institutions can have an impact on public debate far greater than would be possible for most isolated individuals. If such voluntarily organized, collective efforts were prohibited, some voices would be effectively silenced.

Second, the freedom to associate is crucial for the transmission of conscientious views over time—particularly from one generation to the next. Without it, there are some forms of explicit manipulation which may be resisted successfully by isolated individuals in the short term, but which may win out over the long term. In the former Soviet Union, religious sects such as the Pentecostalists suffered greatly from the fact that their children were effectively taken away from them.[16] Even if individuals resist repression of their conscientious beliefs in their own lifetimes, if the values for which they stand cannot be passed on, groups embodying those values in their ways of life may die out. In that way, explicit manipulation can have drastic effects over the long term when it is directed at voluntary efforts at association with like-minded persons to produce and influence the socialization of the next generation.

For this reason, I interpret freedom of association to include the freedom to voluntarily form and maintain families and to have substantial influence over the socialization of offspring in those families. This does not, of course, make the families immune from all forms of coercive interference. First, when the voluntary and consensual character of a family breaks down, there may be grounds for interference by the state (or others) to protect the rights or interests of some members. It is the mutually voluntary formation and maintenance of families that deserves protection within freedom of association. Second, I specified only that families have a "substantial influence" over the socialization of their offspring. Within this framework, there is certainly room for states to intervene when families monopolize the determinants of socialization in ways that do serious harm to the child or that prevent the child from being capable of assuming responsibilities in adult society. Hence, the state could certainly intervene if a child were denied appropriate nutrition or medical care, or the essential educational prerequisites for participation in the political and economic life of adult society.[17] These limitations are modest enough, however, to leave wide latitude for families to transmit their conscientious views from one generation to the next.

Throughout human history, states have engaged in explicit manipulation. One of the earliest *systematic* cases comes to us from China, from a historian writing two millennia ago about the first edict of the Quin (Ch'in) emperor in the third century B.C.:

> All books in the imperial archives except for the records of Quin should be burned; all persons under heaven, except learned scholars in the Academy, in possession of the BOOK OF ODES, the BOOK OF HISTORY and essays of the hundred schools of philosophers should take them to the magistrates and be burned; those who dare to talk to each other about the BOOK OF ODES and the BOOK OF HISTORY should be executed and their bodies exposed in the market; those who refer to the past to criticize the present should be, with members of their families, put to death; officials who knowingly failed to report are guilty of the same crime; after thirty days from time of issuing the decree, those who have not destroyed their books are to be branded and sent to build city walls; books not to be destroyed are those on medicine, pharmacy, divination, agriculture and horticulture; those who want to study edicts should be taught by officials.[18]

The Quin dynasty, despite its brutal suppression of all opposition, lasted only fourteen years. Its most notable mark in history was not the building of the Great Wall, but the attempt to erase all history, all freedom of thought. Our knowledge of these distant events comes from the great Chinese historian Ssu-ma Ch'ien (Si-Ma-Quian), who was himself castrated for contradicting a later emperor (Han Wu-Di).

It was surely this kind of control over freedom of thought that led John Stuart Mill, in the essay *On Liberty,* to conclude that "we have a warning example in China" about the social consequences of suppressing intellectual freedom: "They have become stationary—have remained so for thousands of years . . . . They have succeeded beyond all hope . . . in making a people all alike, all governing their thoughts and conduct by the same maxims and rules; and these are the fruits." [19]

Explicit manipulation imposes penalties, not only on particular individuals, but also, when carried out systematically, on entire societies. In the interests of maintaining those in power, such societies blind themselves to the possibility of self-improvement or self-reflective re-examination. Within our framework, their practices cannot satisfy the conditions for solving the legitimacy problem because any consensus supporting them must be suspect. Any such consensus has not passed the test of self-reflective political dialogue, a test that could give us confidence in the kind of scrutiny it has survived.

Thus far, we have focused only on explicit manipulation. However, public dialogue can be subjected to strong manipulation without any recourse to coercion or penalties. Crucial voices may fail to achieve an effective hearing without it being necessary for any voices to be silenced. The same result may follow without anyone being penalized for speaking: if the relevant voices do not wish to speak, if they do not have an opportunity to be heard, or if the relevant audiences have learned not to listen. In these three main ways, effects similar to those of explicit manipulation may be achieved without any penalties actually being imposed or threatened against anyone within the sphere of political culture. In this sense, avoiding explicit manipulation is not enough to guarantee meaningful freedom of political culture.

To cover these cases, a second form of strong manipulation needs to be specified. Because it concerns the structure of communication, rather than explicit acts of manipulation, I will call it *structural manipulation*. In some ways it may seem misleading to call it manipulation at all, since it may well occur without anybody consciously playing the role of manipulator. But just as some situations may be structured in a coercive manner without anybody consciously playing the role of coercer,[20] some situations may be structured in a manner that has the effect of manipulation, without anyone consciously playing the role of manipulator. With this terminological caveat in mind, we can define structural manipulation.

The basic idea is that *effective voice must be given to interests across every significant cleavage in the society.* When this effective voice is denied, then the political dialogue has been subjected to structural manipulation. An effective voice is one that is widely disseminated and that people are prepared to, and capable of, substantially evaluating on its merits (rather than merely on the basis of the source).[21] The difficulty, of course, is that it is not clear, at least at first glance, how such an effective voice can be guaranteed.

Note, first, that whatever the difficulties of implementation, the criterion at least gives us a notion of what voices are crucial to the dialogue's being self-reflective rather than suspect. Second, the strategy for achieving a self-reflective political culture will often be *indirect*. It will focus on altering background conditions for the development of practices and preferences. It need not be the direct result of policy choice. Clearly, in this case, structural manipulation will only be avoided when the background conditions are adjusted, in an ongoing society, so that a culture of *participatory civility* has been achieved. In such a culture, people will participate and listen (and be capable of listening) on the merits.

Setting aside, for the moment, the issue of background conditions, let us consider the dangers of strong manipulation. Manipulated debate in either of our two senses deserves to be distrusted. What confidence can we have in any political proposition when critics of it have been silenced? Or when crucial interests, reflecting any of the main cleavages in the society, have been shut out? If there is a consensus, under such conditions of manipulation, it must be suspect. It is suspect because we cannot know how it would generally be evaluated if the challenging voices had not been suppressed.

When crucial interests or contrary voices are suppressed, the claim of political institutions to make rational demands upon us has been compromised. It is compromised because, within our framework, the claim to rationality depends upon those institutions and practices being supported by a consensus that *survives* unmanipulated self-scrutiny. We cannot know how a consensus would survive contrary voices if there are none. We cannot know whether, if some crucial interest had been given effective voice, support across a main cleavage might have disappeared. We can-

not know the degree to which acts of manipulation (or the toleration of structural manipulation) are self-serving. The capacity of
the system (and those acting within it) to evaluate itself has been
severely impaired.

The claim of the political practices to survive rational evaluation is only vindicated when threatening voices and crucial interests obtain the requisite hearing. After such a hearing, if we should
conclude that the contrary arguments are mistaken, or even ridiculous, we are likely to have benefited from them, nonetheless. We
would then get what Mill called "the clearer perception and live-
lier impression of truth, produced by its collision with error." [22]

Most important, if the dialogue takes place free of strong manipulation, any consensus that survives has a basis for making a
rational claim upon us. Strong manipulation would rob us of one
of the necessary conditions for reasonably having confidence in
those propositions. While Mill's argument was only formulated
to deal with what we have called explicit manipulation, his general point is relevant: "There is the greatest difference between
presuming an opinion to be true, because, with every opportunity
for contesting it, it has not been refuted, and assuming its truth
for the purpose of not permitting its refutation. Complete liberty
of contradicting and disproving our opinion is the very condition
which justifies us in assuming its truth for purposes of action;
and on no other terms can a being with human faculties have any
rational assurance of being right." [23]

I will rely on this basic insight of Mill's in the argument for
liberty of political culture. However, by the "complete liberty of
contradicting and disproving our opinion," we mean something
more demanding than the liberties of thought and discussion defended in Mill's essay. [24]

Nevertheless, Mill's insight here is central and far-reaching. It
permits a different slant than the one commonly taken on what
we have been calling the legitimacy problem. Instead of arguing
that liberty of thought and discussion are instrumental to truth, in
general, and that truth, in general, is instrumental to utility, [25] we

are arguing that liberty of political culture is necessary if we are to have any confidence in certain particular political "truths," and that having confidence in just those particular political "truths" is part of the solution to the legitimacy problem.

As I noted earlier, political practices that can justifiably determine obligations of all members provide a basis for solving the legitimacy problem. But members are obligated to support political practices only if they are of a kind that it is reasonable for them to accept. I am taking the position here that, at least within ideal theory, it is reasonable to accept only political practices that have passed a certain test of rationality—of self-critical re-examination. That test is that the consensus about them must survive the self-reflective scrutiny of what we have been calling unmanipulated debate. Once the debate is manipulated, then the political practices protected by such manipulation are suspect in their rationality. If the practices are suspect, then it is no longer reasonable in the same way for us to accept them. As a matter of expediency, under less-than-ideal conditions, we may well be forced to accept them. But the claim of the system to provide a full solution to the legitimacy problem would have been undermined.

According to the ideal proposed here, a political culture is "self-reflective" when it provides the collective conditions for its own rational self-evaluation. We should be suspicious of the self-evaluation of any other form of political culture. The hand of the state is heavy on most citizens—demanding moral deference in the name of allegiance and patriotism. The latter qualities may be admirable, even in a self-reflective political culture—but only when care is taken to separate them from unthinking obedience and from the surrendering of self-critical capacities.[26]

A self-reflective political culture defines certain far-reaching conditions of liberty, conditions under which a society's members are free from all forms of strong manipulation of their conscientious political views. That this requirement is distinctive can be seen from comparing it to the most common formulation of liberty of political thought and discussion. Consider what might be called a minimal, or laissez-faire, construction: no significant coercive interference with the liberty of individuals to express political opinions, hold political beliefs, or associate voluntarily together for those same purposes. By "no significant" coercive interference, I do not mean to rule out time, place, and manner restrictions used sparingly enough so as not to affect the basic character of political debate.

The laissez-faire view is a close cousin to the one developed here. The most obvious connection is that coercive interferences with political expression, belief, or association will count as explicit manipulations of the political culture in the sense defined earlier. Penalties imposed on people (individually or collectively) for expressing or holding certain beliefs will either silence voices in the debate through sheer coercion or silence them through intimidation and self-censorship (conducted under threat of coercion). The requirement that a self-reflective political culture forgo explicit manipulation is sufficient, by itself, to yield significant liberties.[27]

Of course, it is not enough that the state refrain from acts of coercion intended to silence people. If the state fails to protect individuals or groups from third-party efforts to intimidate or silence political expression or the holding of certain political beliefs, the same problem of explicit manipulation arises. Vigilante groups may silence unpopular views as effectively as may official action. Less obviously, job discrimination based on political belief or political expression may have equally devastating effects. If I am threatened with firing, or if I am denied the equal consideration I am entitled to in the job market because my ideological views (irrelevant to the job at issue) prompt employment discrimination, my liberty to express and/or hold political opinions has been interfered with, coercively.[28]

However, this minimal, or laissez-faire, construction is clearly insufficient to bring about a self-reflective political culture. Consider the possibility raised forcefully by C. E. Lindblom that democratic systems are vulnerable to "circularity": "It may be that people are indoctrinated to demand . . . to buy and to vote for . . . nothing other than what a decision-making elite is already disposed to grant them. The volitions that are supposed to guide leaders are formed by the same leaders." The key to what Lindblom calls "indoctrination" is its "lopsided" character. It is "not the mutual persuasion of liberal democratic aspiration but a lopsided, sometimes nearly unilateral persuasion by business, governmental and political leadership directed at ordinary citizens who do not themselves easily command, as leaders do, the services of printing and broadcasting." [29]

There is no need for us here to enter the fierce empirical debate about the extent to which this kind of circularity applies to the U.S. or to any other major Western democracy.[30] At the very least, it is, theoretically, a troubling possibility, one that is clearly compatible with the minimal, laissez-faire construction of political liberties. Without any resort to coercive interference in political expression, belief, or association, it is possible for some groups to speak, as it were, so loudly and so much as to deny an effective hearing to contrary voices.

Hence, the negative guarantees embodied in the minimal, laissez-faire conception do not, by any means, ensure the conditions for a self-reflective political culture. They do block the coercive interference that could be achieved by explicit manipulation. However, those guarantees do nothing to prevent the other form of strong manipulation discussed above: they do nothing to ensure an effective hearing for other crucial voices, voices representing interests across the main cleavages in the society.

Somehow, the possibility of structural manipulation has to be ruled out without the remedy itself taking the objectionable form of strong manipulation. The kind of liberty guaranteed by the laissez-faire view would protect individuals, groups, or institutions acting voluntarily, but in concert, so as to drown out all opposing voices. Instead of employing the blunt tool of coercion to silence voices in the chorus that would otherwise predominate, the state should attempt to create forums and positive incentives for political dialogue—particularly for crucial interests that would not otherwise achieve an effective hearing. In this sense, a more activist liberty of political culture is required.

But is not intervening actively in this way itself a form of manipulation by the state? While it might be labeled manipulation by some, it is not a form of strong manipulation in the sense defined here. No voices are suppressed, no crucial interests are shut out of the dialogue. If the state intervenes to create forums or positive incentives for the expression of opposing views, it is not attempting to manufacture consensus around a preferred conclusion. Rather, it is preventing us from adopting views prematurely, before there has been an airing of contrasting voices and of crucial interests.

The term *intervention* should not be misunderstood. I use it only to distinguish the activist conception from the merely laissez-faire, or minimal, conception of liberty of political culture. It does not imply that the government should follow every debate and intervene directly to balance out the dialogue based on its judgment of predominant messages about any particular issue. Not only is such a system not required; it would be extremely unlikely to operate well or to facilitate the goal of a self-reflective political culture. The very fact that public debate was known to be under official scrutiny, for whatever putative reasons, would likely have a chilling effect on the more extreme forms of dissent or criticism. As a matter of institutional design, we should distrust efforts by public officials to explicitly manage or control the content of political dialogue. On any realistic construction, they have too much at stake for their self-interest not to affect the results, covertly if not insidiously. This caution should be applied even if their mandate were to free dialogue from all forms of strong manipulation, both explicit and structural. Rather, the strategy should be to create certain general practices in the operation of the media and of the public spaces open for political debate. Over the long term, these practices should be designed to facilitate the openness of forums and positive incentives in those forums for opposing views and for the representation of crucial interests.

But why limit these general interventions to positive incentives and other adjustments in background conditions? If a self-reflective political culture is so important, why not just threaten or coerce everyone to participate so as to produce one? There are two obvious objections. First, we cannot expect to achieve a form of political culture untarnished by strong manipulation by threatening people with coercive penalties whose application, in many cases, will constitute strong manipulation in the explicit sense. Second, our goal is a political culture that is self-reflective in its political dialogue. By "dialogue" I mean the expression of conscientious, reasoned debate on grounds sincerely believed to be valid and appropriate by its participants. As a matter of institutional design, it is unrealistic to expect coercion, threats, and intimidation to produce much conscientious debate in this sense. Apart from some principled resistance, this kind of brute interference is likely to produce only cynical or self-serving efforts to avoid whatever penalties are feared.

Let us attempt to formulate, in greater detail, what is distinctive about the activist conception of liberty of political culture. Unlike the laissez-faire conception, the activist conception is not merely negative. It does not consist entirely in prohibitions on interferences with the holding or expressing of political beliefs (or of people associating together for either purpose). While the activist conception gives a major role to such guarantees, sole reliance on them would leave the system vulnerable to "circularity," indoctrination, and patterns by which the interests of certain groups or institutions prompt them to drown out their opposition, effectively shutting crucial interests out of the continuing dialogue. For this reason, I have posited the need for incentives, forums, and forms of access for political dissent if a self-reflective political culture is to be achieved—if, in other words, the political culture is to become significantly self-critical as a result of unmanipulated debate.

Of course, this goal may strike some people, at the outset, as bizarre. Why should critics even be permitted, much less encouraged, by official design? A common view is that the state can pursue its goals more efficiently if meddlesome critics are out of the way. But without critics—and the self-reflective political culture they help create—one must be suspicious of the state's goals and of the processes by which those goals have been determined in the first place.

Of course, agonized self-reflection is no substitute for action. But the prescription for a self-reflective political culture does not preclude a design for political institutions permitting swift action when circumstances require it. Of necessity, criticism will often be retrospective rather than prospective. In any case, we have said very little thus far about the structure of political decision making. The self-reflective argument is not intended to produce a blueprint for the best liberal institutions. Rather, it is meant to single out certain distinctive features of an ideal liberal state—features that would permit a full solution to the legitimacy problem.

Suppose, however, that all forms of strong manipulation are eliminated but no criticisms of the system result. Political theorists and social planners finally think up the perfect system and get it adopted. Our definition of a self-reflective political culture requires that it be consistently self-critical through unmanipulated debate. Suppose that unmanipulated debate produces no criticism. Are we then in the position of claiming that such a system must be worse precisely because it is so perfect as to be beyond criticism?

With Mill, I assume that the empirical concomitant of significant freedom of thought is diversity of opinion on the full range of questions touching on our definition of the political. Hence, perfect agreement that a system was beyond criticism would in itself constitute powerful evidence that meaningful freedom of thought had not been achieved.

Hence, without suppression of freedom of thought, we can assume that there will always be critical voices which could be given an opportunity to contribute to self-reflective dialogue, to the system's capacity to examine itself. If we do away with both forms of strong manipulation, then these conscientious criticisms can get aired. If the consensus supporting the system's political practices can maintain itself in the face of the resulting self-critical examination, then that consensus has a reasonable claim to authority over us.

3.5 The Conditions of Activist Liberty

In Anthony Trollope's novel *Phineas Finn,* the protagonist, who has spent his political career arguing for greater democracy, is put up as the candidate for Loughton, a rotten borough controlled by the Earl of Brentford. Trollope describes his first visit to the borough:

> Each individual man of Loughton then present took an opportunity during the meeting of whispering into Mr. Finn's ear a word or two to show that he also was admitted to the secret councils of the borough,—that he too could see the inside of the arrangement. "Of course we must support the Earl," one said. "Never mind what you hear about a Tory candidate, Mr. Finn," whispered a second; "the Earl can do what he pleases here." And it seemed to Phineas that it was thought by them all to be rather a fine thing to be thus held in the hand by an English nobleman. Phineas could not but reflect upon this as he lay in his bed at the Loughton inn. The great political question on which the political world was engrossed up in London was the enfranchisement of Englishmen,—of Englishmen down to the rank of artisans and laborers;—and yet when he found himself in contact with individual Englishmen, with men even very much above the artisan and the labourer, he found that they rather liked being bound hand and foot, and being kept as tools in the political pocket of a rich man. Every one of those Loughton tradesmen was proud of his own personal subjection to the Earl![1]

When Phineas later remarks, "They all seemed to be very obliging," the earl replies: "Yes they are. There isn't a house in the town, you know, let for longer than seven years, and most of them merely from year to year. And, do you know, I haven't a farmer on the property with a lease,—not one; and they don't want leases. They know they're safe. But I do like the people round me to be of the same way of thinking as myself about politics."[2]

The awkward situation in which Phineas finds himself is emblematic of a challenge facing us at this stage in our argument. Trollope confronts us with a political culture distorted by clientalism and deference. Nominally equal liberties are emptied of any meaningful content by the spillover effects of economic and social inequalities. Yet the participants in this drama enjoy, for the most part, formal rights to legal and political equality—rights that are clearly insufficient to yield a self-reflective political culture in our sense. Our problem is to determine what additional adjustments in background conditions would be necessary to banish the specter of the Earl of Brentwood from liberal-democratic institutions.

The earl's remarks suggest the beginnings of a response to this challenge. Using an economic threat directed at his tenants' votes would constitute explicit manipulation in our sense. Just as the "Buy Christian" boycott against the Jewish merchant in our earlier example employed coercive penalties against conscientious religious views, the threat of eviction if one does not vote according to the earl's preferences would constitute a similar intrusion of political manipulation onto market relations. In both cases, the status quo against which penalties are to be judged should be defined independently of one's conscientious views. Once the power of explicit manipulation is removed, it is an open question how long the political culture of the borough can be dominated so easily. A number of other factors in the design of background conditions can be specified that, together, would encourage diversity and meaningful participation. Or, at least, our task in this section is to explore adjustments in background conditions that, together, make it reasonable to assume that this sort of counterexample would be ruled out.

But the example also poses a challenge of a second kind. My contention that the earl's behavior constitutes explicit manipulation depends on an interpretation of market relations that holds political beliefs to be irrelevant. People have a right to be treated in the market in a manner that is independent of their conscientious beliefs in the sphere of political culture.

However, suppose that the right of the earl to dictate politics in the borough was widely accepted, and, furthermore, that similar prerogatives of noblemen were the generally accepted practice throughout the society. Would that legitimate the practice, according to our proposal? Or, at least, would it not vitiate my claim that the appropriate benchmark for judging a penalty was defined by market relations as they would exist without any reference to politics?

The answer to the first question is clearly no. For the ideal of a self-reflective society to legitimate a given social practice, many conditions in addition to its being widely accepted must be satisfied. Among other factors, it should be obvious that our self-reflective condition would pose a major obstacle. Even if such a practice were widely accepted, there is no reason to believe it would maintain its legitimacy in the face of the kind of unmanipulated, critical scrutiny required by our argument.

But there is a second reason for believing that such a practice—let us call it political clientalism—could not be legitimated by a self-reflective political culture. Not only is it not likely to be accepted *after* being subjected to thoroughgoing criticism of the kind required for a self-reflective political culture. It is incompatible with the kind of unmanipulated, critical dialogue required to produce a self-reflective political culture in the first place.

The incompatibility stems from the fact that if clientalism were established as an accepted practice, it would institutionalize strong manipulation in our second sense. It would freeze out any effective voice for the interests at stake in the division between patron and clients. With such a practice in place, people would not be prepared to speak, and those few who would speak would find that their potential audience had learned not to listen. In either case, clientalism would prevent the interests of the subordinate groups from getting an effective hearing.

Hence, if clientalism were institutionalized, it might prevent us from classifying its practices as explicit manipulation (because the practices in question would no longer regard political opinions as irrelevant to the determination of benchmarks against which changes would constitute penalties), but those practices would, nevertheless, count as strong manipulation in our second sense of structural manipulation.

This dramatic but admittedly isolated case brings into relief the fact that, at this stage in the argument, we need to focus on choices among alternative possible practices that might facilitate a self-reflective political culture. We cannot rest content with merely ruling out certain forms of coercion or interference if we are to give content and plausibility to the notion of a self-reflective political culture. Isaiah Berlin's distinction between positive and negative liberty, while in some respects a simplification, helps us focus on the difference between what might be called the laissez-faire and the activist conceptions of liberty.[3] The laissez-faire conception is negative in that it offers freedom *from* certain kinds of intentional interference with political dialogue—freedom from the imposition of penalties through what we have been calling explicit manipulation.

However, without explicit manipulation, a political culture may fail to be "self-reflective" in various ways. Important groups or crucial interests may lack the self-esteem, the resources, the inclination, or the opportunity to voice their interests. The activist conception proposes to attack these problems *obliquely* through adjustments in background conditions.

One reason for attacking these problems obliquely is that it would be virtually impossible to attack them directly without employing some form of strong manipulation. Even then, we should be skeptical about what would be achieved by such an effort. As noted earlier, we must be distrustful of government officials regulating communication according to its content—even if their announced mandate is to produce a more self-critical dialogue.[4]

The oblique strategy of the activist conception is to ensure that background conditions encourage widespread, meaningful participation. By background conditions, I mean the basic social practices in the society determining the distribution of valued goods or characteristics. On this broad definition, background conditions in contemporary American society would include market relations, patterns of family relations, the educational system, and the system of entitlements and obligations (affecting all three of the above) characterizing the modern welfare state. The system of criminal justice, and the practices governing access to the political system and to the mass media, would also qualify as background conditions. They are all social practices that determine the distribution of valued goods or characteristics (jail sentences, political power, social esteem, money, and so on).[5] For our purposes, we need not develop an exhaustive list of the basic social practices defining background conditions; we need only focus on those background conditions that might plausibly play a role in implementing the activist conception.

The activist conception of liberty requires that background conditions be adjusted nonmanipulatively to ensure widespread, meaningful participation in the process of political dialogue and to ensure freedom from strong manipulation (in either sense). By "nonmanipulatively," I mean the adjustments should proceed without employing strong manipulation.

Our task at this point is not to provide a blueprint for the self-reflective society. Rather, it is to address a prior issue: whether the ideal of a self-reflective society is hopelessly utopian, or whether it might be achievable under conditions that are realistic for a modern, developed society, at least under favorable conditions. Defending the latter possibility is the main task remaining to us. I propose to do so by outlining a general strategy for implementation and by introducing two examples of the kind of institutional innovation that would be necessary: the representation voucher and the deliberative opinion poll. My suggestions constitute a research agenda rather than a blueprint, but I hope to demonstrate that the ultimate goal is a reasonable aspiration.

We need to establish that it might be possible to achieve mass engagement with a self-reflective political dialogue, one that gives effective voice to interests across all the main cleavages in the society. For our purposes, the crucial issue is not the level of mass political participation, but whether there is mass engagement with a self-reflective political dialogue, one that avoids manipulation in the senses we have defined.

The required adjustments in background conditions can be considered under three headings: *capacities, incentives,* and *opportunities.* Under the first heading, I will argue that the social conditions for certain essential capacities are required as part of the "essential benefits" (guaranteeing the social conditions of full membership). Under the second and third headings, I will argue that certain incentives and opportunities are required if manipulation, explicit or structural, is to be avoided. If background conditions are adjusted under all three headings, then it may be possible to fulfill the activist conception of liberty of political culture.

First, citizens generally should have the capacity to receive and express political views, both factual and evaluative, on any issues they find salient within the broad domain of "political" culture defined earlier.[6] These capacities obviously include whatever literacy and language skills are necessary for participation in the shared social space of the political culture. They also include whatever knowledge of social conventions and institutions constitutes a minimum prerequisite for political participation. In this country, if I do not understand the role of Congress, or of parties and elections, my ignorance is likely to cut me off from many effective acts of political expression and participation (writing my congressman, helping in campaigns, making contributions, and so forth). In addition, one must be knowledgeable about the shared social conventions of evaluation regarded as appropriate for public policy. This does not mean that one must ultimately subscribe to those conventions. But one must understand what they are in order to receive (and interpret what one receives) and/or transmit (in appropriate form) any response one might be moved to put forward. Hence, by "capacities" we mean literacy, language skills, and knowledge of social conventions. The latter is interpreted broadly to include knowledge of the prerequisites for participation and evaluation, both in formal political processes and in the informal practices available to citizens.[7]

Hence, the entire system of socialization—within which I include families, school systems, the mass media, and private voluntary organizations (ranging from churches to the Boy Scouts)—must be assessed according to how well it ensures these capacities throughout the population. When there is evidence that children are not being provided with the essential capacities—literacy, language skills, knowledge of social conventions necessary for participation and evaluation—then it is appropriate for the state to intervene by causing some adjustment in the relevant background practices, provided that its interventions do not themselves constitute strong manipulation.[8]

This result should be neither controversial nor surprising. For example, accepted notions of family autonomy leave ample room for the state to intervene in the "best interests of the child."[9] While these notions leave families wide latitude to influence the development of their children, it is still appropriate for the state to ensure that, somehow, the child is prepared for adult roles by acquiring the basic capacities necessary for citizenship. Similarly, whatever else we might expect of our school systems, ensuring these basic capacities would seem central to their mission.

But can the state adjust background conditions that determine capacities without engaging in explicit manipulation? First, it should be noted that the state can have a considerable impact without employing coercive penalties. For example, the state can set standards for schools to ensure that the basic capacities are developed in students, and then it can offer matching funds or grants to schools that meet its requirements. Alternatively, it can offer vouchers directly to students—provided that the vouchers are used at schools or at preschool programs meeting standards that ensure acquisition of the required capacities.

It is also worth noting that some of the most dramatic improvements in the cognitive development of children from disadvantaged families have resulted from educational efforts in the home designed to affect patterns of parent-child interaction so as to encourage the early acquisition of various cognitive skills.[10] Such efforts require the voluntary participation of parents; government support to make such assistance available could do a great deal to ensure that children from the "underclass" do not end up effectively disenfranchised as adults for lack of basic skills.[11]

A second point is that even when the state employs coercive penalties, it need not employ them based on the content of conscientious political views. In that way, it can avoid explicit manipulation. The required literacy, language skills, and knowledge of social conventions are all defined independently of the individual's conscientious political views. To a large extent, people may believe what they like but still acquire the capacity to employ certain skills and to understand the social conventions necessary for full membership in the society. There is no presumption that they will subscribe to the view that these conventions or skills are appropriate, but only that they will have sufficient familiarity with those skills and conventions to be able to employ them if they wish.

Suppose, however, that someone resists as a matter of principle. She might, for example, believe that modernity is simply evil and that to acquire the capacities even to understand it is to open herself up to forbidden influences and temptations. To permit her to resist acquiring the skills necessary for participation is to permit her, effectively, to disenfranchise herself from active membership in the political culture. The difficult issue is that the state has to ensure, at some point, that she has the capacities necessary to be able to make the decision (to opt out) competently. This will require that at some stage in her life she be given enough familiarity with the culture to be able to evaluate it. As a result, some exposure to modernity will be unavoidable. After that, if she opts out voluntarily, there is no reason why it must be a concern of the state's.

With children, however, the matter is a bit different. For parents to be permitted to deny their children the essential capacities to participate in adult society (and eventually to make their own decisions about their respective conscientious beliefs) is to impose a penalty on them. We can consider the essential capacities for adult participation something to which everyone is entitled (or to which every normal child capable of acquiring them is entitled).[12] Within our framework, they should be considered part of the "essential benefits" of full membership. Hence, if parents deny their children the conditions necessary to acquire those capacities, they are penalizing their children based on their notions of what the conscientious beliefs of their children eventually ought to be. Their action fits the definition of explicit manipulation offered earlier. For the state to intervene in families merely to ensure that children acquire these essential capacities, one way or another, is to intervene so as to prevent strong manipulation by the parents.

To require the provision of essential capacities for all future members of the society is not to single out the children of any particular group. Of course, if parents object not to their children acquiring the essential capacities, but to one particular manner of acquisition—say, school attendance rather than home instruction—then the state might well have to accommodate alternative methods. The parents would have a compelling case when there was a practical, alternative strategy for fulfilling the same purpose that could be made available to them without imposing a penalty on them (and without imposing a significant penalty on anyone else).

Turning to our second heading, citizens should generally have incentives to exercise the capacities just enumerated. Two kinds of incentives need discussion: negative and positive. By negative incentives, I mean the penalties ruled out by the prohibition on explicit manipulation. This prohibition prevents negative incentives from being imposed (or credibly threatened) because of the content (actual or prescribed) of conscientious political views (to the extent that these are formulated as contributions to political dialogue).

But the mere absence of negative incentives cannot be expected to guarantee participation. We need positive incentives, both for engagement and for participation. Unless citizens are generally engaged by the process of political dialogue, unless they have an interest in conscientiously employing their capacities, the contributions of others effectively will fall on deaf ears. While some apathy and disinterest is inevitable, a self-reflective political culture would be impossible unless there were mass receptiveness to the dialogue.

The first step, but only a minimal one, in providing an incentive for mass engagement in the political culture is to make public opinion consequential. If we institutionalize a regular connection between public opinion and public policy—in short, if we establish some form of *democracy*—then public opinion on political matters is, by that fact alone, rendered consequential. It is differentiated from opinions about fashion or the weather or the upcoming football season. Of course, in large-scale institutions or groups, individual incentives to participate in the provision of public goods may be so small as to be nearly negligible. Those concerned merely with the benefits flowing from policy decisions will often find it rational (in a narrow, instrumental sense of rationality) to be free-riders. They can get the benefits of a public good without going to the trouble of contributing to its provision.

To take the classic example, why should I vote (or otherwise participate) in the politics of a large-scale nation-state? My vote will not, on any reasonable expectation, make any difference to the outcome and whatever benefits result from public decisions are benefits I will receive anyway. Even if my reasons are not self-interested but I am evaluating the consequences of an election on altruistic or ethical grounds, those consequences will result in any case, and my vote is unlikely to make any difference.[13] A similar point can be made about most other forms of political participation available to me in the large-scale nation-state—making small campaign contributions, signing petitions, canvassing in elections, manning the phone banks, and so forth.

It is worth pausing for a moment to consider this familiar line of argument, for it undermines the claim that institutionalizing democracy might, by itself, provide an incentive for people to become engaged by their political culture in general, and by the process of political dialogue in particular. If the notion is that my opinion matters because my vote matters (and I cannot responsibly decide how to vote unless I am engaged by public debate), then this strategy for adjusting background conditions would clearly be undermined if it were rational to conclude that my vote, on any reasonable analysis, simply does not matter.

Hard-headed analysts of probability have found the prospects of individual influence so small that they have only managed to rescue the rationality of voting by positing voter satisfaction with the "ethic" of voting.[14] But that ethic, conceived in terms of its consequences, in turn supports the conclusion that it is irrational to vote, given even trivial costs and the clearly minuscule probability of having any individual effect. Positing satisfaction with the ethic of voting does not save individual participation from the charge of irrationality because it relies on individuals being irrational, not in their calculation of costs and benefits, but in their inclusion, within the benefits, of a duty that is irrational on its own terms.

Of course, for our purposes it would not be devastating if individual participation were irrational—provided that we could count on it in any case. At this point in our general argument, we are concerned with the adjustment of background conditions so as to provide incentives guaranteeing enough participation, or at least mass engagement, to produce a self-reflective political culture. If participation is irrational but we can count on it in any case, then, in some sense, the task has been accomplished. The difficulty is that in a self-reflective political culture we could not count on people continuing to accept an ethic that was irrational on its own terms, because of mere habit or lack of analysis. The forces of inculcation that might permit such an ethic to be widely maintained in some societies would not operate as effectively in one that achieved the level of conscientious and continuing self-examination we are positing here.

This conclusion about the irrationality of the duty follows most clearly when the issue is posed in act-utilitarian terms or in terms of any other clear-headed evaluation of the consequences of the isolated decision to vote (even when the consequences that are valued may be completely independent of utility or preference satisfaction). However, some other main approaches that depart from this assumption do not, thereby, produce more satisfactory results. One approach is to conceive of political participation not in terms of its consequences for the state of the world, but in terms of its expressive function for the individual agent. Just as I may wish to express myself, regardless of whether I influence the opinions of anyone else, I may wish to vote, regardless of whether I have any effect on the outcome. However, while voting is undoubtedly a form of expression, its anonymous and routinized character in the modern nation-state renders this dimension of the act extremely thin. This approach does not seem plausible for a generalized rehabilitation of the rationality of voting in national elections. Many other forms of expression will better communicate to others, will be more intrinsically satisfying, and will involve less inconvenience. Carrying a placard outside the polling booth will better communicate the content of my views to others than will filling out a secret ballot inside. As for satisfaction, even singing political songs in the bath is likely to be more satisfying than pulling a lever on a voting machine.[15]

Another approach to rehabilitating the rationality of voting and other forms of participation in the large-scale nation-state would rely on a principle of hypothetical generalization. Like the expressive-function argument, this approach departs from the assumption that the act of participation is to be evaluated in terms of its (actual) individual consequences. We are to argue instead from a principle of false universalization: what if everyone did the same? I should vote because if everyone failed to vote (or if everyone on my side failed to vote), the results would be disastrous for the institutions of democracy (or for my particular issue). However, as C. D. Broad demonstrated in a classic article, this principle of hypothetical generalization functions as a "moral microscope." It is indiscriminate. While it succeeds in magnifying the trivial effects of my vote to a level of moral significance, it also magnifies a host of other trivial effects, endowing them all with moral significance. Broad's example was that plucking one ear of corn from a field would lead us to imagine a million people doing likewise. Plucking one ear would not do any harm worth considering, Broad concluded, even though a million similar acts would have a devastating effect.[16]

Clearly, this argument gets at the free-rider. Shirking his part in the collective effort will not by itself do any harm, but "everyone" (or large numbers of others) doing the same will prevent the public good from being provided. But this argument also gets at far more than the free-rider. What trivial act in your life or mine would resist enlargement to a level of moral significance through hypothetical generalizations envisaging the consequences of everyone doing the same? After finishing this paragraph, should I go to the library to check out some books? If "everyone" went to the library, the building would probably collapse; and if it did not collapse, the library would be emptied at a stroke by countless others doing "the same."

Perhaps some limitation of the generalized-consequences principle could be designed so as to limit its indiscriminate magnifications, so as to limit the range, so to speak, of the "moral microscope."[17] However, there is no reason for us to require that the motivations for political participation depend on any particular controversial line of revision for the problem of the isolated voter in the large-scale nation-state. Instead, I will focus on adjustments in the background conditions which alter the situation and, in that way, reduce the vulnerability of individual participation to charges of irrationality.

One reason for this focus is that the problem of adjusting background conditions is not primarily a moral problem, but rather one of institutional design. It is a matter of institutionalizing social practices that will *effectively motivate* people, collectively, to create a self-reflective political culture. Morality is only one motivator, and not necessarily the most effective one. In any case, it is arguable that our framework already supplies an answer to the specifically moral problem—why should people participate politically in the large-scale nation-state? According to the ideal of a self-reflective society, if citizens receive the benefits of full membership under all of our conditions (where exit is unimpeded, where the practices are self-reflective, where there is a consensus supporting the relevant practices, and so on), then they are obligated to live up to the duties of full membership. Our variant of the fairness argument can be viewed as a response to the pure problem of political obligation. However, this pure problem—the ethical issue of why I should vote or in any other way participate in the politics of the nation-state—is only a part of the problem of effectively motivating people to participate to the extent required for a self-reflective political culture.

The argument for political participation in the nation-state being irrational depends on group size, on the absence of selective incentives that apply just to those who participate, and on the costs of participation. Background conditions can be adjusted substantially on all of these counts to encourage both engagement and participation.

The charge of irrationality acquires plausibility from a picture of isolated voters in mass society motivated to obtain benefits from collective decisions about the provision of public goods (or motivated to produce consequences they approve of by such decisions, whether or not those consequences benefit them in any egoistic sense). Public goods in the technical sense are available to all members of a given group if they are available to any. The basic intuition, made famous by Mancur Olson, is that it would seem rational not to undertake the costs of participation when the same benefits can be expected in any case. In very large groups, one's own participation will not make any difference to the outcome. Hence, if the public good is to be provided, one will receive it as a free-rider without having to share in the costs. An important premise of the argument is that participation, rather than being valued for its own sake, is valued only instrumentally for its effect on the decision to provide the public good. However, some forms of participation may be valued for their own sake. Olson can assimilate them to his argument by saying that they provide "selective incentives" (incentives specific to those who participate). If adjustments in background conditions provide selective incentives or if they affect the group size relevant to particular forms of participation, the rationality of political participation can be rehabilitated.

The other side of the argument attacking the rationality of participation in large groups is the affirmation of the rationality of participation in smaller groups and institutions. There, it is reasonable for each individual to conclude that he is far more likely to make a difference. For that reason, the strategies of decentralization and organizational pluralism should both weigh heavily in the adjustment of background conditions. Decentralization provides arenas smaller than the large-scale nation-state where an individual can have a far greater effect. Organizational pluralism means that there are many arenas in addition to the formal governmental apparatus in which the political culture can flourish and in which individuals may participate and influence each other on public issues. This point encompasses the full range of voluntary organizations, from those which are explicitly political to those which usually attempt to distance themselves from partisan politics (such as civic groups, religious organizations, and trade and professional associations). In all of these arenas, participation in the political culture can be both instrumentally effective and intrinsically appealing.[18]

The latter point puts the issue of selective incentives in a different light. If one has the capacity to participate in the political culture, and if the forms of participation are not limited to the mass-anonymous variety (such as voting in national elections), then it may become plausible to regard politics itself as a selective incentive. Participation comes to be valued not merely for what it produces, but also for what it means. Formulating, holding, and expressing political opinions become parts of a way of life.

A related factor encouraging participation might be termed the distribution of self-esteem. Of course, "distribution" is misleading if it is taken to imply a centralized or unitary process of decision. It is, nevertheless, the case that the structure of background practices can greatly affect whether self-esteem is so differentially distributed that certain groups would be loath to participate in the political culture in any serious way. As Barrington Moore argues, the sanctions that once applied to Indian Untouchables served "to prevent individual Untouchables from acquiring any sense of self-esteem that could challenge the authority of superior castes."[19] If the essential benefits of full membership are to be provided for everyone, then the practices defining background conditions must provide a basis for self-esteem and mutual respect across all the major social and economic cleavages of the society. In other words, regardless of one's family background, class position, religion, sex, or ethnic group, it should be reasonable and plausible to regard one's own conscientious views as deserving of a hearing along with those of anyone else. Background conditions can encourage this goal by promoting both (a) a variety of formal liberal practices—"process equalities"—embodying and affirming equal consideration, and (b) strategies for taming the effects of economic inequalities on the political culture.

Beginning with (a), I have argued, elsewhere, that the substantive implications of liberalism can be thought of as a series of "process equalities"—social practices implementing equal consideration of everyone's relevant claims or interests in crucial, selected spheres of life. Equality before the law, formal political equality (one person, one vote and other formal requirements about the value of one's vote), and formal equality of opportunity (meritocratic, nondiscriminatory practices of job assignment) are the most obvious. Equality of consideration of one's essential needs by the medical care system would be another. When these liberal process equalities are implemented, they encourage a measure of self-esteem and mutual respect throughout all sectors of the society.[20]

Of course, people can have the same right to equal consideration of their capacities in the job market, the same right to equal consideration of their votes in the electoral system, and the same right to equal consideration of their relevant claims by the legal or health care systems, but still lack the self-esteem to assert or exercise those rights. The difficulty is that self-esteem cannot be distributed directly by government hand-out in the way that food or money can be.

Over time, however, the appropriate background conditions can be expected to do a great deal to encourage a sense of equal worth and mutual respect. When the process equalities are combined with the exposure to diverse views and collective self-criticism that characterize the activist conception of liberty, a basis will be available for criticizing any ideologies that undermine self-esteem. Furthermore, it will be available to persons who are, themselves, guaranteed the essential capacities to engage in that kind of criticism. This combination of factors provides reasonable grounds for expecting that the self-esteem necessary for political self-assertion and participation will be widely available throughout the society.[21] While there will always be idiosyncratic individuals who lack self-esteem, it should be possible to avoid gross maldistributions of self-esteem corresponding to identifiable cleavages in the society. Avoiding such maldistributions would lend plausibility to the claim that the *social* conditions for self-esteem had been made generally available across the society's major cleavages.

The process equalities just mentioned do not deal directly or explicitly with economic inequalities. They single out claims to equal consideration that are meant to apply, in their essentials, regardless of economic differences. But there is no doubt that economic differences themselves, when sufficiently great, can so drastically affect the distribution of self-esteem that some members can be effectively disenfranchised from participation.

There are three obvious strategies for dealing with this problem: insulation, social mobility, and redistribution.

By insulation I mean the strategy of preventing economic inequalities from affecting the distribution of the good in question. To some extent, the process equalities already mentioned serve this function. It is important for the society's social practices to affirm that everyone has the same right to equal consideration of their relevant claims by the voting system, the legal system, and so forth. It is no small matter for state interventions to ensure the same right to an equal vote, to a fair trial, to consideration of essential health needs, to consideration of one's relevant qualifications in the job market—all to be established regardless of one's starting position in the economic hierarchy. If this process—of insulating the process equalities from giving greatly differential consideration to the wealthy and powerful—succeeds, then one of the major threats posed by economic inequality will have been defused. A first step in this direction is to focus on floors rather than ceilings—on guarantees of the minimum acceptable level for everyone. While anyone accused of a crime may not be guaranteed the most talented representation money can buy, he or she can be guaranteed representation at an adequate level of competence. Similar requirements could be worked out for the other process equalities.[22]

We will return to insulation strategies in discussing the distribution of opportunities for expression and participation. For the moment, it is worth noting two other strategies for ameliorating the effect of economic inequalities on self-esteem: social mobility and redistribution.

Even if the economic inequalities are great, if I have substantial prospects (and if my children have them as well) of reaching some of the more highly valued positions, then I can think in terms of my future position as well as my present one. However, if my apparent prospects for social mobility are based on nothing more than false consciousness or class mystification, then these soothing psychological effects cannot be counted on in a *self-reflective* political culture. They will likely be revealed as shams serving an ideological function—keeping the lower orders in their places. Rather, we would require the reality and not merely the appearance of social mobility in order to make this strategy work. In this society the main problem area would be the urban "underclass" that has faced enormous difficulties, from one generation to the next, breaking into the mainstream economy. A concerted policy effort would have to be mounted to improve skill acquisition, initial entrance into the job market, access to capital, and opportunities for entrepreneurship.[23] Another important factor would be to foster conditions for family formation so as to better provide for the next generation. Substantial prospects for social mobility from all sectors of the society are not a utopian requirement, but they might be an expensive one, particularly when one considers that many of the programs we now conventionally identify with the welfare state benefit the middle classes far more than the very poor.

Instead of ameliorating or insulating the effects of economic inequality, one could attack the problem directly by attempting to eliminate or decrease it. Any plausible theory of distributive justice will, no doubt, require a substantial degree of redistribution. However, our concern here is not the development of a full-bodied theory of distributive justice. Rather, it is the much narrower question of what background conditions would facilitate a self-reflective political culture. Assuming that some minimum floor has been guaranteed by the essential benefits of full membership, the issue of economic inequalities arises at two points: one is the effect on self-esteem (which affects the motivations for, and character of, participation), and the other is the distribution of opportunities for participation. There is no doubt that some degrees of economic inequality can have a very substantial effect on self-esteem. Is this effect so great as to prevent political participation? This is a complex empirical question that raises issues of institutional design.

I am already assuming that the essential benefits of full membership would require some socially agreed determination of a minimum acceptable level of economic well-being. Not only would such a floor be required by the notion of essential benefits, it would also be a plausible component of the background conditions necessary for a self-reflective political culture. Those who are on the margins of survival are more easily subjected to strong manipulation. They are too busy attempting to survive, and they have too few of the relevant organizational resources, for their interests to obtain an effective hearing.

Undoubtedly, some minimal economic prerequisites must be satisfied if people generally are to have a sense of independent self-worth. If I face a continuing threat of starvation, I may not feel secure in asserting my opinions and may feel it necessary to defer to those who have economic power over my very survival. For this reason, enough redistribution to ensure an economic safety net, an insurance level for everyone, is the least that is required. In addition, as Michael Walzer has argued, many developed societies have economic prerequisites for a full sense of membership in the political culture. If one lacks access to television or a telephone, or to newspapers, radio, or the postal system, one is effectively disenfranchised from the mainstream political culture of a modern society. This kind of access is useful not only because it facilitates participation, but also because it encourages a sense of full membership in the political culture (particularly when combined with the process equalities mentioned earlier).[24]

Regardless of the prerequisites provided at the bottom, there is no doubt that the *relative* standing of various strata can have an independent effect on self-esteem.[25] However, with process equalities, social mobility, and the safety net all in place, it is an open question how much additional redistribution might be required—at least for the limited purpose of ensuring the universal prerequisites for political engagement and participation regardless of social stratum. Rawls, while not favoring redistribution for its own sake, argues that at some point, if economic inequalities become great enough, envy becomes "excusable" because of the effect of those inequalities on self-esteem.[26] Accepting this point provides independent grounds for limiting the most extreme economic inequalities (through redistribution) regardless of the success of the other strategies (insulation and social mobility) for ensuring a universal basis for self-esteem and mutual respect.

Note that our focus here is on adjustments in the background conditions that would be necessary for liberty of political culture in the activist sense. In such a society, the option of more redistribution would remain open, depending on how other issues of political and economic structure were decided. My contention is that from the premise that we must solve the legitimacy problem for ideal theory, we can get distinctive and demanding criteria for liberty of political culture. These criteria tell us a great deal about the morally preferred state, but they do not, in a context-independent manner, tell us everything.

However, if a self-reflective society were achieved, the institutions and practices solving the legitimacy problem could do a great deal to complete the argument. For example, the norms of evaluation internal to the welfare state, to the market, and to political democracy would, if legitimated by this kind of argument, give substance to the conflict of principles in particular policy cases and institutional decisions. Without a systematic theory, a basis for the system's particular decisions would follow from this theory of legitimacy.

What I am proposing is a theory of fully legitimate political systems, not a systematic theory of justice. If a fully legitimate political system maintained its consensus, remained self-reflective in its evaluation of its own political practices, and satisfied our other conditions, then conforming to the norms of evaluation internal to those legitimate practices would determine specific distributional questions as they arose. After we have specified background conditions for the system to fulfill our legitimacy requirements, many details would still remain open to the political determinations of such a system. It is in that sense that our prescriptions are context-dependent, rather than context-independent in the manner of more systematic theories.

The effects on self-esteem are not the only peril posed by the market economy to the development of a self-reflective political culture. We might imagine commercial messages so dominating mass communications that, in effect, the entire political dialogue is drowned out and its audience dulled or deadened to it. On this scenario, structural manipulation through mass advertising and the encouragement of single-minded consumerism succeeds by completely diverting the citizenry from paying any serious attention to the issues posed for them by political dialogue.

Some accounts of advertising contend that this hypothetical picture correctly applies to our society at present.[27] Other studies argue that this picture is grossly overstated and the effects of advertising overestimated, in part because consumers know that advertising is "propaganda" and they learn, accordingly, to tune it out or pay it little attention.[28]

I will not presume to resolve empirical controversies of this kind about contemporary American society. Note that, for my argument, consumerism does not in itself pose a decisive impediment. There is no requirement that individuals be self-reflective in their choice of life-style, only that the system's collective process of self-examination be effectively applied to its political practices. So long as the system is successful in encouraging widespread engagement in the political sphere, there is room for a mass consumer culture, just as there is room for a host of other personal preoccupations—organized religion, the cult of self-improvement, the quest for salvation, adult education, hobbies, sports, voluntary organizations, and any manner of life-styles.

The special danger posed by advertising is that its ever-present messages might drown out the political dialogue and dull the sensibilities of its audience. However, even if one accepted the most extreme account of advertising's role in contemporary American society, that would not touch the issue of how advertising would compete for people's attention in a society which instituted the rest of our background conditions—which generally provided the capacities, incentives, and opportunities for mass political engagement. Even if one thought that advertising succeeded so overwhelmingly in competition with our present, attenuated political culture, it would still be a completely open question how it would compete once the conditions for a more robust, self-reflective version was in place.

If advertising played the role assigned to it by the worst case—even under the best conditions of ideal theory—then some restrictions or modifications of institutional design could be devised. Presumably, commercial television advertising and the consumerism it fosters, to the extent that they function as diversions from political dialogue, are not themselves contributions to it. Therefore, they have no basis for protection at any fundamental level within this theory. Perhaps restrictions as to sheer volume would be in order. Alternative financing schemes for broadcast television might have to be devised. Entities like the British Broadcasting Corporation, which preserve substantial independence from both government and the private sector, provide one useful model. A greatly strengthened Public Broadcasting Service—combined with strategies for more effectively insulating it from both government and the private sector—would be worth exploring. Cable television, video cassette recorders, and other technological developments render this an area of rapid change in any case.[29] The important point is that we should not expect advertising to pose an insuperable obstacle to mass engagement in political dialogue under conditions of ideal theory. And to the extent that we are mistaken in this hypothesis, restrictions, modifications, or alternatives to our present scheme of commercial broadcasting could be devised.[30]

Thus far, we have focused on incentives for engagement and participation at the mass level. However, in a large-scale nation-state, there will inevitably be a great deal of specialization. We can expect that many of the burdens of political dialogue will be carried by competing specialized elites of one sort or another, particularly public officials, leaders of groups and organizations, intellectuals, reporters, and decision makers in the media. Obviously, the incentives for conscientious political dialogue by occupants of these specialized roles will not be the same as for ordinary citizens. Some additional adjustments in background conditions will be required if they are to have the appropriate incentives.

A promising strategy for implementing a self-reflective political culture at the elite level is to attempt to harness the forces of political, institutional, and economic competition so as to encourage serious and critical political debate. If we accept the argument offered earlier for political equality and some form of democracy at the mass level, then we already will have provided for significant incentives at the elite level. Electoral competition for public office creates an incentive for issue entrepreneurship so that a candidate for public office can make a name for herself as the standard bearer for the preferred side on some policy problem.[31] However, the same forces of competition also create incentives for evasion and ambiguity.[32] Nevertheless, adjustments in background conditions can do a great deal to encourage more serious public dialogue.

When major news organizations compete with teams of investigative reporters potentially critical of government policy, when major research institutes compete to produce findings relevant to public policy, when nonprofit organizations and public interest groups employ experts to support their respective causes, then the forces of institutional and economic competition have been harnessed in the service of a more self-reflective political culture. All of these activities are susceptible to incentives that can be adjusted by the state to encourage or discourage this kind of behavior. Much depends on the state's tax incentives (for the formation and support of nonprofit organizations and foundations interested in supporting research and public debate), on the state's libel laws (which may introduce the risk for the media of large legal fees or costly settlements of suits), on the state's broadcast licensing provisions (which may either encourage serious public affairs programming or introduce the threat of nonrenewal for certain kinds of broadcasts), and on the state's telecommunications policies on new technologies (cable, satellite, videotext, and many other innovations that potentially offer greater diversity and access).

We can divide the question of opportunities into occasions for receiving and for expressing conscientious political views—with or without amplification. In discussing both, I will focus on access to messages that are amplified to a large-scale or mass audience. The ban on explicit manipulation applied to acts of expression or association already does a great deal to protect interpersonal access to messages between individuals or small groups. Of course, even small-group interaction can be facilitated, particularly over significant distances, through policies affecting technological connections, such as computer networks, videotext and, access to (and privacy of) telephones. The problematical issues, however, arise for larger audiences.

Some of the requirements already mentioned should facilitate opportunities for diverse messages to achieve an effective hearing. The capacities we specified earlier for universal development require that people be literate and have a knowledge of the social conventions necessary to evaluate political messages. Furthermore, institutionalizing some form of democracy provides an incentive for those people to be reached. To the extent that competition among candidates and parties can be intensified or made more widespread, the incentives to communicate competing messages to virtually every constituency will also be increased.

I have argued that, in the contemporary social context, access to television, radio, the postal service, telephones, and newspapers should count as part of the required minimum resources necessary for a sense of full membership in the political culture. Furthermore, public policies can increase the significance of this kind of access. When C-Span broadcasts congressional hearings, when cable television in Canada broadcasts the daily Question Period in the Canadian House of Commons, when postal subsidies facilitate delivery of newspapers and magazines, then access to serious political dialogue has been significantly increased. Public policies encouraging or facilitating these innovations can do a great deal to increase opportunities at the mass level to receive politically relevant messages.[33] However, improving access is not, by itself, sufficient to effectively motivate engagement.

In considering adjustments to background conditions, we should aspire to a culture of participatory civility—a political culture where people learn to listen and respond on the merits in an atmosphere of mutual respect. *Participatory civility can be encouraged by patterns of mutual voluntariness* (a) in speaker-audience interaction and (b) in choices of preferred forms of expression (for a given contribution to political dialogue).

By "speaker," I mean the person expressing a message, whether it is spoken or written and whether it is primarily verbal or non-verbal. In the interest of facilitating mutual voluntariness, there would be grounds, on occasion, for restricting the time, place, or manner of expression, provided that the restrictions did not themselves constitute strong manipulation. As a matter of general social practice, two caveats seem advisable. First, time, place, or manner restrictions should be applied in a content-neutral manner whenever they might impinge on contributions to political dialogue. In that way, explicit manipulation can be avoided. Hence, if a public park is opened to private groups for the display of religious symbols, it should be open to any groups who might wish to mount such displays, but the park in question could also, in a content-neutral manner, be closed to all public displays. Second, care should be taken that such restrictions do not have the cumulative impact of effectively silencing a particular opinion or viewpoint. Hence, to take an extreme case, if all public places were closed to expression in a content-neutral manner, then many dissenting voices and fringe opinions might be silenced entirely (while more mainstream opinions could still rely on the mass media). The effect would be objectionable because it would effectively shut out certain groups from the political dialogue and thus amount to structural manipulation.

Mutual voluntariness, when applied to speaker-audience interaction, is intended, first, to permit those who wish to hear (or see or experience) a given message to do so, and second, to permit those who wish to avoid a given message to do so. When speaker and audience both wish to interact, we should aspire to facilitate that connection. But when either wishes to avoid the other, then the interaction is not mutually voluntary. This does not mean, of course, that those who wish not to hear a message should have a veto on the right of others to express it or to hear it. But it does mean that some weight should be given to the plight of captive audiences who may intensely wish to avoid receiving messages of a certain kind or from certain speakers. For example, Joel Feinberg has catalogued three dozen disgusting acts that he imagines people doing on a bus. Many of these acts are not likely to be construed as acts of expression, or at least as acts of expression intended to contribute to political dialogue (copulation and the eating of pickled sex organs of various animals would seem to be in this category).[34] There is no difficulty about restricting such acts before captive audiences because they do not fall directly within our argument, since they do not constitute contributions to political dialogue. However, we might imagine a countercultural theatrical troupe that performs a variety of acts in public considered disgusting by the mainstream society—and that articulates a political message according to which those apparently disgusting acts can be considered symbolic contributions to political dialogue. They are even willing, in the midst of their disgusting acts, to hand out long and boring pamphlets explaining the political significance they attribute to their performances.

I assume that every act of expression which can be considered a contribution to political dialogue has attached to it some actual or possible verbal formulation of that contribution. The most effective strategies of communication will, however, sometimes be "symbolic" or even completely nonverbal.[35] In a given context, acts that may not ordinarily be considered political at all may carry a meaning which dramatizes a given contribution to political dialogue, a contribution which might otherwise have far less emotional or intellectual effect on others. For example, blacks asking to be served coffee at segregated lunch counters had far more effect at the time than any number of speeches. Granting that many important contributions to political dialogue may be largely nonverbal and, in that sense, "symbolic" does not mean that people should have an inviolable right to select their preferred form of expression without considering the effects on others. The system should be constructed so as to give weight to their preferences, but also to the rights and reactions of others. Even when the countercultural theater troupe clothes its performance in the garb of political dialogue, it does not have the right to unilaterally determine that its preferred form of expression be imposed on captive audiences. Mutual voluntariness would permit some modification in the form of expression when its involuntary recipients object strongly. Presumably, sites can be arranged for voluntary viewing. Less offensive forms of expression for essentially the same message might be arranged for captive audiences (political pamphlets being distributed is one thing, public copulation in the interests of political theater is another).

Burning a draft card and assassinating a public official might both be considered acts of symbolic political expression, in certain contexts. The former involves quite minor effects on others, while the latter involves grave effects that should be considered intolerable under most conceivable conditions. The latter would itself be an act of explicit manipulation.

The system should operate so as to give some weight to the speaker's preferred form of expression, but this can easily be outweighed, as in the political assassination case, by the grave interests and rights of others. Presumably, opposition to the target and to the regime can be expressed in many other ways, so that the basic message of a given contribution to political dialogue can be given a hearing, even if it is only through the purely verbal expression of opposition (or through some choice of tactics along a whole range of tamer acts).

The basic point is that practices facilitating mutual voluntariness should serve, in the long term, to moderate the intensity of conflicts and cleavages and to facilitate mutual toleration. For that reason, they may help a self-reflective political culture to maintain itself so as to bring the argument within the feasible set, at least for ideal theory.

Just as freedom of association on the interpersonal or small-group level should be conceived as mutually voluntary (to be forced to attend a meeting I disapprove of is to have a penalty imposed on me), so should communications at the mass level aspire to the same model of mutual voluntariness. If I do not like the messages on channel X, I can turn the dial; if I am offended by certain video tapes, I am under no compulsion to play them in my home; if I do not like materials I receive in the mail, I can throw them away or request that I be removed from certain mailing lists; if I do not like a telephone solicitation, I can hang up or even request an unlisted number. In all of these cases, I cannot be protected from the bare knowledge that messages or materials I object to exist. But that bare knowledge is necessary for the model of mutually voluntary association; it is necessary for me to be able to *decide* whether or not I wish to be on the receiving end. For that reason, bare knowledge should not by itself be considered a penalty.

In all of these cases, there is a twofold reason to be solicitous about captive audiences. First, doing so conforms to the model of mutual voluntariness; departures from that model risk exposing people to penalties because of their views and, hence, to explicit manipulation. Second, consideration for captive audiences helps to contribute to an atmosphere of toleration and mutual respect. Both are relevant because they facilitate an effective hearing for divergent views and also strengthen the system's capacity to survive the rigors of self-critical debate. For all of these reasons, those who wish to avoid messages they find strongly offensive should have the opportunity to do so.[36]

Thus far, we have focused on opportunities to receive but not to express political messages. Opportunities for expression can be considered at three levels: interpersonal, small-group, and large-group or mass-audience. The ban on explicit manipulation applied to beliefs or voluntary associations already provides protection for expression at the first two levels. The difficulties arise with the third. In a technologically complex society, significant speech is seldom exemplified by the isolated man on a soap box, the pamphlet distributed door to door, or the citizen speaking up at a town meeting. All of these activities are important. But they are routinely dwarfed in their influence by television news programs and documentaries, political advertising campaigns, mass circulation newspapers, magazines, and journals of opinion, and cable television channels.

The difficulty is that political dialogue can be subjected to structural manipulation depending on access to mass or large-scale amplification. If we can all speak, but some speak with amplified voices, those who consistently speak without amplification can be effectively silenced. The difficulty can be ameliorated somewhat by a decentralization of arenas for speech. Local meetings, local organizations, local access to cable television stations, radio talk shows, local newspapers willing to amplify the views of small groups—all can make a contribution. Nevertheless, access to amplification to mass audiences remains a crucial issue, particularly for the character of national political dialogue.

Organizations and institutions that have the ability to reach mass audiences can all be considered *amplifiers* of political dialogue. Amplifiers will differ in their magnitude and degree of partisanship (promoting an acknowledged point of view) or nonpartisanship (attempting to be neutral among viewpoints in political dialogue). Both of the latter classifications are simplifications. The nonpartisan amplifiers will have implicit value commitments embodied in their patterns of editorial decision making; the partisan amplifiers will often, as an institutional matter, be more open to transmitting diverse materials than a single label would suggest (consider, for example, the diversity of material broadcast by the Christian Broadcast Network).

Decisions about amplification should be diverse and competing, and they should be institutionalized so as to represent conscientious judgments about the merit, newsworthiness, or importance of the materials amplified. Partisan amplifiers should be balanced by a diversity of competing channels. New technologies, particularly cable, satellite transmission, video, and videotext, offer the promise of greater diversity and easier access.[37] It is important that no group with a significant or intense following that attempts to participate in conscientious dialogue should continually lack access to amplification. Given the diversity of channels, both broadcast and print, this is not an overly demanding requirement.

In the present American context, political action committees pose a problem. As organizations designed to aggregate small contributions, PACs do not threaten to overamplify a few individually wealthy patrons. But the proliferation of committees representing certain ideologies and interests poses a threat not only to the terms of political competition, but also to the prospects that groups without such massive resources can obtain a hearing at all.[38] If background conditions could be adjusted to greatly increase the diversity and ideological balance of PACs, this danger could be averted. Another solution would be to reimpose contribution and expenditure limitations of the kind the U.S. Supreme Court has overturned.[39] While this would place a limit on access to amplification (and in that sense constitute a sacrifice in free expression), if it were imposed in a content-neutral manner, it would not constitute explicit manipulation in our sense. Hence, it would not constitute a sacrifice in the dimensions of liberty as defended here. In fact, to the extent that such limitations would effectively protect political dialogue from structural manipulation, they would be justified by the principles developed here.

However, we need to think more creatively about adjustments in background conditions that might energize competition among groups, institutions, and issue entrepreneurs so as to give voice to the interests of groups that might otherwise be left out of the dialogue. One focus for such innovation is government itself. Institutional incentives can be created to get government to speak in criticism of itself and on behalf of viewpoints or interests that might otherwise be left out. As Charles A. Reich noted in the 1960s:

> Perhaps the most interesting and significant innovation in dealing with freedom of expression is the possibility that government itself can be structured so as to foster differences. A government department could have in it a unit designed to represent a particular point of view, such as a consumers bureau in the Agriculture Department, or a bureau of natural beauty in the highway department. Some of the community-action programs connected with the poverty program find themselves promoting opposition to the policies of other public agencies; thus diversification may grow up naturally within the seeming monolith of government.[40]

Opposing voices can be created within government itself. For example, a government bureau or agency could be charged with monitoring the condition of the homeless or the hungry, or with monitoring and reporting on discrimination against homosexuals. Such arms of government might routinely end up criticizing other parts of government. If they spoke on behalf of groups or interests that might otherwise lack an effective hearing, such innovations could contribute to the prevention of structural manipulation.

However, the success of such innovations would depend on the broader political environment. We need to think about incentives for creating voices and organizational resources for those same groups outside government. Without attention to the broader environment of interest groups and political incentives, there is the danger that new offices or agencies will simply be captured by those they are meant to monitor or criticize. Competitive voices in government are likely to thrive only if they are part of a broader dialogue of organized and competing voices in the political world at large. To create such a dialogue, broader changes will have to be made in the distribution of resources and of incentives for political organizing. We turn to two such proposals in the next section.

3.6 Representation Vouchers and Deliberative Opinion Polls

Representation vouchers offer an innovation addressed to the problem of how resources for political organization are distributed. I have already mentioned the role vouchers could play in education.[1] Philippe Schmitter and others have proposed that they be applied to the general problem of political representation.[2] While Schmitter's theoretical preoccupations are different from mine, his proposal adds plausibility to the notion that background conditions could be adjusted to facilitate a self-reflective political culture.

Suppose every member of society is given a voucher to represent her chosen interests. The voucher must be substantial enough that organizations will want to compete for each voucher. The vouchers can only be cashed in, say, once a year by organizations that satisfy some minimum regulatory requirements ensuring that the organizations are not fraudulent, that they are not-for-profit, and that they act appropriately to represent the interests they claim to represent. If every member has a voucher, then there will be incentives for organizations to compete with each other to speak for the interests of all those who are now unorganized, including the underclass, the dispossessed, the invisible, the quiescent. Some organizations may well be created just to monitor other organizations. Provided that the barriers to entry in this competition are kept low, there will be a continual dynamism in the creation of organizations and, hence, in the creation of effective voices, where before there were only silence and indifference.

Even now, there is extraordinary diversity in the organizations that presume to speak knowledgeably for the interests of Americans: the National Organization of Women, the Sierra Club, Common Cause, the National Urban Coalition, the AFL-CIO, the American Enterprise Institute, the Heritage Foundation, People for the American Way, the Jefferson Institute, the Coalition for the Homeless, the National Right to Life Committee, Beyond War, and the Rockford Institute are only an eclectic list. Even now, some of these attempt to get a hearing for those who lack resources or even self-consciousness. Think how neglected, or merely latent, coalitions could be mobilized by the competition for vouchers.

To create a self-reflective political culture, we would have to overcome several problems. First, the collective action problem stands as an impediment to individual participation. Second, scarcity and maldistribution of organizational resources make it difficult for some groups to engage in the dialogue because they must compete for expertise and an effective hearing. Third, some "groups" may never get to the point where they constitute themselves as groups. They lack the resources and infrastructure to organize; they may lack the collective consciousness even to realize the need.

It is plausible that representation vouchers, when applied in conjunction with all of the other adjustments in background conditions I have specified, would do a great deal to respond to these three basic problems over the long term. I do not propose representation vouchers as a panacea, but as an example of the kind of institutional innovation that could bring about the conditions for a self-reflective society. The central challenge is overcoming the problem of structural manipulation, of giving effective voice to the interests across every significant cleavage in the society. Vouchers would give organizations incentives to take seriously the interests of those who are now left out of the dialogue. Or, if established organizations failed to adjust, issue entrepreneurs would have a strong incentive to fill the gap. Correspondingly, individuals would have no incentive to be free-riders, because the cost of participation is merely the assignment of a voucher that cannot be spent on anything else. In fact, if computerized records were kept about who has assigned her voucher, the system could be organized so that the cost of failing to participate would be the possible inconvenience of continued solicitations and competition for representation. People would have a strong incentive to think about the problem and to make a decision. Attempting to be a free-rider (in the sense of doing nothing) might well be more costly than participating. Nonparticipation would produce its own negative incentive, its own motivation to overcome apathy.

Most important, representation vouchers would alter the present scarcity of organizational resources, a scarcity now skewed in favor of those who have other resources. Just as class action suits and public interest research organizations have partially opened up the representation and advocacy of interests that were previously unvoiced, representation vouchers would create incentives for the continual, competitive creation of new organizations.

Representation vouchers focus on the political environment within which politicians operate. What about the political process itself? I have already mentioned the general argument for democracy—that by making public opinion consequential, democracy creates incentives for interests to be given voice and for people to voice their interests. But I have not said much about the structure of democratic institutions.

One reason for not being more specific is that, on my argument, the appropriate structure will be the one that comes to be accepted self-reflectively according to all of our conditions. Hence, many precise details cannot be determined in advance. However, our task here is to approach a different question: What institutional innovations would facilitate the *development* of a self-reflective political culture in the first place? Representation vouchers would create incentives for interests to be voiced that might otherwise be left out of the dialogue. Institutionalizing public self-criticism within the government itself blunts the force with which a government might otherwise, monolithically, imprint its doctrines on citizens. Yet I have said nothing about innovations *within* the process of campaigns and elections, innovations that might give more effective voice to interests across all the major cleavages of the society.

To make the issue more concrete, let us consider a specific but far-reaching innovation—the possibility of inserting deliberative opinion polls into the presidential nominating process as well as into the nominating process of offices at other levels. An ordinary opinion poll models what the public thinks, given how little it knows or pays attention. A deliberative poll models what the public *would* think if it had a more adequate chance to assess the questions at issue.

Imagine a new start to our season of presidential selection. Take a national random sample of the citizen voting-age population and transport them to a single site where they can interact in person, over an extended period, with the candidates for president.[3] Prepare the delegates beforehand with briefing materials on the issues. Have the candidates respond to questions in small-group sessions broken down by issue areas and poll the delegates about the merits of the candidates, breaking out the results by party affiliation (Democrats, Republicans, and independents).

Such an event would turn the "invisible primary," the period of jockeying by the candidates before the first official events, into a nationally representative and deliberative event. Because it is nationally representative, it would provide the candidates with incentives to address the interests of groups across all the major cleavages in the country, facilitating our effective-voice condition. Because it is deliberative, its results model what would be achieved, hypothetically, if the entire society grappled thoughtfully with the issues in the campaign. While it may be utopian to expect an entire society, even under favorable conditions, to be aroused to active political participation in a large-scale nation-state, it is not utopian for a representative sample to be sufficiently aroused so as to model the conclusions the society's nationally representative deliberations would come to.

Clearly, such an event would constitute an improvement over

our present method of beginning the primary season, the Iowa caucuses and New Hampshire primary. Neither state is representative of the entire country; both states have far less minority and urban populations than the country as a whole. Furthermore, neither event is deliberative at present. They are dominated by repetitive stump speeches, money, political organizations, shrinking sound-bites, and attack videos. Given the demonstrated role of momentum in the presidential selection process, early victories and defeats are greatly magnified in their effect on the eventual outcome.[4] If the first event were representative and deliberative, many of the irrationalities in our present process could be avoided, even if the rest of the process were to continue precisely as does the current system.

The race for the presidency is now the major arena for issue entrepreneurship in American society. If it could be turned into a deliberative process addressed to interests across all the major cleavages of the society, then many of the results of a self-reflective political culture could be approximated. Neither the deliberative opinion poll nor the representation voucher is offered as a panacea for defects in our present political culture. Rather, both of these innovations exemplify the general strategy proposed here: the indirect strategy of changing incentives in the background conditions for political dialogue and participation. These two innovations, when combined with the adjustments in background conditions discussed earlier, give verisimilitude to my claim that a self-reflective society is a feasible ideal for solutions to the legitimacy problem within a modern large-scale nation-state.

3.7 Conclusion

My proposals are intended not to offer a blueprint, but to dramatize the viability of a general idea: that a freely self-examining political culture can provide the foundations for its own legitimacy. Such a political culture would be engaged in a continuing, collective process of self-criticism. Its practices would then have a claim to reasonableness—a claim defined by the fact that its consensus, even if it is merely a procedural consensus on political practices, has survived unmanipulated critical scrutiny.

Such practices represent a self-reflective, collective determination of the distribution of essential benefits and burdens. With exit unimpeded as an option, each member of the society who receives essential benefits incurs a moral obligation to live up to the requirements of membership so long as she remains a member. If all those subject to the authority of the state remain obligated in this way, then the system is *legitimate* in the sense that everyone is obligated to support it.

A legitimate political system defines a range of practices for making decisions in various arenas of life. Some choices may be left to the market, some to individual decision, some to authoritative decision by one institution or another. The general questions posed by the theory of justice will be decomposed into many parts, and in that way relegated to many decision makers in many roles. To the extent that their decisions correspond to the norms of evaluation built into the widely accepted legitimate practices, members of the society are obligated to uphold them.

If my argument has succeeded, then we have found a way out of the three false dilemmas with which we started: absolutism versus relativism, religion versus amoralism, and systematic theory versus intuitionism. First, the argument for legitimacy developed here does not require the truth of absolutist claims of natural rights, but neither does it legitimate all widely accepted social practices in the manner of sheer relativism. On the contrary, its required conditions for the self-reflective development of political cultures would block the claims to legitimacy of many objectionable social practices. Second, it does not import religion into our public dialogue, but neither does it leave us with amoralism. On the contrary, it would determine moral obligations of membership for us all (while leaving all of us free to pursue salvation in diverse, private ways free of manipulation). Third, it does not live up to the expectations of systematic theory, but neither does it leave us with sheer intuitionism. On the contrary, the many public institutions of a legitimate political system would make specific determinations that we were all obligated to uphold.

A theory of legitimacy does not yield a systematic theory of justice. Instead, it yields a theory of the fully legitimate political system. Such a system, in all its many parts, can produce justice defined in all its concrete particularity. It is the justice that comes from people operating in roles whose norms have achieved self-reflective legitimacy. The result is the collective reasonableness of a political system examining—and accepting—itself through unmanipulated dialogue.

Notes

1.1 Introduction

1. See *Citizens and Politics: The View from Main Street America* (prepared for the Kettering Foundation by the Harwood Group, June 1991, Dayton, Ohio).

2. A good indicator of the level of activity can be seen in the massive annotated bibliography about just one book, John Rawls's *A Theory of Justice*. See David T. Mason and J. H. Wellbank, *John Rawls and His Critics* (New York: Garland, 1982).

3. See Leo Strauss, *Natural Right and History* (Chicago: University of Chicago Press, 1953) and Allan Bloom, *The Closing of the American Mind* (New York: Simon and Schuster, 1987). The cannibalism example is from Strauss, "Relativism," in Helmut Schoek and James W. Wiggins, eds., *Relativism and the Study of Man* (Princeton: Van Nostrand, 1961).

4. For a modulated version of this argument (with an assessment of the more extreme versions), see Richard John Neuhaus, *The Naked Public Square: Religion and Democracy in America* (Grand Rapids, Mich.: William B. Erdmans, 1984).

5. The focus of part 2 will be methodological in the sense that it will concern decision procedures for resolving substantive issues.

6. In essence, the priority problem concerns what principles should outrank other principles in determining the basic priorities of a just society. If more than one first principle is proposed, fundamental moral conflicts can be avoided through the device of "lexical" ranking. See John Rawls, *A Theory of Justice* (Cambridge: Harvard University Press, 1971), sections 7 and 8.

1.2 The Problem of Value

1. For more on justice between societies, see Charles R. Beitz, *Political Philosophy and International Relations* (Princeton: Princeton University Press, 1974) and Henry Shue, *Basic Rights* (Princeton: Princeton University Press, 1980).

2. Bruce A. Ackerman, *Social Justice in the Liberal State* (New Haven and London: Yale University Press, 1980).

3. Or, as I note in section 2.7, these difficulties can be avoided for want-regarding criteria, but at the cost of limiting judgments to those changes sanctioned by the Pareto principle. This latter restriction would entail silence on most issues of social importance (whenever some gain and some lose, the change would be considered Pareto-noncomparable).

4. E. L. Thorndike, *Human Nature and the Social Order* (New York: Macmillan, 1940), pp. 170–71. I am indebted to Doug Rae for bringing Thorndike to my attention.

5. See the more detailed discussion of "the calculus of pains, deprivations and frustrations" in Edward L. Thorndike, "Valuations of Certain Pains, Deprivations and Frustrations," *Journal of Genetic Psychology* 51 (1937), pp. 227–39.

6. See, for example, E. J. Mishan, *Economics for Social Decisions: Elements of Cost-Benefit Analysis* (New York: Praeger, 1973).

7. See section 2.7 for more on this issue.

8. For a particularly clear-headed account, see Gerald Dworkin, "Paternalism," in Peter Laslett and James S. Fishkin, eds., *Philosophy, Politics, and Society,* 5th series (New Haven and London: Yale University Press, 1979). I take the terminology of "want-regarding" and "ideal-regarding" from Brian Barry's excellent discussion in *Political Argument* (London: Routledge and Kegan Paul, 1965). For more on these issues, see sections 2.6 and 2.7 below.

9. Appropriate judgment, but not in the sense of systematic theory. The result will, however, satisfy the criteria for an acceptable theory specified in section 2.1.

10. See Barrington Moore, Jr., *Injustice: The Social Bases of Obedience and Revolt* (White Plains, N.Y.: M. E. Sharpe, 1978).

1.3 Future Generations

1. Below, I call the conceptions in question the identity-specific and the identity-independent conceptions of human interests.

2. This section draws on my contribution to Peter Laslett and James Fishkin, eds., *Justice between Age Groups and Generations,* vol. 6 of *Philosophy, Politics, and Society* (New Haven: Yale University Press, 1992).

3. As the majority in a major "wrongful life" case noted: "The normal measure

of damages is compensatory. Damages are measured by comparing the condition plaintiff would have been in, had the defendants not been negligent, with plaintiff's impaired condition as a result of the negligence. The infant plaintiff would have us measure the difference between his life with defects against the utter void of non-existence, but it is impossible to make such a determination" (*Gleitman v. Cosgrove* [1967], 227 A. 2d 689,692).

4. A possible exception would be cases of disability so severe that one might claim such a life is worse than nonexistence. The difficulty of dealing with this kind of counterfactual is dramatized by a Yiddish saying quoted by Nozick:

—"Life is so terrible; it would be better never to have been conceived."

—"Yes, but who is so fortunate? Not one in a thousand." (*Anarchy, State and Utopia* [New York: Basic Books, 1974], p. 337)

5. This argument extends one I made in "Justice between Generations: The Dilemma of Future Interests," *Bowling Green Studies in Applied Philosophy* 4 (1982), pp. 24–33. Derek Parfit has developed a very fertile and original attack on the identity-specific view in his *Reasons and Persons* (Oxford: Oxford University Press, 1984). My discussion here has benefited greatly from reading Parfit's work. In "Justice between Generations" I offer a more extended critique of his advocacy of what I call an identity-independent solution.

6. Thomas Schwartz, "Obligations to Posterity," in R. I. Sikora and Brian Barry, eds., *Obligations to Future Generations* (Philadelphia: Temple University Press, 1978), pp. 3–13, esp. p. 6.

7. See, for example, *Curlender v. Bio-science Laboratories* (1980), in which a limited claim for damages was granted on appeal: "In essence, we construe the 'wrongful life' cause of action by the defective child as the right of such child to recover damages for the pain and suffering to be endured during the limited life span available to such a child and any special pecuniary loss resulting from the impaired condition" (165 Cal. Rptr. 477,489).

Two other notable cases are *Turpin v. Sortini* ([1982], 31 Cal. 3d 220) and *Procanik by Procanik v. Cillo* (New Jersey [1984], 478 A. 2d 755). Note the argument for considering damages to the child rather than merely damages to the parents: "We believe it would be illogical and anomalous to permit only parents and not the child, to recover for the cost of the child's own medical care. If such a distinction were established, the afflicted child's receipt of necessary medical expenses might well depend on the wholly fortuitous circumstance of whether the parents are available to sue and recover such damages or whether the medical expenses are incurred at a time when the parents remain legally responsible for providing such care" (*Turpin v. Sortini*, 238).

8. We will return to interpersonal comparisons in section 2.7.

9. See Parfit, *Reasons and Persons,* part 4.

10. Arthur Koestler, *Darkness at Noon*, trans. Daphne Hardy (New York: Macmillan, 1941), pp. 161–62. I was reminded of Koestler's treatment of this issue by Joel Feinberg's excellent essay "Rawls and Intuitionism" in Norman Daniels, ed., *Reading Rawls: Critical Studies of "A Theory of Justice"* (New York: Basic Books, 1975).

11. Peter Singer, *Practical Ethics* (Cambridge: Cambridge University Press, 1979), pp. 80–81.

12. For an extended discussion of the character and limitations of purely structural principles, see my *Tyranny and Legitimacy* (Baltimore and London: Johns Hopkins University Press, 1979), chaps. 10 and 11.

13. Jonathan Bennett, "On Maximizing Happiness," in R. Sikora and B. Barry, eds., *Obligations to Future Generations* (Philadelphia: Temple University Press, 1978), p. 62.

14. I take the term *harm principle* to refer to any of the standard variations on Mill's "one very simple principle" that "the sole end for which mankind are warranted, individually or collectively, in interfering with the liberty of action of any of their number is self-protection" (*On Liberty*, in *Utilitarianism, On Liberty and Other Writings*, edited with an introduction by Mary Warnock [New York: New American Library, 1962], p. 135). For a systematic account of variations on the harm principle, see Joel Feinberg, *The Moral Limits of the Criminal Law* (Oxford: Oxford University Press, 1985).

1.4 Structure

1. In this section I rely on arguments I developed in "The Complexity of Simple Justice," *Ethics* 98, no. 3 (April 1988), pp. 464–71.

2. For more on the assignment problem, see section 1.5.

3. Douglas Rae, "A Principle of Simple Justice," in Peter Laslett and James Fishkin, eds., *Philosophy, Politics, and Society,* 5th series (New Haven: Yale University Press, 1979). See also his "Maximin Justice and an Alternative Principle of General Advantage," *American Political Science Review* 69 (June 1975), pp. 630–47.

4. H. L. A. Hart, "Between Utility and Rights," in Alan Ryan, ed., *The Idea of Freedom: Essays in Honor of Isaiah Berlin* (Oxford: Oxford University Press, 1979), p. 77.

5. Ibid., p.78.

6. See, for example, Gilbert Harman, *The Nature of Morality* (New York: Oxford University Press, 1977), p. 3, and Judith Jarvis Thomson, *Rights, Restitution, and Risk* (Cambridge: Harvard University Press, 1986), p. 95. See also Philippa Foot, "The Problems of Abortion and the Doctrine of the Double Effect," *Oxford Review* 5 (1967). For some other variations on involuntary

organ donation, see my "Justice versus Human Rights," *Social Philosophy and Policy* 1, no. 2 (Spring 1984), pp. 103–07.

7. Brian Barry, *Political Argument* (London: Routledge and Kegan Paul, 1965), p. 43.

8. See Laurence J. Lafleur, Introduction to Jeremy Bentham's *An Introduction to the Principles of Morals and Legislation* (New York: Hafner Press, 1948), p. xi.

9. See Amartya Sen, *On Economic Inequality* (New York: Norton, 1973).

10. The reference to Rawls is to *A Theory of Justice* (Cambridge: Harvard University Press, 1971). The delightful properties of Ackermanian manna are discussed in Bruce A. Ackerman's *Social Justice in the Liberal State* (New Haven and London: Yale University Press, 1980).

11. For a more detailed argument to this effect, see my *Beyond Subjective Morality* (New Haven and London: Yale University Press, 1984).

12. Rae, "Maximin," p. 640.

13. It also violates the weaker and more general condition of acyclicity (which rules out cycles whether or not they depend on the indifference relation).

14. This cycle should not be surprising to students of the classic voting paradox. In the table below, alternatives W, X, Y, Z can be thought of as chosen by people A, B, C, D or by principles A, B, C, D. Whether we think of them as people or as principles, we can use the rankings at the left to get a cycle (the rankings can be thought of as utilities, with higher numbers being higher).

Rankings (or Utilities)	Principles (or People)			
	A	B	C	D
3	W	Z	Y	X
2	X	W	Z	Y
1	Y	X	W	Z
0	Z	Y	X	W

It does not matter whether we are discussing people voting or the rankings determined by principles. Each of our minimum tests takes three of the principles together as sufficient for an alternative to be morally preferred. On either interpretation, we can go from Z to Y, from Y to X, from X to W, and from W back to Z through support of three out of four in each case. We can move from Z to Y (by principles A, C, D), from Y to X (by principles A, B, D), from X to W (by principles A, B, C), and from W back to Z (by principles B, C, D).

15. For more on this notion of "ideals without an ideal," see the concluding chap-

ters of my *Beyond Subjective Morality* and *Justice, Equal Opportunity, and the Family* (New Haven and London: Yale University Press, 1983).

1.5 Assignment

1. While it is true that we may expect systems of assignment to have complex empirical effects on the structure of distribution, it is nevertheless possible to match structurally identical states of affairs where in one sequence we have no objectionable assignment practices, and in the second we do.
2. I will deal with the assignment problem in this section in terms of equal opportunity, as that is the form the problem takes for the major issues of distributive justice affecting the basic structure of the society. The merit component of equal opportunity raises the issues of desert and of procedural fairness that are essential to any more general discussion of assignment, even for one appropriate to exotic situations such as the one posed in section 1.4 for the patient in room 306. Assignment raises the question: Why me? whether it is for benefits or for burdens. A systematic theory of justice ought to aspire to answer that question for all the problems of distribution that might fit within this framework. For our purposes, it will be sufficient to expose the conundrums applying to the equal opportunity problem. That part of the overall assignment problem is both crucial and inescapable.
3. I have made this argument in greater detail in *Justice, Equal Opportunity, and the Family* (New Haven and London: Yale University Press, 1983).
4. Bernard Williams, "The Idea of Equality," in Peter Laslett and W. G. Runciman, eds., *Philosophy, Politics and Society*, 2d series (Oxford: Basil Blackwell, 1962), pp. 110–31.
5. This is essentially the move John Rawls makes. See *A Theory of Justice* (Cambridge: Harvard University Press, 1971), pp. 72–74, where he explains how "fair equality of opportunity" adds to merit ("careers open to talents") the additional requirement that "those with similar abilities and skills should have similar life chances." After adding some requirements for how abilities and skills are to be acquired, he admits: "The principle of fair opportunity can be only imperfectly carried out, at least as long as the institution of the family exists." He never explains, however, why the family should have the kind of independent moral weight that should stand against realization of one of the principles ranked in lexical order.
6. See, for example, Christopher Jencks, *Who Gets Ahead? The Determinants of Economic Success in America* (New York: Basic Books, 1979), pp. 82–83.
7. Bruce Ackerman's proposals for "liberal education" would go a long way toward fulfilling both of these functions. See his *Social Justice in the Liberal State* (New Haven and London: Yale University Press, 1980), chap. 5.

8. I am assuming throughout this argument that there are background conditions of social and economic inequality in the adult generation. My discussion focuses on equality of opportunities, not equality of outcomes. Equality of opportunities is a rationing of chances to be unequal. If there were no inequalities of outcome, then equality of opportunities would follow in an empty, merely formal sense.

9. See, for example, Rawls's *Theory of Justice*, pp. 34–40.

10. See my *Justice, Equal Opportunity*, section 4.5. Since we are far from the possibility frontier in fully realizing any of these three principles, there is clearly progress of the first sort to be made. The liberty to confer benefits within the family could certainly be increased by changing the incentives for the formation of two-parent (as opposed to single-parent) families. The welfare system, at present, provides an incentive for the formation of families that will confer few benefits. Policies that would lessen minority teenage unemployment would also indirectly improve the incentive for the formation of two-parent families. In addition, more systematic and innovative proposals might be constructed that promote the liberty to confer benefits within the family by providing the conditions for maximizing choice in the institutions to which children are subjected. Educational voucher systems might well be developed to serve this end, so that choice of schools would be not merely a privilege of the advantaged, but an opportunity spread throughout the society.

11. It is also clear that we sometimes sacrifice one of these principles without any corresponding gain in the others (or in additional factors that might be identified). Preferential treatment based merely on race, when it is applied in competitive meritocratic contexts, will sacrifice meritocratic assignment, but will not significantly serve equality of life chances. When preferential treatment is applied to members of a minority group per se, an institutional incentive is created to accept or confer the benefit upon the most qualified members of that group. They will come, clearly, from the most advantaged members of the minority group. Hence the debate about mistargeting of preferential treatment, not to those who are actually disadvantaged, but to those who, symbolically, share racial, ethnic, or other characteristics with those who are actually extremely disadvantaged. This objection applies to preferential treatment for minority groups per se, and not to preferential treatment when it is carefully targeted through income and other criteria to those who *actually* come from disadvantaged backgrounds. In that case, my objection no longer applies, because it may well be that the sacrifice in merit, real though it may be, is made up by an improvement in equality of life chances. On the other hand, when preferential treatment is applied to mere membership in the minority group, no gain in equal life chances can realistically be expected to follow.

12. The position I propose in this book, while compatible with some features of intuitionism, has more precise implications. See part 3.

1.6 Democracy and Progress

1. This account of "Madisonian" democracy has obviously benefited greatly from Robert Dahl's *A Preface to Democratic Theory* (Chicago: University of Chicago Press, 1956). Furthermore, the majoritarian dimension is roughly what he labels "populistic." In labeling the northern dimension Madisonian, I do not wish to limit Madisonian values to that dimension. For example, Madison would have been more sympathetic to the eastern, or representative, dimension of our scheme than to the western, or direct, dimension.

2. However, while impediments to new policies will prevent tyranny through commission, they will not prevent tyranny through omission. For an extended discussion, see my *Tyranny and Legitimacy* (Baltimore and London: Johns Hopkins University Press, 1979). For an identification of the very idea of democracy with "limited majority rule" (limited so as to protect minorities), see Giovanni Sartori, *The Theory of Democracy Revisited* (Chatham, N.J.: Chatham House, 1987), section 2.4. Sartori's point is a useful corrective to common usage.

3. Dahl, *Preface*, p. 132.

4. See Robert Paul Wolff, *In Defense of Anarchism* (New York: Harper and Row, 1970). James Buchanan and Gordon Tullock, in *The Calculus of Consent* (Ann Arbor: University of Michigan Press, 1971), also grant the unanimity rule a privileged status but, unlike Wolff, argue for departures from it based on decision costs.

5. See the discussion below, in section 2.6, of the limitations of the unanimity rule.

6. For some creative proposals along these lines, see Benjamin Barber, *Strong Democracy: Participatory Politics for a New Age* (Berkeley and London: University of California Press, 1984), esp. chap. 10.

7. In terms of recent American experience, the movement of the Democratic party from the McGovern reforms in the presidential selection system back to greater control by party notables is a movement roughly from A to B and back again—a movement supported by differing images of democracy.

2.1 Criteria for an Acceptable Theory

1. For an extended argument that no theory of obligation can satisfy the particularity requirement, see A. John Simmons, *Moral Principles and Political*

Obligation (Princeton: Princeton University Press, 1979). For his definition of the requirement, see p. 43. My claim will be, contra Simmons, that my proposal satisfies the particularity requirement.

2.2 Beyond Intuitionism

1. Maurice Cranston, *Freedom: A New Analysis* (London: Longmans, 1953), p 65. For an incisive tour of the many uses of the term *liberalism*, see Giovanni Sartori, *The Theory of Democracy Revisited* (Chatham, N.J.: Chatham House, 1987), chap. 15.

2. Ronald Dworkin, "Liberalism," in Stuart Hampshire, ed., *Public and Private Morality* (Cambridge: Cambridge University Press, 1978), p. 115.

3. "Government must treat people as equals" in the sense that "it must impose no sacrifice or constraint on any citizen in virtue of an argument that the citizen could not accept without abandoning his sense of his equal worth" (Ronald Dworkin, "Neutrality, Equality and Liberalism," in Douglas MacLean and Claudia Mills, eds., *Liberalism Reconsidered* [Totowa, N.J.: Rowman and Allanheld, 1983], p. 3).

4. See Bruce Ackerman, *Social Justice in the Liberal State* (New Haven and London: Yale University Press, 1980), chap. 1. An excellent selection of writings on utilitarianism can be found in Amartya Sen and Bernard Williams, eds., *Utilitarianism and Beyond* (Cambridge: Cambridge University Press, 1982). See also Peter Singer, *Practical Ethics* (Cambridge: Cambridge University Press, 1979).

5. See John Rawls, *A Theory of Justice* (Cambridge: Harvard University Press, 1971), pp. 34–40. Rawls's central ambition is, of course, to develop a constructive alternative to intuitionism.

6. Brian Barry, *Political Argument* (London: Routledge and Kegan Paul, 1965), pp. 4–8, and Brian Barry and Douglas W. Rae, "Political Evaluation," in Fred I. Greenstein and Nelson Polsby, eds., *Handbook of Political Science* (Reading, Mass.: Addison-Wesley, 1975), pp. 353–57.

7. See Alasdair MacIntyre, *After Virtue* (Notre Dame, Ind.: University of Notre Dame Press, 1981), p. 229, for similar criticisms of the "weighing" metaphor.

8. This claim applies to the production of a full-fledged systematic alternative, but not to the strategy I will develop for a partial alternative in part 3.

9. Ackerman, *Social Justice*, p. 14.

10. If the state of theoretical debate is not actually robust, then the test becomes partially hypothetical: we have to ask whether a theory would differentiate in the required way among alternatives, *if* the state of debate permitted us to identify a broad range of alternatives from which to choose.

11. Rawls, *Theory*, pp. 8–9, 245–47. For further discussion of ideal versus non-ideal theory, see my *Tyranny and Legitimacy: A Critique of Political Theories* (Baltimore and London: Johns Hopkins University Press, 1979), chap. 7.

12. I will also follow Rawls in limiting ideal theory, at least initially, to the nation-state considered in isolation: "I shall be satisfied if it is possible to formulate a reasonable conception of justice for the basic structure of society conceived as a closed system isolated from other societies" (Rawls, *Theory*, p. 8). External threats to the nation-state raise an issue for Rawls of nonideal or partial compliance theory. In applying our argument to the nonideal case, some exceptions for national security may thus be required. For some useful observations on how to draw these narrowly, see Thomas I. Emerson, *The System of Freedom of Expression* (New York: Random House, 1970), chap. 4.

13. I take the term *moderate scarcity* from Rawls, who explains it thus: "Natural and other resources are not so abundant that schemes of cooperation become superfluous, nor are conditions so harsh that fruitful ventures must inevitably break down. While mutually advantageous arrangements are feasible, the benefits they yield fall short of the demands men put forward" (ibid., p. 127).

2.3 Political Thought Experiments

1. Ackerman's theory employs neutrality as a filter. See the discussion below.

2. As we will see in parts 2 and 3, the hypothetical category includes realistic thought experiments as well as purely imaginary cases (such as Rawls's original position). A realistic thought experiment, such as Nozick's argument from the state of nature to the minimal state, is hypothetical because the minimal state is being advocated for us based on the decisions of imaginary people.

3. A good account of these ambiguities, along with specimen illustrations, can be found in Hannah Pitkin, "Obligation and Consent," in Peter Laslett et al., eds., *Philosophy, Politics and Society*, 4th series (Oxford: Basil Blackwell, 1974).

4. Robert Nozick, *Anarchy, State and Utopia* (New York: Basic Books, 1974), p. 5.

5. See section 3.1 below.

6. It is in this sense that the doctrine of primary goods is "ideal-regarding" as explained in section 1.2.

2.4 The Quest for Consent

1. Robert Paul Wolff, *In Defense of Anarchism* (New York: Harper and Row, 1970), p. 23.

2. Ibid., pp. 23 and 24.

3. "The autonomous man, insofar as he is autonomous, is not subject to the will of another" (ibid., p. 14).

4. For further implications of the unanimity rule, see Douglas Rae, "The Limits of Consensual Decision," *American Political Science Review* 69, no. 4 (December 1975), pp. 1270–94. See also my *Tyranny and Legitimacy* (Baltimore and London: Johns Hopkins University Press, 1979), chap. 8.

5. Of course, sunset laws might to devised to limit some of these conflicts. However, given Wolff's complete prohibition on violations of autonomy, differences of degree or in the number of violations would not make any difference to the basic argument.

6. John Locke, *Two Treatises of Government*, ed. Peter Laslett (New York: New American Library, 1965), p. 392.

7. Hanna Pitkin, "Obligation and Consent," in Peter Laslett et al., eds., *Philosophy, Politics and Society*, 4th series (Oxford: Basil Blackwell, 1974), p. 55.

8. I say "some" grounds because the basis might, at best, be viewed as prima facie. Consider Hanna Pitkin's example of the minor official in Nazi Germany who has given his express consent by taking an oath of office ("Obligation and Consent," pp. 64–65).

9. Wolff is at his best in his pungent critiques of the classical arguments for majority rule. See *Defense*, pp. 38–58.

10. See my *Tyranny and Legitimacy*, chaps. 1, 2, and 8.

11. Joseph Tussman, *Obligation and the Body Politic* (New York: Oxford University Press, 1965), pp. 8, 21–22, 37.

12. As Dahl notes, the tyranny problem recurs "like a nagging tooth." See his *A Preface to Democratic Theory* (Chicago: University of Chicago Press, 1956), p. 124.

13. Of course, the unanimity rule, at the extreme, gives even one person a veto and so makes frustrating policy changes from the status quo easiest of all.

14. Later I will employ a solution to the problem of obligation to solve the legitimacy problem. However, my strategy will be very different from that of actual-consent theory. In the terminology just introduced, I will employ a category 4 theory rather than a category 1 theory.

15. Michael Walzer, *Spheres of Justice: A Defense of Pluralism and Equality* (New York: Basic Books, 1983).

16. *Consent* and *choice* are here being used broadly enough to cover not only express acts, but also tacit or implicit acts of agreement to, or acknowledgment of, a shared convention or belief.

17. Ibid., p. 9.

18. Ibid., pp. 312 and 29 (emphases added).

19. John Rawls, *A Theory of Justice* (Cambridge: Harvard University Press, 1971), pp. 302–03.

20. Harold Lasswell and Abraham Kaplan, *Power and Society* (New Haven: Yale University Press, 1950), pp. 55–56.
21. Walzer, *Spheres*, p. 313.
22. My own proposal in part 3 clearly owes a debt to Walzer's book. But that debt takes the form of proposals which take the entire approach out of category 1 and into category 4.
23. Tyranny is defined as crossing the boundaries of the spheres as determined by the shared understandings. See Walzer, *Spheres*, p. 20.
24. Barrington Moore, Jr., *Injustice: The Social Bases of Obedience and Revolt* (White Plains, N.Y.: M. E. Sharpe, 1978), chap. 2. However, Moore, in contrast to Walzer, rejects relativism (see chap. 13).

2.5 Realistic Hypotheticals

1. I interpret a claim that X actually is on at least as high an indifference curve as she was previously as falling within this category of strict agreement.
2. Robert Nozick, *Anarchy, State and Utopia* (New York: Basic Books, 1974), p. 5.
3. Ibid.
4. Ibid., pp. 58 and 331.
5. Ibid., pp. 30–33. The only possibility for exceptions to the side constraints that Nozick mentions is "the question . . . whether they may be violated in order to avoid catastrophic moral horror, and if the latter, what the resulting structure might look like." Rather than deciding this question, he says it is "one I hope largely to avoid" (p. 30, note).
6. Ibid., pp. 23, 117–18.
7. Ibid., pp. 110–14.
8. The argument would then have about the same status as that suggested by the Yiddish proverb "If my Grandmother had wheels, she'd be a trolley car." With sufficiently implausible assumptions, we can find a basis for almost any conclusion.
9. Nozick, *Anarchy*, pp. 25, 113–15.
10. Actually paying compensation makes up for a rights violation. This kind of compensation requirement is, of course, quite different from the hypothetical compensation tests used in cost-benefit analysis (Kaldor-Hicks, Scitovsky, etc.), whose ultimate point is utilitarian but for which the compensation does not have to be paid. For more on the latter, see I. M. D. Little, *A Critique of Welfare Economics*, 2d ed. (Oxford: Oxford University Press, 1957).
11. Nozick, *Anarchy*, p. 63, and also the definition on p. 57.
12. Ibid., p. 66. Suppose, however, that the eccentric attempted to compensate everyone who felt fear as a result of his actions. "This would be so expensive as

to be beyond the means of almost everyone" (ibid., p. 68). There is the further issue of "free-floating anxiety" for which people could not be compensated. Nozick speculates that "market compensation" (what people would consent to, in advance, through negotiation) might be required instead of merely "full compensation." ("Full compensation is an amount sufficient, but barely so, to make the person afterwards say he's glad, not sorry, it happened" [ibid.].) While market compensation is more demanding, the difficulties I am discussing depend only on the weaker requirement of full compensation.

13. There is no provision for educational services in the minimal state as described in Nozick's book. We might, however, consider this an oversight and focus the argument on the extension of other services.

14. Nozick, *Anarchy*, p. 114.

15. Consider some of the independent Alaskans depicted by John McPhee playing this role in Nozick's scenario.

16. Nozick appears to flirt with this possibility in his discussion of the epileptic driver who should be compensated for being prohibited from driving only to the degree to which he is relevantly disadvantaged. Hence, if he were given taxi fare, and so was not really disadvantaged, he would not be able to claim a rights violation, even if he did not like taxis (and hence was not on as high an indifference curve after compensation was paid). Perhaps if the epileptic driver had already been incorporated into the state—and thus had lost the right to self-help enforcement—there might be an argument for less than full compensation (because the state had already been established as the final arbiter of when the epileptic's rights were violated). But for our problem, the independents, by definition, retain the right to self-help enforcement. The very right that is being taken away is the right to judge when and to what degree their rights have been violated. For the state to supplant the judgment of the independents with its own judgment about whether compensation is sufficient is to take away the right to self-help enforcement in the determination of the value of self-help enforcement. Anything less than full compensation should plausibly be interpreted as a rights violation on this issue. But full compensation leads to a more than minimal state. See *Anarchy*, pp. 79–87, for Nozick's discussion of the epileptic driver case.

17. For an application of this general argument to another case in category 2, David Gauthier's *Morals by Agreement*, see my "Bargaining, Justice and Justification," *Social Philosophy and Policy* 5, no. 2 (Spring 1988), pp. 46–64.

2.6 Impartial Decision Procedures

1. See section 2.7 below (for a discussion of Dworkin's notion) and Peter Singer, *Practical Ethics* (Cambridge: Cambridge University Press, 1979), pp. 12–13.

2. Excellent discussions of these ambiguities can be found in Alan Gewirth, "The Golden Rule Rationalized," *Studies in Ethical Theory*, vol. 3 of *Midwest Studies in Philosophy* (1978), pp. 133–47, and J. L. Mackie, *Ethics: Inventing Right and Wrong* (New York: Penguin, 1977), chap. 4.

3. John Rawls, *A Theory of Justice* (Cambridge: Harvard University Press, 1971), pp. 154–56; John C. Harsanyi, "Morality and the Theory of Rational Behaviour," in Amartya Sen and Bernard Williams, eds., *Utilitarianism and Beyond* (Cambridge: Cambridge University Press, 1982). Rawls also develops the average utility argument on pp. 164–65 of *A Theory of Justice*.

4. See Singer, *Practical Ethics*, chap. 1; Rawls, *Theory*, pp. 136–42; and Lawrence Kohlberg, "Justice as Reversibility," in Peter Laslett and James Fishkin, eds., *Philosophy, Politics, and Society*, 5th series (New Haven: Yale University Press, 1979).

5. According to Rawls, the "social primary goods" that are "at the disposition of society" include "rights and liberties, powers and opportunities, income and wealth" (*Theory*, p. 62). In Ackerman's thought experiment, "manna is infinitely divisible and malleable, capable of transformation into any physical object a person may desire" (*Social Justice*, p. 31). For a critique of Ackerman, see section 2.2 above. For a critique of utility, see section 2.7.

6. Thomas Nagel, "Rawls on Justice," in Norman Daniels, ed., *Reading Rawls: Critical Studies of "A Theory of Justice"* (New York: Basic Books, 1975), p. 8 (emphasis added).

7. The moral point of view is formalized in the sense that the assumptions provided (or permitted by) the decision procedure are spelled out with sufficient rigor and clarity to determine a unique ultimate conclusion (or, at least, that is the aspiration).

8. Rawls, *Theory*, p. 395.

9. John Rawls, "Fairness to Goodness," *Philosophical Review* 84 (October 1975), p. 537.

10. Rawls, *Theory*, p. 421.

11. Ibid., pp. 413 and 408. See also pp. 416–17.

12. Ibid., pp. 423 and 432.

13. The maximin formulation of the general conception appears in the final statement of the principle on p. 303 of *A Theory of Justice*.

14. Ibid., pp. 302–03.

15. Ibid., p. 408.

16. How, in other words, is it supposed to yield the maximin distribution of primary goods in the general conception and the lexical priority of liberty over equal opportunity over income and wealth in the special conception?

17. Rawls, *Theory*, p. 155.

18. Ibid., p. 154.

19. I used similar charts in appendix B of my *Tyranny and Legitimacy* to make a different argument.

20. For some of maximin's bizarre implications, see Douglas W. Rae, "A Principle of Simple Justice," in Laslett and Fishkin, *Philosophy,* esp. pp. 150–52.

21. See Brian Barry, *The Liberal Theory of Justice* (Oxford: Oxford University Press, 1973), chap. 9, where the ambitious interpretation of the threshold in terms of a satiation point for wealth is subjected to a sustained critique.

22. Adam Smith defined the "necessaries" as including "not only the commodities which are indispensably necessary for the support of life, but whatever the custom of the country renders it indecent for creditable people, *even of the lowest order,* to be without" (emphasis added). Within the latter category, Smith included a linen shirt and leather shoes as necessary in his own time (because, for example, "a creditable day-labourer would be ashamed to appear in public without a linen shirt"). See Smith, *An Inquiry into the Nature and Causes of the Wealth of Nations* (New York: Modern Library, 1937), book 5, chap. 2, pp. 821–22. For some of the difficulties in evaluating subsistence needs, see my *Tyranny and Legitimacy,* chap. 5.

23. I believe this comparative view of the three features is the most sympathetic and plausible interpretation. In other words, from the original position, compared to the risk of falling below the threshold, we care little, if at all, for increases above it. This line of reasoning naturally leads us to something close to subsistence and a tenable claim to neutrality. Unless this comparative view is adopted, it seems implausible that the very same point at which we become satiated with wealth (not caring for further increments) is the point at which anything less is a disaster. For the satiation view, see Barry, *Liberal Theory,* chap. 9.

24. For Rawls on lexical priority, see *Theory,* pp. 42–45 and 60–65. For some excellent criticisms of Rawls's lexical rankings, see Daniels, *Reading Rawls,* esp. the articles by Daniels, Feinberg, Scanlon, and Barber.

25. The counting principles require only that I choose effective means for realizing my aims, that I choose more inclusive plans, and that I take account of likelihoods (when I have appropriate information). See Rawls, *Theory,* pp. 411–13.

26. John Rawls, "Kantian Constructivism in Moral Theory: The Dewey Lectures 1980," *Journal of Philosophy* 77, no. 9 (September 1980), pp. 515–72. For a useful assessment of the shift, see William A. Galston, "Moral Personality and Liberal Theory: John Rawls's Dewey Lectures," *Political Theory* 10, no. 4 (November 1982). See also Rawls, "Justice as Fairness: Political, Not Metaphysical," *Philosophy and Public Affairs* 14, no. 3 (Summer 1985), pp. 223–51.

27. Rawls, "Kantian Constructivism," p. 524.

28. Ibid., p. 526.

29. See Rawls, "Justice as Fairness," pp. 227–28.

30. In the argument that follows I expand on some points I made in "Can There Be a Neutral Theory of Justice?" *Ethics* 93, no. 2 (January 1983), pp. 348–56.

31. "Rationality," in Ackerman's view, is merely the requirement that questioning not be suppressed and that "reasons" be given instead (see *Social Justice*, p. 4). Ackerman later argues that "the reason advanced by a power wielder on one occasion must not be inconsistent with the reasons he advances to justify his other claims to power" (p. 7).

32. Ibid., p. 11.

33. Once again, the basic difficulty is the dilemma between substantively significant conclusions that lack a firm basis and firm conclusions that lack substantive significance.

34. The general version of the argument yields initial equality of manna or material resources (Ackerman, *Social Justice*, section 14). Once the full diversity of goods available for distribution over time is taken into account, a more complicated conception of "undominated equality" is reached. See *Social Justice*, pp. 28–29, for a full statement.

35. Ibid., p. 48.

36. Ibid., pp. 48–49 (emphasis added).

37. Ibid., p. 56.

38. Recall that in this science fiction scenario, the measurement problems arising from interpersonal comparisons have been set aside in order to give the utilitarian the benefit of the doubt. See Ackerman, *Social Justice,* pp. 45–49, 265.

39. Ibid., p. 49.

40. For a spirited defense of his basic claim that, at the very least, his own proposal clearly passes neutrality, see Ackerman, "What Is Neutral about Neutrality?" *Ethics* 93, no. 2 (January 1983), pp. 372–90. There, however, Ackerman does admit the theoretical possibility that his neutrality constraint might be compatible with radically different metrics for measuring outcomes. "It *may* be possible to produce a nonpreclusive model [one that does not rule out, by definition, the power struggles characteristic of the world as we know it] that analyzed Everyman's power struggle in a *radically* different way—one that did not at all resemble the way I have used the basic descriptors in my model: "genes," "education," "manna," "transactional structure," "Everyman." The outcomes of neutral dialogue in *such* a world would doubtless yield a very different conception of undominated equality—though it is hazardous to predict the differences until the rival model is produced" (p. 383, emphasis added).

   The argument developed here offers no objection to Ackerman's vision of the liberal state (or to Rawls's) once it is considered as part of such a family of liberal first principles—each of which makes symmetrical claims from its own variant of a fundamental thought experiment. The difficulty for our purposes is that when Ackerman's vision is taken in this pluralistic spirit, the basis it might offer for solving the jurisdiction problem will have been lost. Its prescriptions can then be evaded by rival theorists employing the same basic strategy (appeal to an impartial thought experiment). To the extent they provide us with substantive conclusions, Rawls and Ackerman are not alone in reaching this result. I have, however, concentrated on them here because they represent, in my view, the most powerful attempts to employ this strategy of combining an impartial thought experiment with the neutral consideration of interests.

41. For a discussion of justice in the distribution of esteem, see William J. Goode, *The Celebration of Heroes: Prestige as a Control System* (Berkeley: University of California Press, 1978), esp. chaps. 13 and 14.

42. Ackerman, *Social Justice,* pp. 3–4. For a catalogue of contested kinds of power relations, see Robert E. Gooden, *Manipulatory Politics* (New Haven and London: Yale University Press, 1980).

43. See Douglas Rae et al., *Equalities* (Cambridge: Harvard University Press, 1981), for a sustained demonstration of the many substantive inequalities compatible with the abstract idea of equality.

2.7 *Preference, Utility, and the Good*

1. Brian Barry, *Political Argument* (London: Routledge and Kegan Paul, 1965), pp. 38–41. See also my *Tyranny and Legitimacy* (Baltimore and London: Johns Hopkins University Press, 1979), chap. 3, where I borrow this distinction from Barry but develop it in a slightly different way.

2. R. M. Hare, "Ethical Theory and Utilitarianism," in Amartya Sen and Bernard Williams, eds., *Utilitarianism and Beyond* (Cambridge: Cambridge University Press, 1982), p. 26. On the tradition of the impartial spectator, see Adam Smith, *The Theory of Moral Sentiments* (Indianapolis: Liberty Classics, 1969), pp. 22, 31–38, 41, 71, 161–62, 247–49. See also John Rawls, *A Theory of Justice* (Cambridge: Harvard University Press, 1971), pp. 183–92.

3. Hare, "Ethical Theory," p. 30. For more on Hare's grappling with the fanatic, see his *Freedom and Reason* (Oxford: Oxford University Press, 1963), chap. 9.

4. Hare, "Ethical Theory," p. 30. In his *Moral Thinking* (Oxford: Clarendon Press, 1981), chap. 10, Hare claims that pure fanatical preferences such as the Nazi's will necessarily disappear through the process of moral universalization. The Nazi, if he imagines himself in the place of Jews, will necessarily lose his pure fanatical Nazi preferences. This strong claim is a sharp departure from the position Hare took in *Freedom and Reason.* For an incisive critique of this last strategy, see Bernard Williams, *Ethics and the Limits of Philosophy* (Cambridge: Harvard University Press, 1985), pp. 82–92.

5. For more on this kind of counterexample directed at utilitarianism (and rival theories that share certain of its features), see my *Tyranny and Legitimacy,* esp. chaps. 1, 2, 10, and 11.

6. Ronald Dworkin, *Taking Rights Seriously* (Cambridge: Harvard University Press, 1977), esp. chap. 9. For comparable efforts to distinguish private- and public-regarding preferences, see Brian Barry, *Political Argument,* pp. 63–64, and my *Tyranny and Legitimacy,* pp. 26–28. For a critique of Dworkin's strategy to rehabilitate utilitarianism, see H. L. A Hart, "Between Utility and Rights," in Alan Ryan, ed., *The Idea of Freedom* (Oxford: Oxford University Press, 1979), pp. 77–98.

7. Ronald Dworkin, "A Reply," in Marshall Cohen, ed., *Ronald Dworkin and Contemporary Jurisprudence* (Totowa, N.J.: Rowman and Allanheld, 1983), p. 284.

8. Ibid., p. 286.

9. John C. Harsanyi, "Morality and the Theory of Rational Behaviour," in Amartya Sen and Bernard Williams, eds., *Utilitarianism and Beyond* (Cambridge: Cambridge University Press, 1982), p. 56.

10. For some further arguments that utilitarianism cannot consistently be selective among preferences, see Bernard Williams, "A Critique of Utilitarianism," in J. J. C. Smart, *Utilitarianism: For and Against* (Cambridge: Cambridge University Press, 1973), pp. 77–150; see esp. section 6.

11. See my *Tyranny and Legitimacy,* chap. 1.

12. Lionel Robbins, "Interpersonal Comparisons of Utility: A Comment," *Economic Journal* 48, no. 192 (1938), pp. 635–41.

13. Ibid., pp. 636 and 637. Robbins is quoting a remark of Jevons.

14. As I. M. D. Little notes in discussing these Paretian limitations, "If the actual compensation of all losers is required before any economic change can be said to be good, then probably no good economic changes can occur. No change of any significance in the real world could ever be made without harming some people" (*A Critique of Welfare Economics,* 2d ed. [Oxford: Oxford University Press, 1957], p. 120).

15. William J. Baumol, *Economic Theory and Operations Analysis,* 4th ed. (Englewood Cliffs, N.J.: Prentice-Hall, 1977), p. 530.

16. Little, *Critique,* p. 87.

17. For an example of distributional weights, see Burton Weisbrod, "Income Redistribution Effects and Benefit-Cost Analysis," in Samuel Chase, Jr., ed., *Problems in Public Expenditure Analysis* (Washington, D.C.: Brookings Institution, 1976), pp. 177–213. For some difficulties in these economic applications of utilitarianism, see the articles by J. A. Mirrlees and Peter Hammond in Sen and Williams, *Utilitarianism and Beyond.*

18. For a critique of Rawls's doctrine of primary goods along these lines, see

my "Justice and Rationality: Some Objections to the Central Argument in Rawls's Theory," *American Political Science Review* 69, no. 2 (June 1975), pp. 615–29. Brian Barry (who, as noted earlier, originated the want-regarding/ideal-regarding distinction) applies it to Rawls in a somewhat different way, classifying Rawls's doctrine of primary goods as "a want-regarding conception at one remove" (*The Liberal Theory of Justice* [Oxford: Oxford University Press, 1973], p. 22). Here I draw the line differently so as to place primary goods in the ideal category. Rawls classifies his own argument this way, as Barry notes (p. 23).

19. See Gerald Dworkin, "Paternalism," in Peter Laslett and James S. Fishkin, eds., *Philosophy, Politics, and Society*, 5th series (New Haven and London: Yale University Press, 1979), pp. 78–96, for persuasive arguments in favor of some weak paternalistic judgments.

20. An example attributed to Robert Nozick in Dworkin, "Paternalism," p. 92.

21. Barrington Moore, Jr., *Injustice: The Social Bases of Obedience and Revolt* (White Plains, N.Y.: M. E. Sharpe, 1978).

3.1 Toward Reconstruction

1. I set aside the issue whether such strategies can solve the particularity requirement—whether, for example, they lead to an obligation to support a particular just society, or just societies in general.

3.2 The Legitimacy Problem

1. I take the term *ideal theory* from Rawls; see the discussion below.

2. Ronald Dworkin, "The Original Position," in Norman Daniels, ed., *Reading Rawls: Critical Studies of "A Theory of Justice"* (New York: Basic Books, 1975).

3. Everyone may have an obligation without the strength of that obligation always being overriding. Some members may, of course, have even stronger conflicting obligations in special cases. A state may be legitimate and still provide some members with grounds for justified civil disobedience.

4. Note to Wollheim's paradox and to the discussion of it in John Rawls, "Legal Obligation and the Duty of Fair Play," in Sidney Hook, ed., *Law and Philosophy* (New York: New York University Press, 1964), pp. 6–8.

5. I say "acceptable account" because it might be possible to do away with all dissent and disagreement under realistic conditions, but only at a cost in what we termed indoctrination problems.

6. See, for example, John Rawls, "Justice as Fairness: Political, Not Metaphysical," *Philosophy and Public Affairs* 14, no. 3 (Summer 1985), pp. 223–51.

7. See Giovanni Sartori, *The Theory of Democracy Revisited* (Chatham, N.J.: Chatham House, 1987), section 5.4. See also Karl Deutsch, *The Analysis of International Relations* (Englewood Cliffs, N.J.: Prentice-Hall, 1968), pp. 101–10.

3.3 Legitimacy and Obligation

1. "The living cremation of the sati was always in theory voluntary, but if we are to judge from later analogy, social and family pressure made it virtually obligatory on some high-caste widows, especially those of the warrior class" (A. L. Basham, *The Wonder That Was India* [London: Sidgwick and Jackson, 1954], p. 188).

2. "Some medieval writers roundly declare that the sati, by her self-immolation, expunges both her own and her husband's sins, and that the two enjoy together 35 million years of bliss in heaven" (ibid.).

3. In addition, it must be asked whether such a practice could be characterized as providing essential benefits.

4. For an illuminating discussion, see Richard Wasserstrom, "Racism and Sexism" in *Philosophy and Social Issues: Five Studies* (Notre Dame: University of Notre Dame Press, 1980).

5. See the discussion of background conditions in section 3.5.

6. See, for example, George Fredrickson, *White Supremacy: A Comparative Study in American and South African History* (New York: Oxford University Press, 1981).

7. See Barrington Moore, Jr., *Injustice: The Social Bases of Obedience and Revolt* (White Plains, N.Y.: M. E. Sharpe, 1978), p. 61.

8. Adam Smith, *An Inquiry into the Nature and Causes of the Wealth of Nations* (New York: Modern Library, 1937), book 5, chap. 2, pp. 821–22.

9. Karl Marx, *Capital*, vol. 1 (New York: Vintage Books, 1977), p. 275 (book 1, part 1, chap. 6).

10. Moore, *Injustice,* p. 59.

11. Moore concludes: "It was a system of rights and duties that was regarded as legitimate by its victims." He also singles out the "Untouchable caste councils which punished individual Untouchables who failed to live up to their obligations under their own systems" (ibid., p. 60).

12. For a penetrating and ambitious attempt to provide an account of "minimum standards of provision" that is very close in spirit to the notion of "essential benefits" offered here, see David Braybrooke's *Meeting Needs* (Princeton: Princeton University Press, 1987).

13. H. L A. Hart, "Are There Any Natural Rights?" *Philosophical Review* 64 (April 1955), p. 185.

14. John Rawls, "Legal Obligation and the Duty of Fair Play," in Sidney Hook, ed., *Law and Philosophy* (New York: New York University Press, 1964). Rawls defines his principle of fair play on pp.9–10.

15. Additional benefits can, of course, be provided, but the obligation to support the practices in question follows from the receipt of essential benefits (provided our other conditions apply as well).

16. Robert Nozick, *Anarchy, State and Utopia* (New York: Basic Books, 1974), p. 93

17. Ibid., pp. 94 and 95.

18. For a subtle and insightful attempt to reconstruct the fairness argument, see Richard Arneson, "The Principle of Fairness and Free-Rider Problems," *Ethics* 92 (July 1982), pp. 616–33. However, Arneson would require that the collective benefit be "worth its cost to each recipient" (p. 623), a position that I will dispute below.

19. My thanks to Lauren Rosenbloom for suggesting this example in class discussion at the University of Texas. I later encountered an Israeli example applied to these questions in George Klosko, "Presumptive Benefit, Fairness and Political Obligation," *Philosophy and Public Affairs* 16, no. 3 (Summer 1987), pp. 241–59.

20. See note 18 above.

21. Note that the basic character of our argument would not be changed if Arneson's proviso were added. Such a move would simply restrict the range of alternative practices that were both acceptable and feasible.

3.4 Liberty of Political Culture

1. I mean "political" to apply to all three areas—expression, belief, and association. However, the modifier is interpreted according to the broad definition in the next paragraph.

2. For an argument that places similar emphasis on freedom of political expression and association as constituting a core value in the liberal-democratic tradition, see Alexander Meiklejohn, *Political Freedom* (New York: Harper and Brothers, 1948; repr. 1979).

3. Thomas Scanlon, "A Theory of Freedom of Expression," *Philosophy and Public Affairs* 1, no. 2 (Winter 1972), pp. 204–26, and "Freedom of Expression and Categories of Expression," *University of Pittsburgh Law Review* 40, no. 4 (Summer 1979), pp. 519–50. For Scanlon's criticism of his own previous position, see pp. 532–34 of the latter article. In his new position, the "ultimate sources of justification relevant to . . . expression are the relevant participant, audience and bystander interests and requirements of distributive justice applicable to their satisfaction" (p. 535).

4. Berlin only needs to respond to this issue to the extent that his argument is, in fact, a defense of a particular conception of liberty. In revisions of that argument, he qualified the sense in which it could be taken as a defense of liberty. Rather, the argument is really a defense of value pluralism. In a note to the introduction to *Four Essays*, he explains: "I have therefore revised the text to make it clear that I am not offering a blank endorsement of the negative concept as opposed to its positive twin brother, since this would itself constitute precisely the kind of intolerant monism against which the entire argument is directed" (*Four Essays on Liberty* [New York: Oxford University Press, 1970], p. lviii). For Berlin's combination of "pluralism" and fallibilism, see "Two Concepts of Liberty," ibid., pp. 167–72. For a greatly overstated version of this problem in Berlin, see Leo Strauss, "Relativism," in Helmut Schoek and James W. Wiggins, eds., *Relativism and the Study of Man* (Princeton, N.J.: Van Nostrand, 1961).

5. For some general issues confronting the strategy of founding liberty on an ideal of human development, see Frederick Schauer, *Free Speech: A Philosophical Enquiry* (Cambridge: Cambridge University Press, 1982), chaps. 4 and 5. On "autonomy," see John Gray, *Mill on Liberty: A Defence* (London: Routledge and Kegan Paul, 1983), pp. 54–56 and 73–81; and Fred R. Berger, *Happiness, Justice and Freedom* (Berkeley and London: University of California Press, 1984), pp. 232–39. Both, however, incorporate autonomy into a theory that depends on the evaluation of states of affairs. On Gray's version of Mill, this evaluation is ultimately utilitarian; on Berger's, it is fundamentally a theory of justice.

6. See the picture of Mill that Berlin emphasizes in "John Stuart Mill and the Ends of Life" (*Four Essays*).

7. Ibsen's plays are full of compelling cases where truth conflicts with utility and/or justice. See, for example, *The Wild Duck* and *An Enemy of the People*.

8. These observations on Twain and Dos Passos derive from Shelley Fisher Fishkin, *From Fact to Fiction: Journalism and Imaginative Writing in America* (Baltimore and London: Johns Hopkins University Press, 1985).

9. See *Cohen v. California*, where First Amendment protections were extended to the "emotive" as well as purely "cognitive" functions of linguistic expression because, as Justice John Marshall Harlan noted, it is the "emotive function which, practically speaking, may often be the more important element of the overall message sought to be communicated" (403 U.S. 15 [1971], at 26).

10. Hence modest time, place, and manner restrictions do not constitute explicit manipulation provided that (a) they are employed in a content-neutral manner and (b) they do not operate so as to effectively silence an opinion.

11. However, this analysis would certainly support the famous view of Justice

William Brennan in *New York Times v. Sullivan* that the libel laws need to be evaluated "against the background of a profound national commitment to the principle that debate on public issues should be uninhibited, robust and wide-open, and that it may well include vehement, caustic, and sometimes unpleasantly sharp attacks on government and public officials." From our standpoint, that decision was important for the "breathing space" which the libel laws had to leave for political dialogue. See *New York Times v. Sullivan*, 376 U.S. 254 (1964), at 270 and 272.

12. See Murray Schumach, *The Face on the Cutting Room Floor* (New York: Morrow, 1964), chap. 4, for some interesting and sometimes bizarre cases of political blacklisting in Hollywood.

13. One of the key demands in the boycott by blacks of white merchants in *N.A.A.C.P. v. Claiborne Hardware Co.* (a boycott which was granted First Amendment protection for its nonviolent aspects) was that the merchants end job discrimination. Consumers should be free to pursue such an effort because the merchants are not entitled to equal consideration independent from such issues arising from their role in the marketplace. Suppose, however, that the white merchants who are the subject of the boycott do not practice discrimination but are the target of the boycott because it is believed that their personal views are racist. If those alleged racist views do not lead to actions that are the subject of protest, then our analysis could, admittedly, result in protecting the merchants from penalties imposed because of their private racist views, just as we would protect the Jewish merchant from penalties imposed because of his private religious views.

14. Kent Greenawalt, "Criminal Coercion and Freedom of Speech," *Northwestern University Law Review* 78, no. 5 (December 1983), p. 1084.

15. Of course, as in much political debate (and in many works of artistic expression), the reasons may be implicit or oblique, but there must be a basis in the work for uncovering them.

16. I am indebted to James Billington for bringing this phenomenon and its implications to my attention.

17. This argument and its connections to what I call the "private sphere of liberty" are developed in some detail in my *Justice, Equal Opportunity, and the Family* (New Haven and London: Yale University Press, 1983), section 2.4.

18. I am greatly indebted to Zhengyuan Fu of the Chinese Academy of Sciences for bringing this to my attention and for providing me with this translation. The quotation is from Ssu-ma Ch'ien's *Historical Records*. However, the standard two-volume English translation by Burton Watson (New York: Columbia University Press, 1961) begins with the later Han dynasty and thus does not include this edict from the Quin dynasty. For a statement from one of the em-

peror's advisers that matches this edict almost verbatim, see Wm. Theodore de Bary, Wing-tsit Chan, and Burton Watson, eds., *Sources of Chinese Tradition,* vol. 1 (New York: Columbia University Press, 1960), p. 141.

19. John Stuart Mill, *On Liberty,* in *Utilitarianism, On Liberty and Other Writings,* edited with an introduction by Mary Warnock (New York: New American Library, 1962), p. 202.

20. For an extended argument to this effect, see my "Bargaining, Justice and Justification," *Social Philosophy and Policy* 5, no. 2 (Spring 1988), pp. 46–64.

21. They do not, in other words, dismiss claims from particular groups merely because of the source.

22. Mill, *On Liberty,* p. 143.

23. Ibid., p. 145.

24. See section 3.5 below.

25. This is, of course, one of the main strands of argument in *On Liberty,* especially chapter 2.

26. For an incisive critique of the claim that "authority" requires a "surrender" of judgment from those subject to it, see Richard E. Flathman, *The Practice of Political Authority* (Chicago: University of Chicago Press, 1980), chap. 5.

27. For the tortuous history in America of the achievement of liberty in the laissez-faire view (treated as freedom of the press in the "libertarian" sense), see Leonard W. Levy, *Emergence of a Free Press* (New York: Oxford University Press, 1985).

28. For more on nondiscriminatory meritocratic assignment, see my *Justice, Equal Opportunity, and the Family,* sections 2.2, 4.1, and 5.1.

29. Charles E. Lindblom, *Politics and Markets* (New York: Basic Books, 1977), p. 202.

30. The attacks on Lindblom concerning this issue are gathered in Robert Hessen, ed., *Does Big Business Rule America?* (Washington, D.C.: Ethics and Public Policy Center, 1981).

3.5 The Conditions of Activist Liberty

1. Anthony Trollope, *Phineas Finn,* vol. 1 (London: Oxford University Press, 1949), p. 297.

2. Ibid., p. 312.

3. Isaiah Berlin, "Two Concepts of Liberty," in *Four Essays on Liberty* (New York: Oxford University Press, 1970). See Gerald C. MacCallum, Jr., "Negative and Positive Freedom," in Peter Laslett et al., eds., *Philosophy, Politics and Society,* 4th series (Oxford: Basil Blackwell, 1974).

4. I say "self-critical" because, by my proposed definition, such a dialogue could

not be self-reflective (the definition includes the requirement that it be unmanipulated).

5. This notion is meant to apply regardless of whether the goods or characteristics are valued negatively or positively. See sections 2.2 and 2.3 above for a discussion of many of the difficult issues in conceptualizing these values.

6. By "receive," I mean process forms of expression offered by others so as to facilitate successful communication, whether oral or in writing, through standard languages or new artistic forms.

7. This knowledge should be interpreted to include not only the capacity to understand, but also the capacity to employ the relevant conventions.

8. For a further argument to this effect, see my *Justice, Equal Opportunity, and the Family* (New Haven and London: Yale University Press, 1983), sections 2.4 and 3.6.

9. See Joseph Goldstein, Anna Freud, and Albert J. Solnit, *Beyond the Best Interests of the Child* (New York: Free Press, 1973) and *Before the Best Interests of the Child* (New York: Free Press, 1979) for some influential work on both the dangers of and appropriate grounds for state intervention.

10. See Urie Bronfenbrenner, *A Report on Longitudinal Evaluations of Preschool Programs: Is Early Intervention Effective?* vol. 2 (Washington, D.C.: Office of Child Development, 1974) and P. Levenstein, "Cognitive Growth in Preschoolers through Verbal Intervention with Mothers," *American Journal of Orthopsychiatry* 40 (1970), pp. 426–32.

11. I take the term *underclass* from Ken Auletta's vivid portrait *The Underclass* (New York: Vintage Books, 1983).

12. See my *Justice*, sections 2.4 and 3.6.

13. For a provocative application to voting in national elections, see Paul E. Meehl, "The Selfish Voter Paradox and the Thrown-Away Vote Argument," *American Political Science Review* 71, no. 1 (March 1977), pp. 11–30. The general theoretical issue was, of course, made famous by Mancur Olson, *The Logic of Collective Action* (New York: Shocken Books, 1968), chaps. 1 and 2. For some crucial ambiguities in the notion of group size, see Russell Hardin, *Collective Action* (Baltimore and London: Johns Hopkins University Press, 1982), chap. 3.

14. See, for example, William H. Riker and Peter C. Ordeshook, "A Theory of the Calculus of Voting," *American Political Science Review* 62, no. 1 (March 1968), pp. 25–42.

15. Stanley I. Benn offered an account of "political activity as a form of moral self-expression" and used as one of his examples "singing political songs in the bath." See his "The Problematic Rationality of Political Participation," in Peter Laslett and James S. Fishkin, eds., *Philosophy, Politics, and Society*, 5th series

(New Haven: Yale University Press, 1979), esp. p. 310. Benn's notion of moral self-expression cannot, it seems to me, admit considerations of effectiveness in expression any more than it can admit considerations of consequences. It is more a matter of consistency with fundamental beliefs or, one might say, a matter of integrity.

16. C. D. Broad, "On the Function of False Hypotheses in Ethics," *International Journal of Ethics* 26 (1915–16), pp. 377–97.

17. For a discussion of various efforts to deal with this problem, see my *Limits of Obligation* (New Haven and London: Yale University Press, 1982), part 2, sections 13–18.

18. These points about organizational pluralism and decentralization have bene-fited from Robert A. Dahl, *Dilemmas of Pluralist Democracy: Autonomy vs. Control* (New Haven and London: Yale University Press, 1982).

19. Barrington Moore, Jr., *Injustice: The Social Bases of Obedience and Revolt* (White Plains, N.Y.: M. E. Sharpe, 1978), p. 58.

20. See my *Justice,* section 5.1, for a further account of these process equalities.

21. I have been focusing here on how the lack of self-esteem may form an impedi-ment to participation. It is also true, of course, that actual engagement in par-ticipation can be expected, in turn, to contribute to self-esteem and to the civic education of citizens—facilitating the development of the necessary capacities. Mill made strong claims about the educative functions of participation. For an assessment, see Dennis F. Thompson, *John Stuart Mill and Representative Government* (Princeton: Princeton University Press, 1976), chaps. 1, 2, and Conclusion.

22. For each of these process equalities, leveling up for the bottom is a neces-sary first step, but one that inevitably falls far short of equalization. Further efforts at equalization must inevitably conflict with important liberties of the better-off strata. How these value conflicts are to be assessed remains a serious controversy. See my *Justice,* section 5.1.

23. For a penetrating assessment, see William Julius Wilson, *The Truly Disadvan-taged: The Inner City, the Underclass, and Public Policy* (Chicago: University of Chicago Press, 1987).

24. Michael Walzer, *Spheres of Justice: A Defense of Pluralism and Equality* (New York: Basic Books, 1983), chap. 4.

25. Although W. G. Runciman argues that this factor will be greatly ameliorated by restrictions in the range of social vision of the worse-off (postal workers comparing themselves to other postal workers, but not to the very rich). See Runciman, *Relative Deprivation and Social Justice* (Berkeley: University of California Press, 1966).

26. John Rawls, *A Theory of Justice* (Cambridge: Harvard University Press, 1971), p. 534.

27. For a historical account of our consumer culture along these general lines, see Stuart Ewen, *Captains of Consciousness* (New York: McGraw-Hill, 1976).

28. For a careful assessment, see Michael Schudson, *Advertising, the Uneasy Persuasion* (New York: Basic Books, 1984).

29. See Ithiel de Sola Pool, *Technologies of Freedom* (Cambridge: Harvard University Press, 1983) for a useful survey of new technologies of mass communication and their promise.

30. For some inventive but speculative proposals for limiting the influence of commercial advertisers, see Charles A. Reich, "Making Free Speech Audible," *The Nation*, Feb. 8, 1965, pp. 138–41.

31. See David R. Mayhew, *Congress: The Electoral Connection* (New Haven and London: Yale University Press, 1974), pp. 67–69. See also John W. Kingdon, *Agendas, Alternatives and Public Policies* (Boston: Little, Brown, 1984), chap. 8, for a detailed discussion of policy entrepreneurs and their relation to windows of opportunity.

32. See Benjamin I. Page, "The Theory of Political Ambiguity," *American Political Science Review* 70, no. 3 (September 1976), pp. 742–52.

33. In this same spirit, see Benjamin Barber's proposals for a "Civic Communications Cooperative" to harness new technologies for democratic political dialogue and a "Civic Videotext Service" to increase citizen access to information (*Strong Democracy: Participatory Politics for a New Age* [Berkeley: University of California Press, 1984], chap. 10).

34. Joel Feinberg, *Offense to Others*, vol. 2 of *The Moral Limits of the Criminal Law* (New York: Oxford University Press, 1985), pp. 10–13.

35. For a strong argument that symbolic speech should be accorded equal status with verbal speech under the First Amendment, see Melville B. Nimmer, "The Meaning of Symbolic Speech under the First Amendment," *UCLA Law Review* 21, no. 1 (1973), pp. 29–62.

36. I am referring to the full experience of such messages, not the bare knowledge of them.

37. For more on this promise, see Pool, *Technologies*. For example: "With the new technologies, the world is shrinking. . . . There will be less cost constraint to do business, consult, debate, and socialize within one's own region only. There will be more freedom to do so with anyone anywhere with whom one finds affinity. This development, along with the development of multiple technologies of communication and of cheap microprocessors, will foster a trend toward pluralistic and competitive communications systems. With hundred-channel cable systems, videocassettes, videodisks, ISDNs, and network links to thousands of on-line information services, there should be a diversity of voices far beyond anything known today" (p. 229).

38. For an assessment, see Larry J. Sabato *PAC Power: Inside the World of Political Action Committees* (New York: Norton, 1984).
39. *Buckley v. Valeo,* 424 U.S. 1 (1976). See also *First National Bank v. Bellotti,* 435 U.S. 765 (1978).
40. Reich, "Making Free Speech Audible," p. 141.

3.6 Vouchers and Opinion Polls

1. See the discussion of capacities in section 3.5 above.
2. I participated with Schmitter, Claus Offe, Terry Karl, and others in a working group focused on representation vouchers at the Center for Advanced Study in the Behavioral Sciences in 1987–88. In what follows, I do not presume to present Schmitter's proposal, as it differs from the sketch suggested here in many particulars. I am, however, grateful to all the participants in this group for some extremely insightful discussions. Their own respective versions of the idea will, I am sure, be presented in various works.
3. I served as chief academic adviser to station WETA in Washington, D.C., for an effort by PBS to mount a version of the deliberative opinion poll in the 1992 presidential campaign. Funding difficulties forced the event to be canceled, but the proposal has been adopted for 1996 by all ten of the nation's presidential libraries. The event will be held at the Lyndon Baines Johnson Library and Museum in Austin, Texas, and is expected to be broadcast nationally. For more details on the possible role of deliberative opinion polls, see my *Democracy and Deliberation: New Directions for Democratic Reform* (New Haven and London: Yale University Press, 1991).
4. For a general account of momentum in the presidential selection process, see Larry M. Bartels, *Presidential Primaries and the Dynamics of Public Choice* (Princeton: Princeton University Press, 1988).

Index